11 $\frac{50}{5/0}$

D1020175

# MARY DIANA DODS,
# A GENTLEMAN AND A SCHOLAR

## Other Books by Betty T. Bennett

*British War Poetry in the Age of Romanticism: 1793–1815*

*The Evidence of the Imagination,* (co-edited with Donald H. Reiman and Michael C. Jaye)

*"A part of the elect," The Letters of Mary Wollstonecraft Shelley* (Volume I)

*"Treading in unknown paths," The Letters of Mary Wollstone-craft Shelley* (Volume II)

*"What years I have spent," The Letters of Mary Wollstonecraft Shelley* (Volume III)

*The Mary Shelley Reader* (co-edited with Charles E. Robinson)

# MARY DIANA DODS,
## A GENTLEMAN AND A SCHOLAR

Betty T. Bennett

William Morrow and Company, Inc.
New York

Copyright © 1991 by Betty T. Bennett

All rights reserved. No part of this book may be reproduced or utilized in any form or by any means, electronic or mechanical, including photocopying, recording or by any information storage and retrieval system, without permission in writing from the Publisher. Inquiries should be addressed to Permissions Department, William Morrow and Company, Inc., 105 Madison Avenue, New York, N.Y. 10016.

Recognizing the importance of preserving what has been written, it is the policy of William Morrow and Company, Inc., and its imprints and affiliates to have the books it publishes printed on acid-free paper, and we exert our best efforts to that end.

Library of Congress Cataloging-in-Publication Data

Bennett, Betty T.
    Mary Diana Dods, a gentleman and a scholar / Betty T. Bennett.
        p.    cm.
    Includes bibliographical references.
    ISBN 0-688-08717-5
    1. Dods, Mary Diana Biography. 2. Shelley, Mary Wollstonecraft,
1797–1851—Friends and associates. 3. Women and literature—Great
Britain—History—19th century. 4. Authors, English—19th century—
Biography. I. Title.
PR4897.L2Z6    1991
828'.709—dc20
[B]                                                                     90-13473
                                                                           CIP

Printed in the United States of America

First Edition

1 2 3 4 5 6 7 8 9 10

BOOK DESIGN BY M. C. DEMAIO

*To Herbert, Marvin, and Gail Edelman*
*For sharing their lives and*
*their creativity with me*

# CONTENTS

# INTRODUCTION

THIS IS A story about tracking—and sidetracking. It began in 1973, when I decided to edit the letters of Mary Wollstonecraft Shelley to better understand that author, who at nineteen wrote the novel *Frankenstein*. Since *Frankenstein* first appeared in 1818, the obsessed scientist and his abandoned creature have haunted the imagination. But studies all described a diffident Mary Shelley with little life of her own beyond *Frankenstein,* Shelley, and their children. Mary Shelley's works—which include six novels, two travel books, biographical lives, short stories, reviews, as well as the works of Percy Bysshe Shelley, her husband—suggest a far more complex woman than either biographers or critics recognized. The place to find that woman seemed to be in her letters. Eventually this search expanded into three volumes of some 1,267 letters, and Mary Shelley's own voice introduced a new Mary Shelley to the world.

The first step was to use colleagues' suggestions and library directories to locate published and unpublished letters, which resulted in doubling the number of Mary Shelley's previously collected letters. Working with the letters took me to dozens of libraries, record offices, and private autograph collections in the United States, England, Scotland, Italy, France, Switzerland, and Australia over a fifteen-year period. I transcribed letters directly from manuscript to avoid the many mistakes in past publications, to find crossed-out words under their inky camouflage, to gently unfold corners of letters that hid parts of sentences, to piece together faded postmarks that told when a letter was written, and to verify if the letters were authentic. Caught in the life of this important but then largely ignored author, my objective was to establish the basis for a reevaluation of her complexity, independence, and intellect through historical and biographical footnotes. The notes had to be complete enough, alive enough, so readers could place her in the context of her own times and understand her significance then and now.

In February 1978, I promised the Johns Hopkins University Press delivery of the manuscript of the first volume the following September. Eighteen months of copy editing would follow, with a flurry of hundreds of editorial questions until the 1,600 pages reemerged, in May 1980, reshaped into the 572-page Volume 1 of *The Letters of Mary Wollstonecraft Shelley*. With long nights, and endless weekends that ended too soon, I could make the deadline. Except for two men who appeared toward the end of the volume: David Lyndsay, a writer; and Walter Sholto Douglas, the husband of Mary Shelley's dear friend Isabella Robinson Douglas. Because neither was a major figure of the era, it seemed sufficient to find out only enough for a brief footnote's worth of information about each of them—born, died, career.

But it didn't happen that way. Buried in the letters referring to Lyndsay and Douglas was a tale of its own—a tale neither I nor any of the others who had previously worked with the Mary Shelley material ever suspected. The story was intended never to be uncovered and only gradually did the pieces come together to reveal a cross-continental adventure that reshapes both historical and biographical fact.

Finding that story—and its motivations—took some twelve years, in part because my attention was primarily focused on the Mary Shelley letters despite Lyndsay's and Douglas's adroitness in intervening and luring me to them. But it also took that much time because the many pieces were scattered in England, Scotland, France, and Italy, for the most part hidden in archives covered with dust and long forgotten.

In many ways, the story is about the unexpected—and what may occur when generally held beliefs are played upon by imaginative, daring people in order to shape their own lives. These events happened mostly in the early part of the nineteenth century, and though publicly enacted and documented, were undiscovered and so passed into "fact." What might contemporaries have made of all this? Would it have forced them to rethink their social codes? And, perhaps more important under the circumstances, what about us and our social codes?

In the course of assembling this story, numerous friends and colleagues have assisted in various ways. Alice G. Fredman, Donald H. Reiman, Charles E. Robinson, and Emily Sunstein have my special gratitude for their important part in untangling this story. Bruce Barker-Benfield of the Bodleian Library; Alan S. Bell, then at the National Library of Scotland; the late Robert Yampolsky, Mihai Handrea, and Doucet Fischer of the Carl H. Pforzheimer Shelley and His Circle Collection; and Hilton Kelliher of the British Library, generously and repeatedly assisted me as I sorted through the collections for which they were responsible. I remain deeply indebted to Lord and Lady Abinger for permitting me to work with their collection of Shelley circle manuscripts over these many years.

For their kind assistance, I wish also to thank: Austin Barron, David J. Brown, Iain G. Brown, Rodney Dennis, Wilfred S. Dowden, Les Duff, Donna Evleth, Irwin F. Fredman, James D. Galbraith, Christina M. Gee, Milton Greenberg, Kathleen Kennedy-Corey, Edward Kessler, John Manners, Celia Morris, William St Clair, Romeo Segnan, Thomas Southall, Harry Watson, Charles E. White, and Josette Wisman; as well as a number of colleagues at The American University who provided bibliographical suggestions.

Permissions to work with their collections, as well as other courtesies for which I am grateful were given by: Archives Nationales de Paris, Bibliothèque de l'Institut de France, the Bodleian Library, the British Library, the Houghton Library, the Huntington Library, the National Library of Scotland, the family of the late Cecilia Payne-Gaposchkin, the Carl H. Pforzheimer Shelley and His Circle Collection of the New York Public Library, and the Scottish Record Office.

I am indebted to Bruce Lee, formerly a senior editor at William Morrow, and Jane Cushman of JCA (literary agency), for their support and enthusiasm for the story; to Lisa Drew of William Morrow, for picking up where Bruce left off; to Ingeborg F. Dim and Joan Ruch for their special assistance in the assembling process; to Mary Mintz and other librarians at The American University for assisting in the "dig"; and to The American University for its support of this book.

Finally, as ever, I thank my parents, Meyer and Jennie Edelman, and my sons, Matthew and Peter Bennett, for their love and care as I wander out into unknown worlds.

—Betty T. Bennett
Washington, D.C.

# PROLOGUE

# YOU ARE CORDIALLY INVITED

THE PLACE IS LONDON. The year, 1825. A hackney coach turns the corner off Tottenham Court Road onto Warren Street, toward Dr. William Kitchener's[1] house. It clips along quickly on this cold January evening, its two horses spurred on by the coachman's anticipation of an extra one penny if they arrive before seven P.M. The impact of wheel on cobblestone makes the ride none too comfortable for the gentleman and young lady inside. But the passengers do not complain. They are guided by as strict a time rule as Cinderella by her fairy godmother: Kitchener, physician, inventor, culinary expert whose book *The Cook's Oracle* is a best-seller, requires his guests to be in attendance by seven. The opening hour of his salon he keeps as punctually as the closing, announced on a board hung in the foyer: "Come at seven: go at eleven." All obeyed. For conversation, music, and sheer oddity, Kitchener's Tuesday gatherings promised amusement for the evening and a week's worth of gossip. As important, in an era when formal introductions are mandatory, Kitchener's is a valuable meeting place. There, publishers, editors, musicians, and writers, as well as that new breed of affluent businessmen and even the occasional lord, mix freely in Kitchener's special amalgam of eccentricity and hospitality. By the close of such evenings, many a writer has no doubt left for home satisfied at having impressed a publisher or, equally important, one of the wealthy who, through cultural societies and private patronage, have so much power over which music, art, or writing is admired and bought.

The coach slows as it approaches Number 43. An abrupt stop on a cobblestone road could topple the carriage. Mr. Joshua Robinson, gentleman, and housing developer, understands from the pace they are almost arrived. He pulls a pocket watch from his vest. It is five minutes to seven. He replaces his watch, making certain not to tangle its gold chain, and pulls from another pocket several coins. His daughter, Miss Isabella Robinson, recognizes the meaning of her father's actions. She adjusts her bonnet and, when her father looks away, pinches her cheeks. The bright pink highlights her deep complexion and dark, flowing hair.

When the coach stops, Mr. Robinson steps out first, avoiding the ditch water that streams in the gutter at the edge of the sidewalk. Safely anchored, he turns and assists his daughter to the walkway. Because London's roads and alleys are polluted with the wastes of its citizens, great care must be taken lest a gentleman's silk hose or, worse yet, a lady's dress and petticoat, be stained and fetid.

The two-and-a-quarter-mile ride from Paddington costs two shillings, six pence,[2] plus the promised one penny for speed. Mr. Robinson thanks the driver, reminds him to return at eleven sharp, and hands the coins up to him. A pound of bread, considered expensive, costs two pence.[3] The two shillings, six pence doubled by the return fare will buy the coachman three days' food for his family of four. He touches his top hat in gratitude. Even as he gestures, his passengers hurry toward the door. Mr. Robinson uses the large brass knocker to summon attention. Within moments the young housekeeper, said to be a relative, opens the door. The Robinsons hand their cloaks to the waiting servant and walk quickly down the foyer leading to the back drawing room. They enter as the clock strikes seven, to find themselves among some fifty other guests already engaged in lively conversation. Across the room, they see Kitchener and make their way to greet their host.

It is easy to see Kitchener even in a crowd. Most gentlemen of the age wore the fashionable dark coat with tails and large-collared shirts with elaborately tied cravats, over tight, often contrasting, breeches met at the knee by boots or silk stockings.

The unusually tall, gangly Kitchener, on the other hand, always dressed in a suit of black, shiny material, with long stockings buttoned to the knee and a waist-length jacket. In keeping with his own conservative attire, he asked that his female guests be spare in finery. For the women writers, often short of money, this was a welcome request. The basic evening fashion just then called for dresses open at the neck, full sleeved, cinched above the waist, and draping to the floor, with some ruffles or other trim at the neck and hemline. A gauze scarf or wrap, as much for modesty as variety and fashion, could dress up a meager wardrobe.

To reach Kitchener, the Robinsons make their way through the groups of threes or fours, who discuss the arts, politics, and international events. One of the several male servants who wander the room handing about trays of small sandwiches, tea, and coffee offers them some refreshment, but they will not partake before greeting their host. Mr. Robinson nods to acquaintances, gestures he will return, and moves on. Isabella Robinson follows, curtsying pertly, sometimes smiling, now demure, now flirtatious. Off in a corner, she sees the friend she particularly planned to talk with that night, and is tempted to break away toward her, but she knows better. She trails behind her father as they weave forward around the stuffed tigers, gazelles, and chamois that serve as seating, past the grand piano, to Kitchener.

At that moment, he is conversing with a woman in her late twenties. Her bright-golden hair, fair skin, and large gray eyes contrast with her black mourning dress. Poised but reserved, she is introduced by Kitchener to the Robinsons: Mary Shelley. With the name comes a history well known in literate circles. Her mother was Mary Wollstonecraft, the radical writer whose 1792 *Vindication of the Rights of Women* is considered the inaugural declaration of the women's rights movement; who shocked all but the avant garde of her own era with her radical political views and with her first, illegitimate daughter; the mother Mary Shelley worshiped, who died in giving birth to her in 1797, leaving her a legacy of idealism and notoriety. Mary Shelley's father was William Godwin, radical writer-philosopher, whose 1793 treatise *Enquiry Concerning Political Justice* and 1794 *Adventures of Caleb Williams,* the first mystery novel in the English language, both argued that unchecked political power and private property should be supplanted by universal education, communal property, and minimal government. The father Mary Shelley revered, though British radicals were cast from the limelight by the mid-1790s when, under Napoleon's leadership, the French turned from a revolution for rights to a twenty-two-year war for power at the same time turning Godwin to a private life of financial struggle.

Mary Shelley, the author at nineteen of the novel *Frankenstein,* had scandalously eloped at sixteen with the married poet Shelley, more noted then for his radical politics and atheism than for the poetry that would years later earn him an honored place among the great writers of English literature. That elopement had taken place almost twelve years earlier. In the interval, Mary Shelley witnessed the publication of her own books and Shelley's, their eventual marriage, the deaths of three of their four children, and, when she was almost twenty-five and Shelley almost thirty, his drowning in the Gulf of Spezia. At twenty-eight, struggling as a writer to support herself and Percy Florence, her one surviving child, she is both young and old.[4]

The Robinsons are introduced, and Mr. Robinson, a graduate of Oxford University, a man whose circle includes musicians and writers, is delighted to converse with this famous author. Who, even then, did not know *Frankenstein*? For her part, Mary Shelley is struck by the remarkable beauty and brightness of the young Miss Isabella Robinson. But Miss Robinson grows quickly restless, and looks around the room. One might think she wished to see which celebrated figures were there that evening. The handsome writer Lord Dillon? The poet Thomas Campbell? The actor Charles Kemble? The singers Mr. Braham, Mr. Sinclair, Miss Cubitt? Or perhaps women writers she already knew, Miss Rennie, Miss Benger, Miss Roberts, who can give her suggestions about her own writing aspirations. It is a long list, the famous in this crowded room, and for the most part, their names are known today only to historians and scholars. But Isabella Robinson has met celebrities before. Thomas Moore, the Irish tenor, songwriter, and close friend of Lord Byron, often visits at her family's home, as do many others whose names fill the social and arts columns in the daily newspapers. She sees in Mary Shelley's eyes that she has made a conquest, and later will take full advantage. Now, she excuses herself and crosses the room to join the two women nearly hidden in the corner.

The women look to be made from the same mold, but the one, Mrs. Georgiana Dods Carter, appears to be the second try, the one that came out right. Miss Mary Diana Dods, of the same mid-height, dark curly hair, and black eyes, is misshapen in figure, pale and sickly in complexion. Nor is her almost gnomelike appearance enhanced by her tight-fitting white dress, with rows of tucks to the knee, topped by a short green jacket. Only when she speaks does her grotesque appearance fade, eclipsed by her extraordinary intelligence and learning. With a perfunctory nod to Mrs. Carter, it is to Miss Dods that Isabella Robinson addresses herself. Mrs. Carter, accustomed to the erratic ways of her sister, and the egocentric ways of her sister's protégée, takes her leave. Isabella Robinson moves closer to Miss Dods, and whispers her story.

No one notices. They continue their tête-à-tête for some while, interrupted only when Kitchener himself approaches with Mrs. Shelley, and informs Miss Dods that he wishes to introduce them. "Though you are quite the conservative, and she of the liberal persuasion, yet I believe you will much like her," he tells Miss Dods. And like Mrs. Shelley she does. The three spend the remainder of the evening together. The *conversazione* continues until ten o'clock, when Mr. Braham gives them a small recital. First, to satisfy their host's ego, he sings some of Kitchener's own lyrical compositions, then some Handel and Mozart. By ten-thirty, partners search each other out in the room in preparation for departing.

Mr. Robinson finds his daughter in the company of Mrs. Shelley, Miss Dods, and Mrs. Carter. Might he be permitted to see them home in his carriage? They gladly accept his generous offer. Bidding good night to their host as they don their cloaks, they join the stream of exiting guests. At eleven sharp, the coachman appears at the door and Mr. Robinson helps the

ladies in. First to Kentish Town and then back to Paddington, he
tells the driver, who, already feeling the extra three shillings in
his palm, turns the carriage and sets off. Behind them,
Kitchener's house grows silent. The doctor climbs to his obser-
vatory at the top of the house to see if the sky is clear enough
for his telescope to explore the universe. Within the carriage,
the new friends converse, already planning when and how they
should next meet.

Kitchener held these salons on Tuesday nights without fail.
And without fail, the famous and would-be-famous attended.
Reports I have pieced together from contemporary memoirs, di-
aries, and letters first place Mary Diana Dods in Kitchener's circle at least by 1823, and in Mary Shelley's circle in 1825, when
both Mary Shelley and Isabella Robinson attended Kitchener's.
Now, I do not know for certain if this is exactly how Mary
Shelley first met Robinson and Dods. They had other acquaintances in common and might have come upon each other some
other way than at the salon of the cook's oracle on Warren
Street. What I do know, however, is that in the early winter of
1825 Mary Shelley began what would grow into a very close
friendship with Isabella Robinson and Mary Diana Dods. And
during the next two and a half years, one of these women arranged false passports for her two confidantes, the second became an unwed mother, and the third became a man.

## CHAPTER 1

# THE SEARCH BEGINS

THE YEAR 1825 is significant in this story, but not in British history. True, John Nash redesigned Buckingham Palace; horse-drawn buses first clattered through the teeming streets of London, its population newly increased to more than 1,200,000; the building industry flourished, turning manored estates into squares of handsome, costly homes for the prosperous; villages adjoining London were unofficially annexed; and 225 miles northwest of London the 38-mile Stockton and Darlington Railroad modernized passenger travel with the first steam locomotives. But for the most part, 1825 fades into the decade of the 1820s, which itself seems to be no more than transition years between the heady Romantic Era and the seemingly staid world of the Victorians. To give the year some larger importance than it acquired itself, we may think of it as almost midway between the final defeat of Napoleon at Waterloo in 1815 and the ascent to the throne of Queen Victoria in 1837.

Napoleon's imprisonment on St. Helena ended some twenty-three years of almost continuous war with France, a war that began with British radicals dreaming that the French Revolution of 1789 would successfully inspire democratic government in their country as well. But under Napoleon, democratic ideals were displaced by the quest for empire. The British, under attack, largely closed ranks, and set back the cause of internal political reform for some thirty years. The end of the war, instead of bringing peace and prosperity to Britain, opened an era of inflation and intense social conflict. A rapidly expanding working class demanded relief, sometimes violently, from its impoverished living conditions. At the same time, the expanding middle class of industrialists and merchants became vocal in their bid for a share of political power from the aristocracy. International war gave way to domestic war. In the face of aroused working-class protests, organized meetings, and large, frequent marches in London and other major cities, the upper and middle classes united. Together, they suppressed the working class using both the legal system and armed force.[1]

Not until the later 1820s were relatively calmer years ushered in. During this period, under continuing pressure for reform, the British began their gradual evolution into a more representative form of government, slowly but increasingly responsive to middle- and working-class voices. In 1832, Parliament passed the first of the great reform bills. Five years later, Queen Victoria's rise to the throne accompanied an era of British empire building abroad and industrial empire building at home. But it is the years between that concern this story, the period of transition that established new social conventions to suit a new middle class. During those years of gradual change, still haunted by the ghosts of revolution and war, two seemingly contradictory social tendencies competed. On the one hand, society found some measure of control through establishing the sexual repression that would mark the remainder of the century. On the other, that same society preserved its belief in the rights of the individual as well as a tolerance for eccentricity and dissent.

Historically, of course, the rights of the individual and dissent were understood to refer to men. Most women complied, but not all. Some found themselves torn between what society declared to be their restricted roles—obedient wives and daughters, doting mothers—and their own intellect. Even Victoria herself provided an ambivalent role model: the Queen, who might defer at times to her beloved Prince Albert and her ministers, and who bore eight children, was nevertheless the ruler and a woman. It is not surprising that the era that cherished her should have nurtured women as well as men dissatisfied with the limitations imposed by their social and legal status. Perhaps it was the very flux of the 1820s and its uncertainty about itself that allowed the events in this story to happen at all.

The eleven-year-old future Queen Victoria, in 1830, pledged to her nation: "I will be good."[2] This story is about three women who took no such pledge. Had they taken one— the dark-haired, coquettish teenager, the golden-haired, reserved widow in her late twenties, and the crop-haired, oddly shaped fortyish woman—their oath would have been, "I will be." And history, in the name of the truth it reveres, must forgive its embarrassment at the many mistakes it made because of them and, however shame-faced, correct its books. For beginning in 1821, Mary Diana Dods, joined eventually by Isabella Robinson and Mary Shelley, left a trail of deceptions that fooled man, woman, and child as well as official government records and historical, biographical, and literary works for the next 157 years. Their secrets were not even suspected until 1978 when, also one of their innocent victims, I hunted for information to complete my first Mary Shelley volume. But there were two problems. One was named David Lyndsay, the other, Walter Sholto Douglas.

Both men entered Mary Shelley's circle after Shelley's death: Douglas, the husband of her beloved friend Isabella Robinson; Lyndsay, a writer of some accomplishment. What irked me was how much I knew about them but still couldn't find the basic facts of their lives. What were their backgrounds? When did Lyndsay meet Mary Shelley? Why such relatively brief when seemingly intense friendships? This information should have surfaced in the course of locating previously unpublished letters, tracing hundreds of other previously unidentified friends and facts in Mary Shelley's life and capturing them in footnotes. But in February 1978, seven months before the press deadline, Lyndsay and Douglas remained biographical mysteries. The thought of the failed footnote, "No biographical information located," taunted my scholarly pride—and my curiosity.

That February I assembled the pieces of the puzzle in hand, concentrating the hunt on David Lyndsay. He wrote. He published. So public a figure could not appear and vanish with no other traces. Of the two letters written in October 1826 and the June 1828 letter in which Mary Shelley referred to Lyndsay, the first was to Alaric A. Watts, an up-and-coming publisher of the period.[3] Watts was editor and proprietor of *The Literary Souvenir,* one of the many successful annuals of the 1820s and 1830s that brought short stories, poetry, and brief memoirs to an increasing middle-class readership anxious to expand its knowledge.[4] Contributed to by leading and aspiring authors of both sexes and illustrated with etchings that often inspired the stories, the annuals were published for Christmas gift-giving and eagerly purchased. Basically, they were "safe" reading, especially for women. Whatever the strange or unhappy fate of a particular hero or heroine, the implicit message stressed home and family. For the reader, the annuals offered harmless adventures with moral lessons in prose and poetry; for the publisher, an impressive income; for the author, publication and payment of five pounds or perhaps ten pounds. Little wonder, then, that Mary Shelley opened her letter to Watts by apologizing for the delay in her response to his invitation for Lyndsay to submit material.

Lyndsay was out of the country. In his stead, Mary Shelley now sends a packet of writing he consigned to her care for Watts. As for submitting "small pieces" by either Shelley or herself, she has nothing just then to offer and is too busy to take on any. She has a short story that would fill nine pages, and two short mythological dramas, but does not send them because she assumes them too lengthy for his needs at that point. She would be glad if he were interested in them for the next year's annual. Finally, she thanks him for sending a gift volume, but refuses his request to include her signature among the autographs he will publish. By habit, she tells him, she withdraws her name from public notice. No need to mention that Shelley's father, disappointed and scandalized by his son, only agreed to her allowance in 1824 to support Percy Florence on the conditions that she repay it when she eventually inherited from the Shelley estate and that she kept the Shelley name out of public notice. Because of this fiat, her own publications had to be credited not to Mary Shelley, but simply to "the author of Frankenstein." In the preface to *The Literary Souvenir* for 1827, Watts regrets that the articles received from Mr. David Lyndsay and the author of *Frankenstein* were too late for inclusion.

What did this reveal? That the author David Lyndsay is abroad somewhere; that he is interested enough in publishing to forward material; that Mary Shelley and Lyndsay were sufficiently close for her to represent him to a publisher. It also suggests that perhaps Mary Shelley placed Lyndsay's stories "The Three Damsels: A Tale of Halloween" and "The Bridal Ornaments: A Legend of Thuringia" in Rudolph Ackermann's[5] competing *Forget-Me-Not* annual for 1827. Not a great deal of information.

Mary Shelley's second Lyndsay letter was to Henry Colburn, the publisher of her novel *The Last Man*.[6] Written at about the same time as the Watts letter, this one is a proposal, an attempt to sell Lyndsay. Mary Shelley assumes that Colburn has of course heard of Mr. Lyndsay as the author of *Dramas of the Ancient World* and *Tales of the Wild and the Wonderful*. The earlier work, especially, was successful and highly spoken of in literary circles. "It is indeed a production of genius," she says, somewhat escalating her April 1822 opinion of *Dramas* when she first read them and wrote to a friend:

. . . by a strange coincidence, the author (one David Lindsey [*sic*]) has chosen three subjects treated by Lord Byron; Cain, the Deluge and Sardanapalus. The two first are treated quite differently. Cain begins *after* the death of Abel & is entitled the Destiny & death of Cain. I mention them because they are works of considerable talent, and strength of poetry & expression; although of course in comparison with Lord Byron as unlike as Short life and Immortality.

Now, Mary Shelley announces that Lyndsay's new work, almost complete, will also be a collection of dramas, even more poetical, including *The Revolt of the Wilderness, The Festival of the Earth,* and *The Wedding of Undine.* In addition, he is translating a lengthy German drama of the highest poetic imagination, *Der Zauber Liebe—Magic Love* by Alarn. She would be very glad if Colburn would enter into a negotiation with her friend.

Mary Shelley sent the third Lyndsay letter in June 1828, just after she returned from Paris. Again, she represents Lyndsay to an editor, forwarding articles and verses for the author who was himself then in Paris. She describes him as the successful author of *Dramas of the Ancient World* and a contributor to *Blackwood's* and other annuals. If this material does not meet the editor's needs, Lyndsay would welcome suggestions as to topics. Apparently, Mary Shelley and Lyndsay were friends between 1826 and 1828 and Lyndsay appears to travel a good deal.

It was Mary Shelley's second David Lyndsay letter that opened the trail that February. Because of the books mentioned, I began a search of library catalogs to see if they revealed anything more about the author: From the largest collections, like the British Library, Oxford's Bodleian Library, The Library of Congress, to small holdings, all they listed were *Dramas,* and one or two short stories. Oddly, none appeared to note *Tales.* The *National Union Catalog* indicated that *Dramas* was available only in a handful of rare book collections, the closest a distance of 150 miles from my home. Though curious, I decided that reading Lyndsay at that point seemed an overexpenditure of time for a relatively simple matter. Surely Lyndsay would surface some other way.

The *Dictionary of National Biography (DNB),* that twenty-two-volume compendium that lists the personages of Britain from ancient times through the nineteenth century, contained nine David Lindsays or Lyndsays, among them a renowned Scottish poet who lived between 1490 and 1555. Clearly, not Mary Shelley's David Lyndsay. But in March, rereading the letter and some notes, I realized not only that Lyndsay had the same name as the Scottish poet, but that the book catalogs indicated *Dramas* was published by William Blackwood, the prestigious Scottish publisher. I hadn't found Lyndsay in England or the United States. Perhaps Scotland was the answer.

In March, Alan Bell, a colleague and then assistant keeper

at the National Library of Scotland in Edinburgh, responded
with exciting news: In addition to *Dramas,* Blackwood had also
published some of Lyndsay's contributions to *Blackwood's Magazine* in 1821–2; the library owned a number of letters from
Lyndsay to Blackwood dated 1821–29, typical of "literary aspirant's," mailed from a variety of in-care-of addresses in London.

Alan had glanced at the letters and sent brief summaries of
a few, among them one that mentioned Lyndsay's acquaintances
included Mrs. Shelley, the author Charles Lamb ("but not as
Lyndsay"), and Dr. Kitchener. The most interesting information
for Alan was a Lyndsay letter of May 5, 1825, indicating that
Hurst and Robinson were publishing Lyndsay's *Tales of the Wild
and the Wonderful.* This proved that *Tales,* published anonymously, was not an early work of the important Victorian author
George Borrow, as literary critics believed. The *Tales* would
now rightfully be attributed to David Lyndsay. Lyndsay's cover
was blown. And now it was clear why *Tales* was not listed under
Lyndsay's name in library catalogs; it was listed among the many
works of George Borrow. Reading *Dramas* and *Tales* moved
from the bottom of my list to close to the top.

Alan also arranged to send a photograph of a four-page,
undated letter in which Lyndsay sent Blackwood gossip about
Mrs. Shelley and her friends. For Alan, finding these answers
provided "a Friday afternoon's pleasant employment." For me,
hooked on the passing comment that Lamb, a friend of Mary
Shelley and her father, knew Lyndsay "but not as Lyndsay,"
Alan's answers transformed my interest in David Lyndsay from
a brief footnote to a twelve-year search. Meanwhile, I began my
search for the even-more-elusive Walter Sholto Douglas.

## CHAPTER 2

# OLD FRIENDS

WALTER SHOLTO DOUGLAS and Isabella Robinson Douglas first appear in Mary Shelley's letter of July 28, 1827, to her friend Jane Williams Hogg. Mary Shelley, her son Percy Florence, eight, and her friends' thirteen-year-old daughter, Mary Hunt, had just left London for Sompting, a seaside town on England's south coast, to take up residence with "sweet Isabel," whose health just then had improved. But Isabella's condition was undermined by her extreme anxiety about "D," from whom they received melancholy letters. Mary Shelley's letter indicates that the Douglases' fate was tied to the funeral of a certain Lord M on the next Monday and the reading of his will that follows. With that event, "certainty will come." Her letter also suggests that the Douglases are newlyweds. Why else did Mary Shelley explain that "Isabel is M^rs Douglas here" and that Mary Hunt will write to her parents "of M^rs D." Until mid-October, Mary Shelley remained in the south of England, preoccupied with the affairs of the Douglases.

Compassion and involvement in the troubles of a dear friend are not unusual for women, then or now. Recent studies show that networks of middle-class women, some relatives, others close friends, gained particular importance in the nineteenth century.[1] Men in the newly emerging middle class, feeling in their hands the gold dust of industrialization, spent more and more time away from their families. Wives, sisters, and daughters, relegated to remain at home, turned to other women for aid, comfort, and advice. Kept within proper limits, charitable acts for friend or impoverished stranger were among the few areas outside the home considered acceptable for ladies of the middle class. Ladies might carry a basket of food to a laborer's starving family. They might rush to the side of a beloved friend to nurse and restore. It was understood, of course, that all such deeds were not to divert the woman's attention from the management of her own household, her servants and nursemaids, her children, and, above all, the needs of her husband.

The demands on Mary Shelley were far different. Widowed in July 1822, she struggled to establish a life for herself and her young son. Before leaving Italy in 1823, already the author of three published books, she confidently found "something inspiriting" in her future ability to support herself and Percy Florence through her own writing and Shelley's manuscripts even if Sir Timothy Shelley, her wealthy father-in-law, "behaves ill."[2] Within the four years since her return to England, she published her edition of Shelley's *Posthumous Poems* and her third novel, *The Last Man,* a grim story of the end of civilization, as well as shorter works. Despite these successes, the reality of her struggle was harsh. Though she and Percy Florence were heirs of Shelley's then-ample estate, while her father-in-law lived, her income entirely depended on her own writing and Shelley's father's whims. If displeased, Sir Timothy held a sword over her through his threat, carried out several times over the years, to stop the repayable allowance—a loan against the estate—he grudgingly provided for his unwanted grandson. Sir Timothy also refused ever to meet Mary Shelley, depriving her of any comfort she might have found within Shelley's family. Only to her own father could she look for family closeness, though unfortunately, not for financial relief. On the contrary, Mary Shelley, always short of funds herself until Sir Timothy's death in 1844, often supplied money to her beloved, ever-strapped father. Still, through Godwin's circles and what remained of her own, she reestablished old friendships and made new ones.

The challenge for Mary Shelley, both socially and financially in the London of the 1820s, was to work around the many restrictions English life was placing on ladies. By necessity and inclination, she had the courage to reject some of these restraints, but many remained. Lacking the apartments, food, and servants necessary to invite mixed company in a stiffening culture, she "could not dream of society" being "un-dinner giving."[3] For the most part, her limited means only allowed her to serve tea or simple dinners for relatives or close women friends. She also found a welcome social outlet through John Howard Payne, the American playwright and actor now remembered for his song "Home, Sweet Home," who unsuccessfully courted the young widow. Though she rejected his suit, they remained friends. Over a number of years, he provided Mary Shelley with free theater passes. With these, she could invite a female friend for an evening out, provided they could find the almost mandatory male escort. When Payne was abroad, his absence as "Cavalier to escort" her and Jane Williams to the theater forced them to remain "like good housewives at our several homes."[4] On a rare occasion when Mary Shelley and Jane Williams attended the opera without a "shadow," they spoke only Italian, a foreigner not being subject to the same rules as an Englishwoman.[5] Indeed, ladies were expected to be accompanied by someone, a man, a child, a servant, even when walking on the street or riding the public, horse-drawn trams.

The practical challenges of Mary Shelley's life were compounded by tormented memories of her lost life with Shelley. From earliest childhood, she had an acute sense of isolation, perhaps because her mother died in giving birth to her or perhaps because she never got along with Godwin's second wife, whom Godwin married when his only daughter was four. Mary Shelley's family life, with her stepmother's two children, Claire and Charles Clairmont; her mother's child from an earlier love affair, Fanny Imlay; and William, a half brother from the new marriage, was always unsettled as much by family jealousies and her own precocity as by her father's inability to make enough money to support this variegated household. However these reasons coalesced, though Mary Shelley loved her father and the memory of the mother she never knew, she carried with her when she eloped with Shelley not only copies of her parents' books but also her childhood hunger for both love and a sense of belonging. With the adored and adoring Shelley, despite their eight years of wandering in England and then Italy, despite the deaths of three of their four children, she found an emotional center. Now Shelley was gone. Italy was gone. More isolated than ever, she had to find a path of her own in a society that increasingly demanded a woman's place be within the home. But she had no real home, only a series of rented lodgings she labored to maintain. In July 1827, she notified her landlady she would permanently leave her Kentish Town apartment. Her reason to live in that village was gone.

Jane Williams, her beloved friend, had moved with her young son and daughter from Kentish Town to Maida Place sometime in May. There, already three months pregnant, she took up residence as Mrs. Thomas Jefferson Hogg. It was a "marriage" unsanctified by church or state. So, too, was her earlier marriage to Edward Williams, who drowned with Shelley. She had to enter common-law arrangements; her first, and only lawful husband, reputedly a man given heavily to drink, was in London and very much alive.

In that era, each divorce required a separate act of Parliament. Jane Williams lacked the qualifications: One had to be very rich; one had to be a man. Even if cruel or adulterous, men were financially protected. They also retained full custody of the children. Only in 1840 did the first changes in these one-sided laws occur, brought about by Mary Shelley's friend Caroline Norton. A writer and herself deprived by a vindictive husband for four years of even visiting her children, Norton led the fight for reform. Her tracts *Observations on the Natural Claim of a Mother to the Custody of Her Young Children* (1837) and *A Plain Letter to the Lord Chancellor* (1839), published under the name Pearce Stevenson, persuaded Parliament in 1839 to change England's custody law, allowing children under the age of seven to remain with their mothers and giving mothers subsequent visitation rights. In preparing her tracts, Norton turned for suggestions and comments to Mary Shelley, who knew firsthand about the court's commanding power and the custody laws.

Mary Shelley learned those lessons in 1817, three years

after she eloped with Shelley, when Harriet Shelley, Shelley's first wife, pregnant by a lover she believed had abandoned her, drowned herself. After a long legal battle, custody of the two children of that marriage was given to a court-appointed guardian because it deemed Shelley an unfit father. The case against Shelley was not the abandonment of his wife. Nor was the issue financial: To her father's yearly two hundred pounds he provided two hundred pounds a year in support for wife and children.[6] Rather, it concerned itself with Shelley's philosophical belief in freedom within relationships that brought him to invite Harriet Shelley to live as a friend with him and his new soul-mate, an offer she refused.[7] And it concerned the atheism expressed in his poem *Queen Mab* and his pamphlet on *The Necessity of Atheism.* The Court of Chancery's judgment, drawing its own fine line, ultimately pronounced its decision to deny Shelley custody of his children based not on what they considered to be Shelley's renegade religious or moral opinions, but because the Court held that his immoral views led to immoral conduct.[8]

After Shelley drowned, Mary Shelley herself had reason to fear the power of the courts. Her father-in-law tried after Shelley's death to prove she was not his legal wife. When this failed, he offered to raise Percy Florence but only if Mary Shelley gave him full custody. Left with only this one living remnant of her life with Shelley, having "endured the agony of knowing that those forms whom I had borne & nourished had before me, decayed,"[9] Mary Shelley adamantly refused. Nor would she give up her fight for financial assistance from Sir Timothy. It was this fight that forced her back to the England she loathed a year after Shelley's death. Her only consolation was that she would at least be in the company of her beloved father and her idealized, angelic Jane Williams. But now the angelic Jane was twice transformed.

One of these transformations centered in Thomas Jefferson Hogg, who played an earlier, important role in the Shelleys' lives. Shelley and Hogg had met at Oxford and become fast friends. When Shelley papered the campus with his pamphlet *The Necessity of Atheism,* the outraged authorities called him in, demanding to know if he was the author. He refused to answer.

They then called in Hogg, and asked him about the pamphlet's authorship. He, too, refused to answer. The two, to the fury of both their fathers, were expelled. Hogg subsequently redeemed himself with his family by becoming a lawyer. Shelley only continued to anger his father. First, he eloped with Harriet Westbrook, the seventeen-year-old daughter of a wealthy innkeeper. Then after two years, he left her with one child and expecting a second, and eloped to the Continent with Mary Godwin, the daughter of the radicals Godwin and Wollstonecraft. To add to the gossip, they took with them Claire Clairmont, Mary Shelley's stepsister, giving rise to the rumor that Godwin had sold his daughters to the wealthy young heir.[10] At this point, Sir Timothy Shelley totally disavowed his son.

Hogg and Shelley remained close friends until Hogg made unwanted advances toward Harriet Shelley. She complained to Shelley, who broke with his college friend. The issue was not that Harriet Shelley was his wife. Rather, Hogg broke Shelley's code by secretly trying to force himself on her after she made it quite clear she was not interested. Shelley renewed his friendship with Hogg only after the elopers returned to London, and Hogg readily accepted Shelley's new companion. Soon after they met, encouraged by Shelley, Mary Shelley and Hogg began a lovers' courtship though she was already pregnant with Shelley's child. That Mary Shelley's pregnancy almost certainly prevented their relationship from going beyond the verbal. A short time after her child was born and within ten days died, Mary Shelley withdrew from the experiment. Eventually, irritated by Hogg's extremely self-centered nature, she came to dislike him. But their rocky friendship endured, tied by their mutual love for Shelley and then for Jane Williams.

When Jane Williams left Italy soon after Edward Williams drowned with Shelley, she carried with her Mary Shelley's letter of introduction to Thomas Jefferson Hogg. After a secret courtship, Jane Williams united with Hogg until the end of their lives. It was not Jane Hogg's new union that disturbed Mary Shelley, or even the secrecy of the courtship. Mary Shelley realized her friend, unlike herself, could not exist independently. What disturbed and tormented Mary Shelley in the summer of

1827 was learning that dear Jane, beloved Jane, angelic Jane, had betrayed their friendship. For some time, Jane Williams had been gossiping about the Shelleys' relationship in Italy in which she cast Mary Shelley as cold and unloving to their dead friend. True, there had been a period when Mary Shelley had felt estranged from Shelley. In August 1818, Shelley had left Mary Shelley and their two children at Lucca to accompany Mary Shelley's stepsister Claire Clairmont to Este, some 105 miles away. Allegra, Claire Clairmont's illegitimate child by Byron, was at Byron's Este villa. The two journeyed there so the mother could visit with her child. Once there, Shelley wrote to Mary Shelley, asking her to pack their household and join them. During the six-day journey, their one-year-old daughter Clara was taken ill with dysentery. On September 24, Clara died. The following June, after another period of travel in Italy, their remaining child, William, also died of dysentery. Bitterly, Mary Shelley wrote in her Journal on August 4, 1819:

> I begin my journal on Shelley's birthday—We have now lived now five years together & if all the events of the five years were blotted out I might be happy—but to have won & then cruelly have lost the associations of four years is not an accident that to which the human mind can bend to without much suffering

It is not at all unusual for couples who suffer the loss of a child to feel estranged. And in the case of Mary Shelley, complex, introspective, it is not surprising that, having lost both her children within ten months, in mourning she returned to her childhood sense of isolation. Some of the pain was relieved with the birth of their son Percy Florence in November 1819, but the rift between the couple was slow to mend.

Even when their relationship was strong, Shelley was occasionally interested in, and inspired by, other women. Biographers speculate about whether those relationships ever went beyond the platonic. There is no evidence to prove they did or that these friendships caused a rift between the couple. But the deaths of their children had a profound impact on both parents.

Shelley, cut off from Mary Shelley by the inwardness of her mourning, no doubt suffering with his own emotions of loss and guilt, felt himself painfully alone. He complained to friends. In the last weeks of his life, he attached himself to Jane Williams, for whom he wrote a series of poems. But the Shelleys' letters and journals make one realize that the period was far from one of complete estrangement. There were shared times, shared closeness, shared problems. In fact, in the spring of 1822, Mary Shelley was again pregnant. When Mary Shelley suffered a life-threatening miscarriage, Shelley rescued her by putting her in an ice bath to stop the hemorrhaging. Two weeks later, Shelley and Edward Williams drowned. What might have happened to the Shelleys had he lived? Perhaps separation. But complete reunion between this couple, given both their natures, was more than possible.

When Shelley drowned, Mary Shelley not unnaturally forgot the difficulties of living with him. With his death, his shortcomings disappeared. She remembered only the poet, the philosopher, the lover. Grief-stricken, she turned to her sister-widow whom she had earlier dismissed as pretty but superficial: Following Shelley's lead, she attached herself to Jane Williams. Mary Shelley aided her, comforted her, and expressed to her her own deep sorrow. No doubt she added to Jane Williams's knowledge of the Shelleys' relationship by blaming herself, in her sorrow, for all their differences. Jane Williams's stories about the Shelleys four years later, perhaps because she was as superficial as Mary Shelley originally believed, took away from Mary Shelley everything fine about her relationship with Shelley, and concentrated only on how she had hurt their revered, lost poet. When Mary Shelley learned of these whispered tales, she grieved as if a beloved friend had died. For her, one had. But she continued to address her friend as *dear girl* and *dear angel,* probably as much out of sensitivity to her friend's delicate pregnancy as her own pride and hurt. In October, Jane Hogg gave birth to a girl; Mary Shelley was asked to be godmother. Finally, after months of grief, provoked by Jane Hogg, a confrontation: abject, emotional apologies from Jane Hogg; and reconciliation. But their relationship was never again the same. Mary Shelley's involvement with Mr. and Mrs. Walter Sholto Douglas in the summer of 1827 began in the midst of her acute suffering at this betrayal and loss.

# CHAPTER 3

# NEW FRIENDS

UNTIL THE LYNDSAY LETTERS arrived in mid-May, I concentrated on reviewing the Douglas-Robinson connection. Hunting in the Mary Shelley correspondence for overlooked Douglas clues, I was drawn more and more deeply into considering Mary Shelley's psyche.

Clearly, in comforting Isabella Douglas, Mary Shelley also took comfort. She filled the vacuum created by the break in her emotional tie to Jane Hogg with the practical and emotional needs of Isabella Douglas, whose health and finances were equally distressed. Had Mary Shelley not suffered herself? Was she not suffering again even then? Who better to know the meaning of affliction, to want the wholehearted aid of another?

Apparently, Jane Hogg knew the details of Isabella and "D's" situation, and it was to her that Mary Shelley confided the progress of the couple's affairs. And who better to demonstrate the meaning of true friendship to than to Jane Hogg? Mary Shelley's letters from July through October chronicle her concern and sympathy as they trace Isabella Douglas's wavering health and her husband's financial distress until he at last is able to join them in the south of England and, after several more months, they leave for France. The letters also trace Mary Shelley's deepening attachment to Isabella Douglas.

Mary Shelley expresses her pleasure from that attachment in letters to other friends as well as to Jane Hogg. To Teresa Guiccioli, Byron's last lover, she writes in Italian of her joy "with a friend of mine who I dearly love and who feels the liveliest affection for me . . . But within a few weeks her husband is coming—they are leaving for Paris."[1] John Howard Payne she warns: "take care of your heart" if he visits them, "for though my friend is a sweet little girl—she is married."[2]

From Payne she "commissions" on September 23 an extraordinary favor. Her friends plan to go from Brighton to Dieppe. Though she is fully aware that "they wont give passports in London except to the persons themselves," would he procure a passport for them? Payne agrees. Her letter two days later sends a physical description of the travelers. "M^rs Douglas is short, i.e. an atom shorter than I—dark, pretty with large dark eyes & hair curled in the neck . . . M^r Douglas is my height—slim—dark with curly black hair—the passport must be drawn out for M^r & M^rs Sholto Douglas." It must also include Mr. Douglas's sister, Mrs. Carter and her two sons as well as Mary Shelley, who had decided to join them as far as Dieppe, and Percy Florence. She also appends two signatures in addition to her own: "Isabel Douglas.—Sholto Douglas." Payne, and a "double" of Isabella Douglas, whose "signature alone is a miracle," obtained the falsified passports.[3]

This unusual deceit could have been an effort to save the financially pressed couple the expense of a London trip. But there were several other things—brief phrases—that puzzled. When Mary Shelley and Isabella Douglas were evicted from their Sompting rooms because the landlord found a higher-paying tenant, Mary Shelley complained they must "go tomorrow to look for lodgings, & remove *without milk*."[4] Before Douglas joined them at their new seacoast location of Arundel, he pleases Mary Shelley because he "now seriously thinks of les culottes."[5] "Without milk"? Slang expressions of the period offered no explanations. "French pants"? Perhaps they had considered somewhere other than France and this indicated that Douglas had given in to his wife's wishes. He would wear French trousers, i.e., they would go to Paris.

And to Paris those passports took them in October 1827. Mary Shelley, traveling with Isabella's father and sister, visited them there in April 1828. Still adoring the lovely Isabella Douglas, Mary Shelley left England "pining"[6] to see her. But on arrival, disaster struck. Mary Shelley fell ill with smallpox, and remained bedridden and quarantined for some two weeks of her month stay with the beloved Isabella and her *sposo*. Eventually sufficiently recovered, she also made new friends in prominent Anglo-French society, including General Lafayette, renowned for his part in the American war for independence as well as his role in the French revolutionary period; the already famous writer Stendhal; the Garnett sisters; a Miss Clarke; the critic and historian Claude Fauriel; and the young Prosper Mérimée, now world-famous for his libretto for the opera *Carmen,* then just beginning his career. Prosper Mérimée provided another, far less attractive perspective on Mary Shelley's beloved Isabella Douglas.

Mérimée, then twenty-five, appears to have fallen in love with Mary Shelley. Mérimée often fell in love. Perhaps Mary Shelley sensed this when she returned his letter, one that appears to have proposed marriage, because it contained "the expression of sentiments which you will probably repent of later."[7] Though rejecting his amorous advances, she kept open the way to friendship. She promised to write to him. Hopefully, they would meet again in Paris or London. Neither side of this correspondence had been found, until 1976 when I discovered seven letters from Mérimée to Mary Shelley.[8] Mérimée's half of their exchange, sometimes petulant and self-centered, almost always lively and flirtatious, tells of both their literary aspirations. The letters trace Mary Shelley's active contribution—through translations and book reviews[9]—in bringing Mérimée's early works to the attention of the British public. The letters also sent reports of Mary Shelley's Paris circle after she returned home in May 1828—particularly of her close friends, the Douglases.

Mérimée's first letter, July 5, 1828, describes Isabella Douglas as bored at least twelve hours a day. He judges her less severely now because he considers her the victim of ennui, which might invite unusual behavior. His letters of July 28 and September 6 merely mention seeing her. But his October 5 letter sends the unexpected story that Claude Fauriel regularly womanizes with Isabella Douglas. At that point, Mérimée launches

into a lengthy, cutting critique of Isabella. He is surprised that
Mary Shelley chose such a friend. True, Mrs. Douglas is amiable
but she is not suited for the role of beloved friend that Mary
Shelley gives her. Mary Shelley herself has the qualities for this
role; Isabella Douglas has not. Mérimée rarely sees her, and is
bothered when he does. With heavy irony, he describes the conditions that would best suit Mrs. Douglas's character, which he
regards as coquettish and flighty. He prescribes for her a quick
and rich widowhood. Then she would be even more amiable,
even more the toast of the town. She would attract many fashionable young men, which would be her proper role, if everything were for the best in the best of all possible worlds.
Mérimée's next two letters make no mention of Isabella Douglas, but in his last letter to Mary Shelley, dated February 4,
1829, protesting against the institution of legal marriage, he indicates that the marriage of the Douglases is a "bel argument"
against the so-called good that occurs within the bonds of marriage.

Mérimée's disparaging remarks about Isabella Douglas dramatically conflicted with Mary Shelley's own image. If anything,
her sympathy for her friend seemed to expand after her visit. In
June 1828, she considered Isabella a "victim" whose sufferings
are matchless. As for Isabella's husband: "What D. now is, I
will not describe in a letter—one only trusts that the diseased
body acts on the diseased mind, & that both may be at rest ere
long."[10] Apparently, Mary Shelley felt Walter Sholto Douglas
was the source of his wife's problem. With this, commentary
about the Douglases in Mary Shelley's letters end. But the trail
continues in Mary Shelley's *Journals*.[11]

Mary Shelley began her *Journals* on July 28, 1814, one
month before her seventeenth birthday, on the day she and
Shelley eloped to the Continent. She ended her fifth, and last,
*Journal* on October 2, 1844, seven years before her death. The
first *Journal* was to be a joint project with Shelley, but soon
became hers. In that, and the next, she kept abbreviated, almost
daily accounts of what the Shelleys wrote and read, their travels,
friends, and major family events. After Shelley's death, the
*Journals,* kept less frequently, were primarily a means for Mary

Shelley to express privately the anguish she suffered in her widowhood as she struggled to keep her independence, to nourish her imagination, to provide for herself and her son. In these pages, she expressed her pain when "proper" society so often turned its back on her because of the Shelleys' scandalous elopement. And resentment, that for her son's sake Shelley's disapproving father held so much control over her life. Most of all, the introspective, cerebral, passionate Mary Shelley used these pages to express her loss, and yearning, for the special kind of love relationship she shared with Shelley.

It is no surprise that Isabella Douglas should show up in Mary Shelley's *Journal*. On September 26, 1827, still with the Douglases at Arundel, in the south of England, she speaks of having shaken off the dead calm of her life "interesting myself deeply for one whose destiny is so strange . . ." wishing to "hover a good genius round" her lovely friend's path—her destiny to form ties of friendship rather than love. On December 5 of that same year, alone and unhappy in London, she expresses her sorrow that she has lost one friend (Jane Hogg) and is divided from another (Isabella Douglas). On February 12, 1828, she records that her otherwise monotonous life is brightened by some friends, including the Robinsons. And on April 11, Mary Shelley notes that she leaves for Paris, in the company of Mr. Robinson and Isabella's sister Julia, who has become Mary Shelley's new young companion. At the time, Mary Shelley is "sick at heart" but pines to see Isabella Douglas. The next entry, July 8, explains her sickness—she had smallpox. Still she records that "The Parisians were very amiable & a monster to look at as I was—I tried to be agreeable to compensate to them." The Robinson family continue to appear in the *Journals,* until the early 1840s, when Mary Shelley broke with them.

But only two other *Journal* entries refer to Isabella Douglas. On May 13, 1829, a melancholy Mary Shelley feels that all she loves flies from her. For a moment, she vows to bury herself in nature's deepest recess and live in her single sensations, but immediately she undeceives herself: She cannot live for herself alone and be happy. With Isabella, she might have been happy but "that dream is over." Finally, an extraordinary *Journal* entry on December 1, 1830, that appears to reverse all past reveries about Mrs. Douglas. Having just seen her, Mary Shelley's words echo Mérimée's: "Good heavens—is this the being I adored—she was ever false yet enchanting—now she has lost her fascinations—probably, because I can no longer serve her she take[s] no more trouble to please me—." Still unwilling to give up that past dream, she adds: "but also she surely is not the being she once was." What caused this change of heart?

Someone else's journal completed the picture I then had of Mary Shelley's relationships with the Douglas-Robinson family. Mary Shelley's father kept a daily log from 1788, when he was thirty-two, until two weeks before his death in April 1836. Year after year, Godwin briefly noted what he wrote and read, whom he visited with, and—cryptically—major family events. A number of entries referred to the Douglas-Robinsons, providing otherwise unavailable information. On November 12, 1827, Godwin dined at Mary Shelley's, joined afterward by "Robinson, père de Douglas;" Godwin joined a Miss Figg and Miss Robinson at Mary Shelley's house on March 2, 1828; eight days later he goes to a gallery with Mary Shelley and Miss Robinson; on June 25, 1828, he visits Mary Shelley and Julia Robinson at Hastings; three days later, Mr. Robinson arrives; on August 31 Godwin dines at the Robinson's Park Cottage home with Mary Shelley; on September 21, he dines there without Mary Shelley; on May 15, 1829, Godwin dines at Mary Shelley's home with Julia and Eliza Robinson; on June 5, 7, and 14, October 6, October 22, and November 18, Godwin sees Mary Shelley in company of one or more Robinsons; on May 10, 1830, he dines at the Robinsons' with Mary Shelley and a number of others, including Rothwell, the artist who would later paint her portrait; June 7, 1830, tea at Mary Shelley's with Thomas Moore and three Robinsons; on April 24, when Godwin visits Mary Shelley, Julia Robinson and a friend call; July 8, 1831, dines at the Robinsons' with Mary Shelley; February 12, 1834, dines with "Jos R" and others, including Mary Shelley; May 21, 1834, again dines with "J Robinson," Mary Shelley, and others.

It appeared every piece of information carried with it new problems. Why did Godwin refer to Mr. Robinson with the

French "père de Douglas" instead of simply describing Isabella Robinson Douglas's father in English? Perhaps his way of indicating the Douglases had gone to France? And who was this Miss Figg, who would show up again in the second volume of letters when Mary Shelley invited her to the theater?

To the Douglas-Robinson facts accumulated, I now added new details received in an ongoing information exchange with Emily Sunstein, then writing a biography of Mary Shelley. It appears the Robinsons are mentioned in a number of memoirs of the age. The editor Cyrus Redding wrote about the pleasant, convivial after-dinner conversations on poetry, philosophy, economy, politics, sometimes religion at the Robinson home in Paddington, near Maida Hill.[12] At these old-fashioned repasts, he first met Lord Dillon and a number of contributors to the *New Monthly Magazine*. Eliza Rennie recollected in her book *Traits of Character* meeting Thomas Moore at her friends the Robinsons' cottage-style house, with its tasteful, large garden. Thomas Moore's *Journal* notes visits to the Robinson cottage and its "little nest of beauties." On one occasion, he "Drove to Hampstead to see Miss Robinson; strange scene."

According to material found for Emily Sunstein by a researcher in England, Joshua Robinson was an Oxford graduate, gentleman, a builder, married to Rosetta Tomlins Robinson, and had a large family. Mary Shelley's letters indicated that there were at least five daughters and four sons. Most important for this search, the *Dictionary of National Biography* identifies Henry Drummond Wolff (1830–1908) as the husband of Adeline, the daughter of Walter Sholto Douglas. Also, possibly from Wolff's autobiographical *Rambling Recollections,* the wedding took place at the consulate in Leghorn on January 22, 1853.[13]

All the Robinson references in these accounts might not refer to Mary Shelley's Robinsons, though her letters confirmed the Paddington cottage location. Particularly interesting were Eliza Rennie's recollections about the Robinsons from her book *Traits of Character* because she tied the Robinsons and Thomas Moore together. Of all the material, the most important was the new trail opened by the *Dictionary of National Biography:* Adeline Douglas was the daughter of Isabella Robinson and Walter

Sholto Douglas. Now I had something missing in the letters, the journals, and all the other sources: a family picture.

Unfortunately, none of Isabella Douglas's letters to Mary Shelley exist among the Shelley papers or, it appears, elsewhere. Undoubtedly they would shed light on husband and wife. With so much still missing, I turned again to Mary Shelley's correspondence and the first references to her new friends on June 27, 1827, to try to trace that mysterious Lord M whose will would determine the Douglases' fate. The first stop was the pages of the London *Times* or the *Morning Chronicle,* the newspaper Mary Shelley read daily. On July 23, a small announcement had appeared in the *Times.* George Douglas, sixteenth earl of Morton, died on July 17 and was to be buried on July 30—the Monday following Mary Shelley's letter. Aged sixty-six, and leaving no issue, his estates were to go to his cousin, George Sholto Douglas. Here was a combination of names that led me to believe I was close to the end of the hunt. True, the sixteenth earl had left no heirs. But Isabella's husband was a Douglas. And George Sholto Douglas, a cousin, was to inherit the estates. Surely Walter Sholto Douglas was a nephew, or cousin.

To find out, I turned to *Burke's Peerage.* Since 1829, these thick, red books have listed those who married, who begat, who died, who inherited among the British aristocracy and landed gentry. Where *Burke's* failed in reliability was in omitting the birth year of females, and even in omitting females in some families altogether. If Douglas was a common name in Britain, surely Sholto was not. On the contrary, it turned out that Sholto Douglas is an old Scottish name used in combination with other names by a large number of families. Still, it was easy to locate the earl of Morton in *Burke's.* The listing confirmed and added to the details of the obituary. No heirs. I searched every branch of the prodigious Morton line for my man. I found nothing, and thought either I had the wrong family or Sholto Douglas was someone's illegitimate son and therefore not included in *Burke's.*

In April 1978 I wrote to Bruce Barker-Benfield, a colleague and assistant librarian at Oxford's Bodleian Library. In 1975 when Lord James Abinger, heir to the Shelley family papers, put his collection on deposit at the Bodleian, Bruce was put in charge. I informed him of the new Douglas clue. The *Dictionary of National Biography,* while it omits the father, does list the daughter in the context of her marriage to Sir Henry Drummond Wolff. And R. Glynn Grylls, in her 1938 biography *Mary Shelley,* mentions Isabella, afterward Mrs. Sholto Douglas, as the mother-in-law of Sir Henry Drummond Wolff.[14] Had Bruce any ideas about searching out Mr. Douglas?

Bruce confirmed that Sholto with or without another Christian name is common in the vast Douglas family. He tried to find the husband by searching under his wife's name in the four-volume *Douglas Book* and *Fingland (Kirkcudbrightshire) and their Descendants.* She appears in neither. He had "only one positive piece of negative information." Sholto Douglas was *not* one of the (legitimate) brothers of the sixteenth earl of Morton.

Whoever Walter Sholto Douglas was, it appeared certain that his fate and his bride's would be determined by Morton's will. The Royal Commission on Historical Manuscripts in London referred me to the Scottish Record Office, which fortunately had the sixteenth earl's will in its holdings. The responding librarian also conjectured that the Sholto Douglas I was searching for was "in fact Sholto George Douglas, George Douglas's eldest son, later 17th earl." The will contained many provisions for his benefit, as heir. Perhaps Sholto Douglas was in a special bequest in a deed dated June 6, 1835, and registered separately on June 23, 1858, that left his son a Bassandyne Bible and a "badge or jewel" of the Order of the Thistle, both formerly the property of the fourth earl, James, the Regent Morton. The librarian offered copies of both.

The dates on the will and the deed seemed odd. Why so late, when the earl died in July 1827? I assumed the will would explain that, too, and felt confident that the Douglas search was at an end. Surely the will would reveal all. Not bad. I had only begun to work on the Douglas puzzle in April. Clearing it up would allow me to concentrate on Lyndsay. That concentration was much needed because in the intervening months, the David Lyndsay microfilm arrived from the Library of Scotland and I learned from it that David Lyndsay was not David Lyndsay.

## CHAPTER 4

# YOURS VERY TRULY, DAVID LYNDSAY

THERE WERE THIRTY-TWO of David Lyndsay's microfilmed letters spanning August 1821 through September 1829, all to William Blackwood, Lyndsay's first publisher. Lyndsay had a reasonably legible nineteenth-century educated handwriting, distinguished by his preference for extraordinarily ornate capital letters. The *D* and *L* in his own name received particularly special flourish. But because microfilmed letters are the third copy of documents—from original to film to viewer screen—they present special challenges for deciphering: Words from one side of the page blur words on the reverse; dust specks add to punctuation; unnumbered and often undated pages had to be placed in logical order through content, postmarks, or other clues. But the hurdles were unimportant. One of those precious letters said David Lyndsay was not David Lyndsay. Perhaps another would tell who he was.

Lyndsay's first letter, dated August 27, 1821, introduced Blackwood to an urbane gentleman, much flattered by Blackwood's intention to publish the unknown Lyndsay's work in the prestigious *Blackwood's Edinburgh Magazine*—*"Maga."* Happy to receive Blackwood's "pecuniary acknowledgement," Lyndsay implies he really may not need money. He is delighted that Blackwood invites him to become a regular contributor to *"The Magazine"* and wants to publish a volume of his works. Lyndsay enthusiastically promises to prepare the volume at once. He follows this, and other respectful compliments expressed in the highly polite style of the era, with a question that suggests the aspiring author also has business acumen: "I do not know which you consider the best season for publishing in Edinburgh, here it is early in the Spring, but all that of course I leave to you." In closing, he asks Blackwood to write to him, as before, in care of Mrs. Carter at 5 Sloane Street, Brompton. It is clear that Lyndsay lives in London. What is unclear is whether Lyndsay directly approached the publisher—where then is that first letter?—or used an intermediary to bring his works to the attention of the Edinburgh house.

A *Bibliography of Articles in Blackwood's Magazine 1817–1825*[1] cites six certain, and one possible, Lyndsay publications:

> *Death, The of Isaiah—a Fragment;* Aug. 1822, XII, 205
> *First Murder, The; or, the Rejection of the Sacrifice . . .*
> (?) (doubtful) Oct. 1821, X, 321
> *Horae Gallicae. No. I. Raynouard's States of Blois;*
> May 1822, 539
> *Mount of Olives, The;* Dec. Part II, 1821, X, 654
> *Plague of Darkness, The: The Last Plague* Aug. 1821,
> IX, 955
> *Ring, The and the Stream;* Jan. 1822, XI, 50
> *Vigil of St. Mark,* X, 341;

This list indicated that Lyndsay's *Plague of Darkness* was the piece that impressed Blackwood sufficiently to invite its author to be a *Maga* regular. Such offers, of course, depend as much on sustaining the quality of the work submitted as reader reaction. Lyndsay was to discover this for himself.

Lyndsay's second letter, written on November 17, finds the author hard at work. Three months have passed since he agreed to prepare a collection, and Blackwood has just written to him with "friendly encouragement" apparently couched in a request for a progress report. The tone of Lyndsay's response is respectful, but also indicates he is his own man. His *Death of Cain* is in outline, but should be completed in about a fortnight. Originally, Lyndsay thought *Cain* would open his second volume (a project never fulfilled) but will send it for the first if Blackwood wishes. Lyndsay is also glad that his *Plague of Darkness* will be reprinted in the collection. He indicates that his *Deluge* and *Sardanapalus* are longish, that his *Foscari* is a sketch to be considered "hereafter," and the subject that most interests him at the moment is a tragedy about "Soul." As to the title of his volume, he first invites Blackwood to title it as he pleases, but then says he would "rather have them called Tragedies of the ancient World." Please let him know soon if he can have the extra fortnight he requires—he would be glad not to be obliged to hurry much. "Yours dear Sir, Very truly David Lyndsay."

Cain? The Deluge? Sardanapalus? Foscari? Anyone familiar with the works of Lord Byron would recognize these subjects not as Lyndsay's but Byron's. Though self-exiled to Italy in the wake of marital and sexual scandal, Byron continued to send his writings to John Murray, who published them in London. Celebrated or attacked, his works sold as quickly then as the recordings of superstars do now. His four dramas—*Cain, The Deluge, Sardanapalus, Foscari*—were announced to be separately published in London, beginning in December 1821. Did Lyndsay know?

His letter of December 1 proved he did. The pace of his writing has quickened. He sends the opening of *The Destiny of Cain*. He has finished *The Death of Cain*. He is not hurrying to finish the "waters of jealousy" because he will turn "heart and Soul" to writing a piece for *Maga*. He asks Blackwood to send the proofs the sooner the better: "*Lord Byron's Cain* is announced for Tuesday next—the 4th." He is pleased with the title Blackwood gives his volume—it is better than Tragedies or Scenes—he will send Cain by post on Monday—"Yours my dear Sir sincerely David Lyndsay."

The fact that Lyndsay knows about Byron's works does not prove he imitated them. In that era, there were countless instances of authors writing on the same subjects at the same time. Mary Shelley's novel *The Last Man* appeared amid a number of other works by that title; and her novel *Perkin Warbeck* was published within weeks of another author's *Perkin*. Byron himself gives us an instance of duplication of topic when his good friend Thomas Moore rushed his poem *The Love of the Angels* into print in 1823 because he had just learned that Byron was preparing to publish a drama on the same subject.[2]

The race is met. Lyndsay's *Dramas* is published mid-December. His letter of December 26 thanks Blackwood for the beautiful appearance of his volume and for the flattering review already published in *Maga*.[3] He asks Blackwood if he should try to get reviews in London papers, having "friends who can Serve me this way." He does, however, dread more than "severest criticisms" the "injudicious praises of friends." Blackwood should decide the matter.

Business matters attended to, Lyndsay, by invitation or inclination, now feels acquainted enough to talk more openly about himself and the literary world of London. He informs Blackwood he is several years younger than Byron and confesses that until recently he has been an "Idler." Now his ambition is to use the years before him to make the literary world speak of him. As to Byron's *Cain,* he read it with mingled "wonder admiration and regret." Lyndsay calls himself a David who expects the critics to cut him into "mince meat" for writing on the same subject as "this Goliath of Tragedy," calling Byron's work superb, the work of a daring spirit—such an antitraditional interpretation of Cain as a figure who can be admired for questioning his father's ways and setting his own standards may occur occasionally even to the most pious but few would publish them—for his daring, Byron is already attacked in the morning newspapers.

Lyndsay sends his opinion of other works as well. Thanking Blackwood for the gift of several volumes by other authors, he compliments the publisher on the last two copies of *Maga* as the best yet. He continues his literary survey with comments on an excellent article in the *Edinburgh Review* that carves up Percy Bysshe Shelley, indicating that he formerly knew Shelley's father-in-law. Finally, returning to his own writing, Lyndsay asks to hear quickly from Blackwood again as his friends are leaving their house (where he receives mail) and he himself is going to the south of England to avoid some weeks of the severe London frosts. "I am my dear Sir—Sincerely yours."

Lyndsay's next letter, circa January 8, 1822, returns to the subject of "puffing." Blackwood's response indicates he agrees with Lyndsay on the dangers of getting one's friends to write reviews of one's works. But Lyndsay will try to get someone to persuade Gifford, editor of the important *Quarterly Review,* to give *Dramas* a notice. Perhaps James Weale, one of Lyndsay's best friends, may be able to do this, as Weale knows many in the literary world. He hopes the sales will go well, and is grateful for compliments sent by Blackwood about the book. As for payment, rather than awaiting the sale of the edition and receiving seventy-five pounds, he would be "perfectly satisfied" with fifty pounds now. Again, he wishes an early reply as he intends to leave town as soon as possible, for his is a "constitution much weakened by suffering." In a postscript he adds he has been translating works by Raynouard; if Blackwood likes, he will send the first act for the February *Maga.*

A summary of the first five letters began to shape a profile of David Lyndsay: about thirty in 1821 (several years younger than Byron); health, poor; receives mail at the address of Mrs. Carter (unidentified) and James Weale (his friend); newly turned to writing; very talented, very lucky or both, to be picked up so readily by Blackwood; sufficiently well-read and self-confident to give Blackwood his opinion of other writers; sufficiently educated to be able to translate from French; polite or politic enough to defer to Blackwood's wishes; ambitious enough to be concerned with reviews and future publications; worldly enough to have friends in the literary circles of London. I could almost see him, fashionably dressed in top hat, tail coated at a literary salon, exchanging literary gossip or trying to appear indifferent as he is introduced as the author of that wonderful new collection of *Dramas.* Mr. David Lyndsay. Author.[4]

The letters that followed picked up the initial themes of the Lyndsay-Blackwood correspondence and expanded them. Lyndsay's next letter, January 15, thanks the publisher for sending the fifty pounds, as requested, for *Dramas.* He didn't see Dr. Stoddart's notice of the volume, but heard of it from several persons. He believes "we shall do well here." And, as if to describe some of the reasons for his confidence, he tells Blackwood that a friend is giving a copy to the great actor Charles Kemble, who is passionately fond of this sort of poetry. If Kemble, according to his custom, reads it aloud in company, it will be the best kind of advertisement. Another friend asks a famous pianist to set one of the passages to music. Lyndsay also confirms that he will follow Blackwood's plan regarding the translation of Raynouard, confiding that he has learned French and Italian "under the best Masters, and to speak them in the best Company." Blackwood apparently informed him that his works not only compete with Byron but with two other writers of the era: Bryan Waller Procter and George Croly. Lyndsay assures Blackwood that he had no idea of the new competition, dismissing it as "whimsical" and the old competition—Byron—as a means that will make his work more read. "I remain dear Sir Sincerely yours" . . . henceforward, send letters not addressed to me "but to James Weale Esq, putting my initials D.L. in the corner."

Three weeks later, February 8, a business letter gives Blackwood a progress report on the Raynouard translations. Procter is in a towering rage, believing some friend had told Lyndsay of his planned *Deluge*. Again, good reviews. Again, hopes of inducing Gifford to publish a review. Again, commentary on the Blackwood publications sent as gifts to Lyndsay. But Lyndsay also sends a complaint. When Blackwood published Lyndsay's drama *The Ring and the Stream* in *Maga* of January 1822, the compositor made many errors . . . if not disagreeable, could those blunders be mentioned in the next issue . . . "I am dear Sir, Very truly and sincerely yours."

Almost two months go by before the next, briefer letter of April 1. Lyndsay returns proofs (of *Horae Gallicae. No. I. Raynouard's States of Blois*); happily it had only one error. Among the customary comments about new and old reviews of *Dramas,* and observations about other authors, Lyndsay introduces two important biographical details. He didn't answer Blackwood's last letter sooner because he was "obliged to try Cheltenham waters during the last few Weeks, as a complaint in the Liver leaves me unhappily seldom entirely Master of either my time or purposes." Another piece of new information follows: He refers to the parsimony of "our Nation." As the name Lyndsay suggests, he is Scottish.

The next letter is undated. A clerk at *Blackwood's* docketed it as received in June 1822, but the content of the letter proves it was written sometime in early May. It is a cranky letter. Lyndsay's translation of Raynouard was not in the April *Maga*. He concludes Blackwood thinks it too heavy for *Maga*, and therefore, as these translations are exceedingly troublesome anyway, he will discontinue the project unless Blackwood particularly wishes it. Instead, he will send something of a lighter complexion for the May issue. Now he proposes to send an article each month on the subject of the London theater. He is an ideal person to do so, as a passionate lover of the drama, a constant attendant at theaters, and an intimate acquaintance of highest ranks of performers, "by whom I am accounted a good Judge." Then, more of the personal. He takes it that his friend Weale had told Blackwood that Lyndsay, like many others of his rank in life, is obliged to make a respectable appearance upon a very moderate allowance from his Father—he asks for an early response on the theatrical criticisms, please—regrets that the *Dramas* have had such poor sales—hopefully, Blackwood has not lost money by the publication—"I am dear Sir, Very truly yours, David Lindsay." Spelled with an *i* not a *y*; not the kind of mistake one makes with his own name.

No theatrical notices by Lyndsay appear in Blackwood's. But in May, his translation of Raynouard's *States of Blois* is published. Lyndsay's June 10 apology for not completing the translations still owed makes clear that Blackwood requested the project be completed. Unfortunately, very particular business had of late engrossed the whole of Lyndsay's attention. The work will be forthcoming, but in the meanwhile he sends a poem. Will Blackwood accept it? Also, he should like to dedicate his drama on Isaiah to the poet laureate. Is that acceptable? And he has other works, gathered during his travels, that he wishes to translate and send. Again, he thanks for words of encouragement, and for books sent ". . . with best acknowledgements dear Sir for all kindnesses I remain, Sincerely yours."

On June 29, Lyndsay wants to review *Halidon Hill,* a drama by the great Sir Walter Scott for the July *Maga.* Shall he? Lyndsay's tragedy on the *States of Blois* will be mailed in a few days. A very brief note, in a scrawled handwriting that suggests either haste or illness.

On July 13, another brief note, enclosing the review. It is his first attempt at this kind of writing, so Blackwood should with no ceremony omit part or all—he thanks for the reprint of Sir Thomas Browne—he has loved him from infancy—and thinks he "becomes Edinburgh . . . I am dear Sir, very truly yours." The review never appears in *Maga.*

Undaunted, in early August Lyndsay sends a lengthy early letter—and a confession. He opens with the offer of a new project, enclosing part of a work by a clever satirical friend written originally as a journal which he intended to continue and publish. Lyndsay's friend proposes the journal become a joint volume: the friend's part, letters and observations; Lyndsay's, tales and poetry. What does Blackwood think? Is he too dispirited by the middling success of Lyndsay's first publication to venture a second? His friend is a clever man but bitter, and Blackwood may think the writing too personal. If Blackwood likes the letters, they will continue them from France where they go, the friend to divert himself at the expense of Parisians and Lyndsay to collect materials for serious subjects, verse, and prose.

Then follows the passage I was looking for about being known as Lyndsay—and more. The information from Alan Bell that Lamb didn't know him as Lyndsay opened at least two possibilities: One, he used a pseudonym with Lamb and possibly others; two, "Lyndsay" was itself the pseudonym. This letter removes all doubt. He hopes "dear Sir and kind Countryman" that Blackwood is not offended by the incognito which he is for strong reasons obliged to keep. He is bound by a promise that compels him not to acknowledge his authorship, but that restraint will not last forever. Though he may not put his name to his volume, it shall be known to Blackwood. He flatters himself that Blackwood will not be ashamed of having called him forward to a literary existence—and reminds Blackwood that a sum is still owing him for one of his published articles, a trifle he would not mention but he is going abroad for a short time and Blackwood knows "Riches is not one of the characteristics of the gentry of our dear Country." Then the Lamb reference. Lyndsay, referring to Lamb by his well-known pseudonym, indicates he is well acquainted with Elia, "though as Lyndsay he does not know me." But no more. Instead, he adds some further discussion about trying to increase sales of *Dramas*—"Let me hear from you as early as convenient. . . . I am my dear Sir Yours very truly, D–Lyndsay."

Was there a Scotsman who could be Lyndsay mentioned in Lamb's letters? No Lyndsay in the old editions of Lamb's letters. No Lyndsay in the new edition then going to press. I continued to read the microfilm, hopeful that Lyndsay's revelation about his name would be the first of many.

Early November 1822; the longest gap yet between letters. Lyndsay—for Blackwood and me, he is still Lyndsay—offers a new proposition. He encloses part of a tale he adopted from childhood reading—"The Yellow Dwarf" as perhaps more suited for *Maga* than his graver, more poetic works. As to *Dramas,* he has heard them much admired in Paris, and booksellers have orders to send for them. Has Blackwood heard how Byron reacted to this rival publication? A friend has assured Lyndsay that Byron was greatly annoyed—but Shelley admired the work, particularly *Cain.* Whether this report was accurate cannot be confirmed. Mary Shelley's letter[5] only indicated that *she* admired *Cain.*

Lyndsay goes from taking pride in Byron's and Shelley's responses to his work, to a long, self-righteous attack on Byron's writings as treasonous and blasphemous. He complains that critics ignore the "question of the morality, to discuss that of style." They carefully avoid comparing Byron's dramas to the "Lindsay Dramas" (the occasional misspelling of his own name is now understandable). Following his caustic remarks on Byron, he sharply takes on the *Liberal,* a new literary journal that was to be published in Italy by an extraordinary trio: Byron, Shelley, and Leigh Hunt. But before it began in September 1822, Shelley was dead. Byron and Hunt continued the project; Mary Shelley prepared Shelley's and her own contributions for the first issue. Byron, Shelley, Mary Shelley, Hunt, and others of their circle—liberals, radicals. Clearly, not people Lyndsay admired. He assures Blackwood ". . . we need not have been frightened to death about it." He hardly knows which is the worst article in it—wanted to say something else about publishing—will defer it . . . "I am, dear Sir."

Now, an even longer gap; February 23, 1823. Lyndsay's and Blackwood's relationship has apparently changed. The author is disappointed. He again has not heard from the publisher. Can he spare a few minutes merely to reply to Lyndsay's wish to publish *Popular Tales of the English*? (There is no letter making this offer, again suggesting there may be an intermediary involved.) Lyndsay has lately written other tales, romantic and in prose, one chivalrous dealing with Spanish and Moorish contentions in Granada; another, a tale of the "Upas Tree." (The name is one of the titles listed under Lyndsay's name in library catalogs—but not published by Blackwood.)

And then, a proposal for yet another new project. Always an admirer of the German muse, he has long been translating German works (another language added to French, Italian, and Latin) into English blank verse. Among the works Lyndsay wishes to publish are Schiller's *Robbers, Don Carlos, the Minister* ". . . allow me the pleasure of soon hearing from you and believe dear Sir, truly Yours." A postscript ensures that Lyndsay is not entirely cut off from Blackwood. He thanks the publisher for the gift of books sent—such counterblasts, Lyndsay tells Blackwood, will "blow the P.P.P. (Paltry Pisa Periodical) as you very justly call it, into tatters." Again, a hit at the Shelley-Byron Italian circle and their *Liberal*. But, at the same time, his offer of German translations is a tie to Mary Shelley's 1826 letter to Colburn.

On March 23, Lyndsay acknowledges Blackwood's rejection of his German translation idea—he tells the publisher his play is now in Charles Kemble's hands, to be produced early next season . . . and asks Blackwood to have his London friends support his first appearance as a playwright. As for the tales, he continues to work on them, some based on English tales, others, like the "Orange Tree," on German. The entire collection he offers Blackwood to publish as *The Upas Tree and Other Tales*—sends the "Upas Tree," hoping for publication that season—thanks Blackwood for books sent but makes a point of withholding his sympathy for the heroine whose family has died because he believes the "bitterest trials we can receive are through the sufferings of those we love . . . dear Sir I take my leave, expecting the fulfillment of your promise to write soon."

Not waiting to hear, on April 7 Lyndsay sends a sheet of varieties for *Maga* and will send the "Orange Tree" in a day or two. He has whole sheets of biographical essays by different hands, done at a time when it was a favorite amusement among a few wild friends—if you like them you shall have more.

Lyndsay's next letter of June 11 returns to his February 23 proposal of German translations. He has been concentrating on these—the *Gespensterbuch* of Apel and Laun—the *Spectre Book* with stories of goblins, spirits, devils, ghosts, and wild beings of every description. Will Blackwood promise to take it off his hands? If so, he will go on. He can send one of these for *Maga* ". . . with your earliest convenience . . . and should like to know what you think of the 'Upas Tree?' . . . Yours dear Sir very truly."

On July 2, Lyndsay thanks Blackwood for the good news: He rejects the "Upas Tree" but is interested in the German Goblin translation project. There are eight or nine German volumes to translate, which would make three English volumes. *Maga* shall have the best. Lyndsay believes Blackwood is now in London, where Weale will assist in the hospitality. (It is Weale whose address Lyndsay uses to receive mail. Now, Weale will actually see Blackwood. Not much later, the suspicion that Weale is Lyndsay's intermediary will be confirmed.) As for Lyndsay's whereabouts, he is at that time "really far away, being in close attendence upon my Papa, who now and then draws largely upon my filial piety." . . . "Goblins" for Christmas publication? . . . Blackwood's editor Christopher North (i.e., John Wilson) has done the *Liberal* in for good, but Leigh Hunt is going to weary them by publishing the *Indicator* again.

A month later, August 3, 1823, Lyndsay's twentieth letter in the sequence. Only twelve left. There is still hope Lyndsay will keep his word and tell Blackwood who he really is. Instead, he sends a "goblin" story for *Maga*—has changed the title from "Freischütz," in English "Free Shooter," to "Magic Balls"— Blackwood should decide. This leads to a reference to another literary figure of the day, Dr. William Kitchener. Lyndsay is glad the last issue of *Maga* has some nice words to say about "my old friend Kitchener" after earlier attacks. Blackwood dined with Kitchener, didn't he? After all, Kitchener is an honest fellow and a sound Tory, so Lyndsay could not understand how another Tory ally could kick him down—"but I am very *new,* particularly to the literary World"—in these "days of private publicities, one ought to be careful how one writes"—but he writes "in perfect confidence to you" as he cannot consider "either of us as merely 'Gentlemen of the Press.'"

Though they are gentlemen, gentlemen may disagree. Lyndsay takes issue with Blackwood's opinion about someone else's translation of *Faust* and demonstrates his point by quoting some of the lines he regards as carelessly translated. "My footman" would have done better— As for Byron's social satire *Don Juan,* "Faugh!"—Let him hear soon— He hopes his tragedy will appear next season, but is not certain. One must butter the actors and actresses—"accept assurances" of his high regard, and "believe me truly Your obliged S$^t$." On second thought, he sends another goblin story so Blackwood may choose.

On September 1 Lyndsay sends a letter of apology and with it, more biographical data. Blackwood having taken offense at his comments causes Lyndsay to explain he meant nothing more than, in common with "every Man of honour to express my abhorrence of the Scoundrel who could be guilty of an act at once so base and cowardly." The man is Patmore. What he did to Blackwood is unclear. But to make clear the extent of his regret, Lyndsay explains he is a young man, thoughtless perhaps, but "a true Gentleman," and he has too much of the "noblest, yes the very noblest of old Scotland's blood" in his veins to permit him to offer impertinence to Blackwood. If this apology is insufficient, Lyndsay invites Blackwood to command him to apologize in any way Blackwood pleases. He implies even a duel is not out of the question, as he deserves a bullet at ten paces for his thoughtlessness. Then to business. It appears Blackwood has informed him that someone else has already published the German collection Lyndsay intended for Blackwood. Can Blackwood send him a copy? Is the "Magic Love" also translated? Mr. Weale being away, and Lyndsay very anxious to hear from him, he asks him to be addressed at "Mrs. Carter's Duke Street Manchester Square . . . Yours dear Sir."

On September 9, just days after Lyndsay's apology, he writes again, relieved that Blackwood accepted his apology. As to the "Tales" sent, they are *not* Lyndsay's collection; his, he argues, are far superior. There is only one duplicate between the two, "The Marksman." Actually, Lyndsay knows the author. His name is Browning, a good sort of man but Lyndsay didn't expect much from his works of fancy as Browning is a "thorough pac'd Hum-drum." Lyndsay will therefore send some of his translations to *Maga:* He will of course abide by Blackwood's opinion—"I am dear Sir."

Not hearing from Blackwood, on October 10, he sends a goblin tale; the original was very long and some parts bordered on the ludicrous, so he has altered the story accordingly. He has also changed its name to "Shade of the Bridegroom." Again, he offers to send samples of the stories he wishes Blackwood to publish for a Christmas volume.

A brief, disappointed note on December 30, 1823. He has not heard from Blackwood, nor seen his goblin story in print. He concludes Blackwood did not like it. And if they are not fit for *Maga,* will he please return to Lyndsay the "Upas Tree" and the "Orange Tree" ". . . wishing enjoyment of this Merry Season . . . I am dear Sir."

Lyndsay does not hear from Blackwood into the new year. On February 16, 1824, another brief note to remind the publisher of his last, with its request to return his stories if not suitable. Return them to Weale, as usual . . . with thanks for the gift of books sent . . . Blackwood has "furnished me with a delightful light Library . . . expecting the pleasure of hearing from you soon."

March 17, 1824. Still no response from Blackwood. May he trouble Blackwood, "my dear Sir," to indulge his request—he is "anxious to show them to a friend—How do the *Dramas* get on? and is there any hope of a second edition—have I any chance? Yours dear Sir &c."

Even briefer contact on May 1. A few lines enclosing a drama about an incident in the life of the Duke of Guise . . . "if too long omit what part you please"—if entirely useless return it to him.

Silence until January 16, 1825. The twenty-eighth letter in the sequence. The tone of this, and the next two, returns to the self-confident Lyndsay who first wrote to Blackwood in 1821. It also introduces Mary Shelley into Lyndsay's life. Lyndsay thanks his "first Friend in Literature" for *Maga*'s kind mention of him last November,[6] crediting that commendation for the good terms received from Hurst and Company, who will shortly publish his book of goblin tales. May he dedicate the volume to Blackwood? If such a work doesn't deserve Blackwood's name, he should not hesitate to say so.

Next, he wants advice. Some friends are trying to establish a quarterly magazine for young persons. Several talented people want to assist, but not have their names come forward. They have given their works to Lyndsay. He in turn sends an essay to Blackwood for his opinion. If good enough for *Maga,* keep it. Otherwise, he will publish it in the new quarterly. Also, he has some essays on phrenology (reading character through analysis of the shape of the skull, a long-standing popular fad)[7], on poetic language, and a short history of Olney, home of William Cowper. Is Blackwood interested?

Just then, there is much gossip in London about Byron, Robert Southey (the poet laureate), and Thomas Medwin, Shelley's friend and cousin. Byron had died in Greece the previous May, prompting Medwin and Robert Charles Dallas to write memoirs. Readers now argued about what was true, what not; who was mentioned, who implied. Lyndsay says Byron seldom spoke truth, except by chance. He then informs Blackwood that he is slightly acquainted with Lady Byron and intimately acquainted with many of her connections and friends. To prove how balanced his opinion is, he also announces that he is now "well acquainted with M^rs Shelley." From neither side has he ever heard a difference of opinion on the subject of Byron's veracity. He doesn't know Medwin, but his book appears prudent in omitting many of Byron's stories; Dallas's book, on the other hand, is the work of "a twaddling old Gentleman" who gives "little of Byron, and an immense load of himself." That Byron endured Dallas so long as a friend is testimony to the "natural kindliness of his heart and temper"—"I am dear Sir."

On May 5, a briefer letter. Please announce in the June *Maga* that Lyndsay's *Tales of the Wild and the Wonderful* is published. He does not put his name to the book. Nor does he, in compliance with Blackwood's wish, dedicate *Tales* to him. Blackwood should include an "absurdities" column in *Maga*. London itself could supply him—take the example of the actor/manager Elliston and his behaving as if he were the King— "I am dear Sir."

Finally, three letters from the end of the sequence, the now-loquacious Lyndsay expands on his close association with Mary Shelley and her circle. The letter is undated, but three internal clues certainly place it sometime after mid-October and late November: (1) Lyndsay has not heard from Blackwood for a long time; (2) He speaks about Leigh Hunt's return to England, which took place October 10, 1825; (3) Lyndsay says if Blackwood publishes the short story he encloses, it would add money to his Christmas box.

This important letter begins and ends on the subject of Lyndsay's writing. He includes a copy of his *Tales* for Blackwood, which suggests it was published much later than the anticipated June date. His next book will be better—would Blackwood send a copy of the volume to Joanna Baillie, to whom he dedicated it, but whose address in Edinburgh he does not have.

Then he turns from his own literary matters to lengthy anecdotes stemming from his friendship with Mary Shelley. With this "fine creature," who is too good for the party to which she is unlucky to belong, Lyndsay is "intimate." She is publishing now with Colburn. Lyndsay "imagines" Mary Shelley wants to dispel the idea that she cherishes the same opinions as Shelley. She believed Blackwood had been severe on Shelley, but Lyndsay proved to her by "whole pages of *Maga*" that Shelley was treated as "a Scholar and a Gentleman," which gratified her. As to their review of her 1823 novel *Valperga*,[8] *Maga* was wrong. Napoleon, "whom she hated," did not at all figure in her delineation of the character of Castruccio. "She has a very powerful mind, and with the most gentle feminine manner and appearance that you can possibly imagine."

Lyndsay follows with information he has almost certainly had from Mary Shelley. Has Blackwood heard of the row between Byron's friend Hobhouse "Hobby O" and that blockhead Thomas Medwin? Though he has the story in confidence, he sends it along. Medwin, still abroad but angry at Hobhouse's attack on his book in the *Quarterly Review,* intended to challenge him to a duel. Mrs. Shelley wrote to Hobhouse, ridiculing the idea of fighting for any literary subject with anybody. Hobhouse's response treated Medwin rather roughly, but didn't declare his intention either to fight or leave it alone. Medwin then wrote to another lady of his intention to challenge. Lyndsay believes Medwin never intended to fight, and is using the ladies for protection.

And more gossip, Mary Shelley apparently the source. Leigh Hunt, whom he has not seen, is returned. From all he has heard from his friends, he is himself infinitely better than his writings. Edward Trelawny, who went with Byron to fight for the Greek cause, is expected. Does Blackwood know that Trelawny fought, married a sister of a Greek leader, and was shut up in a cave by the Greeks after they murdered his brother-in-law? But he escaped, and is en route home. Then stories about Hunt's brother John Hunt, also a publisher. And he expects to be amused by Hunt himself, who no matter how good he is is too much of a coxcomb not to furnish rich food for mirth— farewell—and will the enclosed story suit *Maga*?—"very truly my dear Sir."

Because Mary Shelley was unusually reticent except with those closest to her, it is clear that by fall 1825 Lyndsay had become an accepted member of her inner circle. No doubt Mary Shelley would have been mortified if she found out that Lyndsay repeated these stories to Blackwood. Nor did Lyndsay's high spirits and talented gossip bring publication offers from Blackwood. Hearing nothing, he sent a brief letter to the publisher in the following March simply asking for the return of the story sent.

Lyndsay's last letter to Blackwood—September 11, 1829—more than three years later, is both disappointed and strange. Lyndsay had sent material a month before, signing himself "X." Though Blackwood returned it, Lyndsay feels the ice is broken between them and wants to submit a lengthy poem celebrating a Scottish historical event. The work was written fifteen years earlier, but there were so many great poets writing then, he laid his aside. Now that the "fiery edges of all the lately reigning Bards" seem a little worn off, will Blackwood consider it? The poem is on 171 sixteen- by thirteen-inch pages. He now sends the "Induction" to it; if Blackwood would let him know either by mail or when he sends the next *Maga*—he would oblige "your very obedient servant David Lindsay." *Lindsay,* again spelled with an *i*. And this time, the handwriting is also different.

What had I learned about David Lyndsay from these thirty-two letters? His father is alive, Scottish, upper class—perhaps an aristocrat. He is himself a well-educated gentleman, about thirty-four in 1825, in poor health because of a liver ailment. He hobnobs with literary and social elites. He first published with Blackwood and despite early intimations otherwise, he needs the money earned from writing, perhaps suggesting a change of fortune. By the end of the 1820s, he has two books and a number of miscellaneous pieces to his name. Politically a Tory, he nevertheless socializes with liberals and radicals. By fall 1825, he and Mary Shelley are close friends. A man of plans and projects, he has enough confidence to try to get Blackwood to publish his works despite many rejections, and an edge of arrogance that shows itself even in politely couched letters. The picture of a gentleman, family fortune lost, who struggles to maintain social position; the picture of an ambitious writer. But the picture crumbles. A gentleman keeps his word. Lyndsay never kept his word to tell Blackwood who he was. Except for his friendship with Mary Shelley, and the publication of his works, there is no way to know if one statement he has made about himself is true.

# CHAPTER 5

# SOME PROGRESS?

IT WAS JULY 1978. I believed that the Douglas search was almost at an end. As for Lyndsay, a month and a half of reading microfilm had formed a picture of a man that might or might not be accurate. The next step was to search through my inventory of Mary Shelley published and unpublished material to try to find a Lyndsay by some other name. Comparing the "facts" about him to all of her friends and acquaintances yielded nothing. But after days of sifting through files, notes, and biographies for some match, a candidate surfaced based not on facts but on handwriting.

In a file labeled "Problems," along with other miscellaneous papers, were stored photocopies of two letters to Mary Shelley from a man named M. D. Dods.[1] I was aware of the Dods letters. The problem was finding where he might fit in Mary Shelley's life. But now I was looking for someone who was Lyndsay *and* someone else. A quick glance at the Dods signature told all. It seemed almost too easy. The letter *D*, the extraordinarily elaborate *D*—the unmistakable *D* used over and over again in the signature "David Lyndsay." I placed a Lyndsay letter next to a Dods to compare the handwriting, isolating the individual characters by looking at them through a small punch-hole in an index card.[2] First, I worked character by character. Then I located the same words in both Lyndsay's and Dods's letters. They matched. There was no question that Dods's and Lyndsay's letters were written by the same person. But who was Dods?

His letters are undated, but Mary Shelley's address—
5 Bartholomew Place—fixes them sometime between June 1824
and July 1827. In rereading his letters, I suddenly realized how
intimate this Dods was with Mary Shelley. Otherwise, how
would he dare take so familiar a tone with her in an era in which
first names were reserved for one's closest circle. Dods goes
beyond first names. To him, Mary Shelley is "miene Liebling"
and "my pretty." Are these love letters? Dods confesses that the
night before, in Mary Shelley's company, he felt, "like a Child
looking forward to its promised holiday," the pain of knowing
he would not see her for five days. "Wilt thou, miene Liebling
of thine own graciousness shorten this period one day?" Tell
Jane Williams a change of plans requires it. He will meet
her on Wednesday and accompany her to visit Jane Williams
". . . thine—D—"

The second Dods letter contritely asks that "my Pretty" remind him of the time they are to meet because so many exceedingly disagreeable things have occurred to him that week, he has
forgotten. He thanks her for showing him Shelley's letters.

> Why do you not publish them? they would do more
> good to his memory than all that Friends can say—they
> contain in themselves such perfect and decided refuta-
> tion of many of the silly calumnies floating abroad—it
> is to be *wish'd* for his own sake and yours—it is
> *necessary* for your Son's—[Shelley's] Plato's Ban-
> quet—but that shall be talk for us anon . . . ever my
> dear Pretty's Admiring Friend MD Dods

The letters are among the most personal in the Mary
Shelley papers. Was Dods Mary Shelley's secret lover? The extent of Mary Shelley's friendship with Mérimée had been hidden
for one hundred and fifty years. Why not this relationship as
well, preserved only in these two brief letters from an unidentified correspondent? Or was Dods an older man, playing the role
of a courtly beau to the young widow? One Dods listed in the
*Dictionary of National Biography* (*DNB*) might fit: Marcus
Dods (1786–1838), the Reverend Marcus Dods, theological

writer, born in England, educated in Edinburgh; in 1810, ordained Presbyterian minister at Belford, Northumberland, and
incumbent there until death. A man of "deep theological scholarship" and of "irrepressible wit," a monument at Belford at-
tests to his truthfulness and his artistic powers: "A man of noble
powers, nobly used . . . vigour and gentleness, gravity and wit
. . . delight of his household . . . helper of the poor . . . captivated friend by rich converse and edified the church by his
learned and eloquent pen." His occupation might well explain
the pseudonym. Lyndsay had said his father "now and then
draws largely upon" his filial piety.[3] Might father be "Father,"
an example of the Reverend's irrepressible wit? Or was the
pseudonym necessary for another reason, attached to the phrase
"the delight of his household." The *DNB* also listed another
Marcus Dods (1834–1909), Presbyterian divine and biblical
scholar, who was Marcus Dods's youngest son. Was Dods a married minister who strayed as a writer and personally? And did
Mary Shelley know any of this?

A few days later, new Lyndsay information arrived from
Charlie Robinson. It appears that William Blackwood was as
curious as I about David Lyndsay. On learning about Lyndsay's
pseudonym, he wrote to Charles Ollier[4] in January 1822, asking
if he knew about Lyndsay. On February 12, Charles Ollier answered saying he knows a good deal about David Lyndsay's
*Dramas*—"The gentleman who has conducted the business with
you is in our shop everyday." Ollier assures Blackwood the gentleman is much gratified by the liberal manner in which Blackwood behaved regarding the publication. Curiosity even more
aroused, on February 22 Blackwood asks for more information
about Lyndsay. Ollier responds on March 11 that a gentleman
named Weale, "who has a considerable situation in government,
is the individual who has conducted the correspondence with
you relative to the Dramas of David Lyndsay." Mr. Weale is a
very clever man with considerable literary knowledge. Ollier
would be happy to introduce Blackwood, when he comes to
town. But Weale says he is not David Lyndsay and that no one
will ever know who he is. The Ollier letters are in the National

Library of Scotland and I wondered what else could be found there.

Charlie has concluded from Ollier's letters that all the Lyndsay letters to Blackwood were written by Weale. If he is correct, then Weale also wrote the letters signed "MD Dods." Is Weale Dods? Lyndsay? Or is Dods Weale?

I wrote again to Alan Bell, asking if he had anything on the Reverend Marcus Dods, and at the same time, I contacted Bruce Barker-Benfield: Among the Abinger papers on deposit at Oxford there are two letters that may be from Marcus Dods . . . are there any other Marcus Dods letters at the Bodleian? Is it possible to get a sample of his handwriting . . . and on the topic of handwriting, have they anything by or about a James Weale, 19 York Buildings, c. 1820s. To Bruce I went so far as to state my belief that Lyndsay was probably Dods.

Having planted these seeds, I left for three weeks of research that would include the Pforzheimer Library—mecca for Shelley scholars in Manhattan; the Huntington Library in San Marino, California; and The University of Texas Library at Austin. En route, I was finally able to read Lyndsay's *Dramas of the Ancient World* and *Tales of the Wild and the Wonderful*.

*Dramas* opens with a disclaimer by its author: David Lyndsay asserts that his having chosen for his dramas two subjects also selected by Byron is "entirely accidental." Lyndsay claims—and his letters appear to verify—that the *Destiny of Cain* and *Sardanapalus* were both written long before Byron's works were announced—before he had any idea that Byron's brilliant pen was engaged upon the drama—the inferiority of Lyndsay's execution may lead him to regret he selected the same subjects but otherwise he cannot regret any coincidence with the admired author of *Manfred* and *Childe Harold*. Lyndsay follows with an invocation to the spirit of Aeschylus to inspire him with "one beam" of his "ethereal fire . . . on the rapt soul of thy worshipper" that "he may become such part" of the great playwright "As is the atom to the universe!" A humble preamble to eight poetic dramas, all written in blank verse: *The Deluge, The Plague of Darkness, The Last Plague, Rizpah, Sardanapalus, The Destiny of Cain, The Death of Cain,* and *The Nereid's Love.*

The dramas proved remarkable for their scope of learning. Footnotes indicate that the author has drawn on the Bible, Greek myth, and Diodorus Siculus's *Bibliotheca historica,* originally a forty-volume account of the history and myths of ancient civilizations; Plutarch; rabbinical writing; as well as comments by contemporary scholars. Lyndsay's *Dramas* told stories of the destiny of nations; love; heroism; evil and self-indulgence; angels married to humans; magic and rituals; dreams and nightmares; wise men and women; and villains. The language is dramatic, perhaps overly so at times. But scattered throughout are strong, poetic lines and passages. The works are complex and cannot be evaluated quickly, but even this first reading shows that Lyndsay had produced a remarkable first book, which is *Blackwood's*[5] reviewer's opinion as well.

Setting *Dramas* against the works of living playwrights including Joanna Baillie and Byron—and discounting Baillie's works because she "is a woman, and thence weak in many things," the review praises the *Dramas* author as "a man of talents and of genius . . . and that is all we know of him, except that he once or twice sent us some dramatic sketches for this Magazine." The reviewer feels at times Mr. Lyndsay might have been more powerful, but in "other passages redeems himself nobly," sometimes "bordering on extravagance" but "not without sublimity":

We do not fear to say, that he is a poet with much feeling and no little imagination . . . chief fault is a dim and misty splendour indiscriminately flung over all his conceptions . . . no simplicity . . . neither is there much curious or profound knowledge of passion . . . But Mr. Lyndsay conceives situations very finely and originally; his diction is often magnificent, and his imagery striking and appropriate; he seems to write in a sort of tumult and hurry of young delight . . . bad passages bombastical . . . [have quoted enough] to prove, that if a young writer, which can scarcely be doubted, high hopes may be justly formed of him who, in a first attempt, has produced so much poetry true to nature, and belonging to the highest province of imagination.

A very fair critique, in general, and in accord with Mary Shelley's own comments in 1821 when she first read Lyndsay's *Dramas*.[6]

*Tales of the Wild and the Wonderful* offers a different Lyndsay voice. From the historical mythic, Lyndsay moved into the shadowy world of the gothic and the fairy tale. Mediating the transition, Lyndsay interjects a passage from the Renaissance on his title page: "'Messer, dovete havete pigliate tante coglionerie?' quoth the Reader," given as a remark made by the Cardinal Ippolito d'Este to Ariosto. What has Ariosto, the great Italian poet-lawyer, and his powerful patron and employer, the cardinal, to do with Lyndsay? Could Lyndsay expect his readers to be familiar with the story of Ariosto's refusal to follow the very political cardinal into yet another sojourn in a foreign nation, thereby causing the angry cardinal to permanently break with the poet and, spurned, ask Ariosto: "Sir, how have you made such nonsense?" Or is this Lyndsay's way of displaying his wide knowledge and at the same time referring to himself as a diffident author worried about his reception?

Are *Tales* nonsense or is their author anxious, given the sales of *Dramas*? Lyndsay asks his "gentle Reader" to "Pause one moment" while he replies to a common accusation against authors that there is nothing new in his book. With some humor, he remarks that if Solomon found all things under the sun to be aged in his time, "what can be expected from a poor scribbler" like him some three thousand years after? To further protect himself, he reminds his "dear reader" that this is the first time he appears as a storyteller—he is timid—nervous—easily discouraged. He offers an international selection of stories: "Der Freischütz" is from the German; "The Fortunes of de la Pole," "The Prediction," "The Yellow Dwarf," and "The Lord of the Maelstrom" are original, though the last two owe something to every fairy tale written since King Arthur's days. "The Lord of the Maelstrom" is his vehicle for presenting the "beautiful mythology of the North, and the introduction of Odin and his exploits—whose history, by the way, I believe, has been extracted from the Talmud, or from the rabbinical traditions of the events previous to the creation, and the deeds of Moses and others."

Lyndsay appeals to his readers to treat him kindly both because whether he writes another volume of stories depends on his reception; and because there has been a "sad sweep lately among those who used to cater for your diversion: many who were most deserving have been snatched from your admiration and regard. 'Shelley is not—Lord Byron is not—and Maturin have they taken away.'" Then, identifying with those recently deceased writers, Lyndsay gives his readers a warning: "For myself, I am not a long-lived man, and therefore advise you to make much of me while I am with you."

This "short-lived man" tells a good story. In "The Prediction" he spins the strange tale of Ruth Tudor, who defies the despotic power of a fraudulent village seer, eventually leading her to murder her own daughter. Combining the motifs of the grail-quest, the owed-child fairy story, and a good dose of anticlerical, antiaristocracy, antifather commentary, "The Yellow Dwarf" tells the story of a dwarf who is eventually done out of the princess Brunilda, his virgin bride, by the noble knight Ludolph. Through the scissors of fate and a good gnome, the lovers Ludolph and Brunilda overcome the dwarf and are reunited. Two passages in this lengthy saga are particularly striking: One, that rails against rank, appears not to mesh with Lyndsay's report of his own "finest Scottish blood"; the other describes the shock received by the dwarf when the princess mocks the ugliness of his long beard, short legs, and large head. This passage certainly reflects the traditional fairy tale's ugly creatures, but as in Mary Shelley's *Frankenstein*, Lyndsay describes how wounded the outcast creature felt about this attack on his appearance.[7]

"Der Freischütz" is a retelling of Apel's German tale of the forester Bertram and the destruction to his family when he insists that his daughter marry the man he selected rather than the man she loves. "The Fortunes of de la Pole" returns to the aristocracy with a story of fratricide and punishment, replete with vengeful ghosts; and "The Lord of the Maelstrom" is about death and destruction among the Scandinavian nobility.[8]

Within one cover Lyndsay brought together stories from a variety of sources, in time and place. He appears to enjoy telling his stories as much when he depicts the veiled side of people as of otherworld creatures. For most transgressors, he has a compassion that goes beyond their ill deeds, giving them perspective through the larger context of the human condition. Even when conventional justice prevails at the end of a story, Lyndsay is far more concerned with exploring the shadows of human motivation, often in the form of defiance against authority of one form or another. Throughout, he relishes interweaving humorous, often satirical, commentary. It is easy to understand how the anonymously published *Tales* were attributed to the highly respected Victorian writer George Borrow.[9]

The question remained whether Lyndsay was that other respected Victorian, the Reverend Marcus Dods. Since none of my inquiries had turned up anything about the reverend, I decided to see if his former Vicarage in Belford, Northumberland, might have some material and wrote a short letter seeking information about Dods in connection with an edition of the letters of Mary Shelley—because Dods was minister at Belford from 1810 through 1838 perhaps they may have suggestions about locating papers belonging to Rev. Dods—or any other information . . . would greatly appreciate any assistance. I also wrote to the University of Edinburgh Library. Dods's son attended New College, Edinburgh; any information about elder Dods—or descendants? No need to explain that the reverend may have used a pseudonym to publish secular literature or that, though married, he appears to have courted Mary Shelley.

## CHAPTER 6

# THE COUNTDOWN BEGINS

THE EARL OF MORTON'S WILL arrived on September 19. Forty-four pages long, dated April 12, 1858, it devises, deposes, disposes, and trusts. A glance at the first page told me something was wrong. The will talks about George Sholto, earl of Morton, and Frances Theodora, countess of Morton, who, by mutual assent and consent, consider it a duty incumbent upon them to settle their affairs in the event of their deaths and for the love, favor, and affection they have and bear to each other and to their children. It is the wrong will. Or rather, the right will, but the wrong earl. This was the cousin who inherited from Walter Sholto Douglas's earl of Morton. I read through the entire document, hoping to find some references to the right earl and his will. It is a very wealthy family and a very long read. The Morton estates in Dalmahoy, Aberdour "and others," along with hundreds of thousands of pounds, linens, plate, books, china, are duly dispersed to sons, their sons, or their sons' sons. Executors and substitute executors are designated. A five-page codicil dated June 23, 1858, separately disposes of the Morton's Bassandyne Bible and the badge or jewel of the Order of the Thistle. The name Sholto Douglas, with a variety of first or middle names, is sprinkled through the text—but not Walter Sholto Douglas.

That same evening, I wrote to the Scottish Record Office,

indicating the documents sent appeared to be a problem. The material requested was the will of the *sixteenth* earl of Morton, who died in July 1827. The documents sent seem to refer to the *seventeenth* earl and do not hold the information required for my Mary Shelley research.

The Record Office responded on September 27, confirming that the document sent was indeed the will of George Sholto Douglas, sixteenth earl of Morton, as requested. However, from the dates in my recent letter, it now appears the earl actually of interest is George Douglas, fifteenth earl (1761–1827). The writs made by the fifteenth earl which bear on the query sent are a bequest to his wife, a disposition to his trustees of his whole estate after death, a bequest for an annuity to two married daughters, and two codicils amplifying the bequest to his wife, all recorded in 1827. Of these, they inform that the "disposition is the most relevant," in that "Grahams time-piece, the screen worked by Queen Mary, the original portrait of Queen Mary, the Keys of Loch Leven Castle, the portrait of the Regent Earl of Morton" were to remain as heirlooms, and to go to the sixteenth earl of Morton—sorry this problem has arisen—they had no reason to believe it was not the 16th Earl who was the subject of the earlier query.

On October 25, I wrote again to the Belford Vicarage looking for Lyndsay, alias Dods, repeating the inquiry about material regarding the Reverend Marcus Dods. On October 26, I returned to the Douglas hunt with a letter to the Scottish Record Office, thanked them for their explanation that the earl who lived from 1761 to 1827 was the earl I wanted to know about— specifically about an annuity to someone other than the next earl.

As it turned out, there are two methods of numbering Scottish titleholders: Scottish guides and English guides do not always agree in numbering the Scottish nobility. According to *Burke's Peerage,* I wanted information about the *sixteenth* earl. According to *The Scot's Peerage,* he was the *fifteenth* earl and the Scottish Record Office, of course, uses *The Scot's Peerage.* Looking for Walter Sholto Douglas, I had also asked them if George Sholto, the *sixteenth* earl, had any brothers. It appears he had both brothers and sisters: Charles, Edward, and Arthur; and Edwin, twin of the *sixteenth* earl who died in infancy; and Frances, Anne, Harriet, Charlotte, Emily, Emma, and Caroline. Among them, not a Walter Sholto Douglas.

After a few exchanges of letters, on January 8, 1979, the right will, dated August 14, 1824, registered on August 10, 1827, arrived. The first page attested that the Honourable George Earl of Morton for certain good Causes and Considerations did present Give Grant Assign and Dispose to and in favour of the Right Honourable Susan Elizabeth countess of Morton. This was the correct name of the fifteenth earl's wife. I read late into the night, working through the elaborate handwriting that deeded, disposed, assigned, lands in Warriston, Dalmahoy, Aberdour, Alderstone; houses, marshes, meadows, fields, yards, orchards, mosses, stocks, wardrobe, diamonds, jewels; Grahams timepiece, Queen Mary's screen, the portrait of Queen Mary, the keys of Loch Leven Castle, the portrait of the regent earl of Morton. Heirs, trustees, and substitute trustees for the estates of the apparently very wealthy *fifteenth* earl were duly appointed. The only annuity mentioned was to the Honourable Alexander Maconachie and Sir William Rae, trustees. I decided to reread the will on the chance I had missed a clause or a sentence that referred to an annuity for Walter Sholto Douglas.

Clause by clause, I worked through the twenty-nine legal-size sheets that disposed of his enormous wealth, and grew increasingly discouraged. By late afternoon, I reached the last page with not a hint of a bequest to Walter Sholto Douglas. Mary Shelley's July 28, 1827, letter certainly stated that "Lord M. is to be buried on Monday—the will will be read—& certainty will come." Again, Mary Shelley's August 15 letter, saying that in "the midst of melancholy a letter from D." gives them "some life . . . Small indeed is the thing done . . ." followed by a full line carefully, irretrievably scratched out by Mary Shelley, then ". . . in some way I suppose the plan of going abroad will be put in execution . . . as yet the mere fact of the continuance of the Annuity and a possibility of something more years hence is all we know." Despite the evidence to the contrary that lay in the twenty-nine pages, there had been an annuity to Walter Sholto Douglas.

A new idea had come to me while rereading the correspondence from the Scottish Record Office. They had mentioned an annuity to two married daughters, but it was missing in the disposition. Perhaps Walter Sholto Douglas was the son of one of these married daughters? I wrote to the Scottish Record Office again—have read disposition sent but find no reference to bequest for annuity to two married daughters "(which you note as on p. 416 in your 27 September letter)"—am I missing this or was it never sent? That Sholto Douglas received some sort of annuity is certain; "whether directly or indirectly, I do not know."

During the next days, I prepared the fourth and final section of volume one of the Mary Shelley letters, removing from the sequence the two October 1826 letters in which Mary Shelley tried to get works by David Lyndsay published and the eleven Douglas-Robinson letters, beginning with July 28, 1827. The 1827 letters, among the last in the first volume, included the letter it seemed fitting to close with. On August 30, 1827, her thirtieth birthday, Mary Shelley wrote to Jane Hogg about Isabella's health, about their need to move to Arundel, and asked if she might borrow ten pounds to see her over because Sir Timothy's lawyer has not sent her allowance as promised. To this, she added a postscript in Italian, perhaps to remind Jane of the glorious days gone forever: "Oime i venti son omai passato sono gia vecchia!" [sic] "Alas" she wrote, "the twenties have now passed I am already old!"

With Mary Shelley's discovery of Jane Hogg's deception, her last deep dependency on the Shelleys' Italian circle ended. Wounded, she would create a new life on her own, one that included the Douglases. Though Mary Shelley's affection for Isabella Douglas could not erase the pain of losing Jane, with her special ties to beloved Shelley and Italy, it did ease it. It seemed fitting to end this first volume as Mary Shelley stepped from one part of her life into another, now accompanied by the Douglases.

A letter from Scotland on January 23 from Edinburgh University Library: —regret no information—doubtless National Library told me to contact Presbytery at Belford, Northumberland—eldest son Marcus died 26 April 1909—Scots Ancestry Research Society may be willing to do some research on descendants.

A second letter from Scotland arrived on January 26, this from the Scottish Record Office. There are five separate deeds of a testamentary nature of which disposition sent me (RD5/345, p370) is only one—clause in disposition I received concerning delivery of articles at Dalmahoy to heir succeeding earl of Morton seemed to be sole bequest fitting description I gave.

The librarian's letter was clear: No Walter Sholto Douglas was mentioned in the remaining documents, only material pertaining to two daughters and to the earl's wife. There was no point in following up. I was more than disappointed. I was defeated. But my lethargy was short-lived.

In mid-February, I made a decision about Lyndsay and Douglas. I added a footnote to the Lyndsay letters, indicating that from materials in the National Library of Scotland, it was apparent that "David Lyndsay" was a pseudonym. I also added the conjecture that, based on handwriting, it seemed possible he might have been the Reverend Marcus Dods of Belford, Northumberland. As for Douglas, I put a brief note in Mary Shelley's letter of July 28, 1827, identifying him as Isabella Robinson's husband, and possibly a blood relative of the *fifteenth* earl of Morton. Then I referenced the remaining ten Douglas letters to this first one. Not very satisfactory.

A full year had passed since I began looking for the two men. Certainly, I now had more information about Lyndsay. But the information that Lyndsay wasn't Lyndsay added to the problem. And I had a Mr. Walter Sholto Douglas who unquestionably received an annuity from the earl of Morton—but he wasn't in the earl's will. More than at any other time in this search, I felt that Douglas and Lyndsay were my enemies; and they had beaten me.

## CHAPTER 7

# THE QUESTION OF A PRONOUN

THEN SOMETHING HAPPENED. Because of the difficulties identifying Lyndsay, I had worked with Mary Shelley's two 1826 David Lyndsay letters out of sequence. I had also worked with the eleven Douglas letters out of sequence. I thought of them as two distinct problems. But I had given colleagues reading the draft of the volume the Lyndsay and Douglas letters in their chronological order, and included the conjecture that Lyndsay was possibly the Reverend Mr. Dods. Based on this speculation, an extraordinary question came back in the margin of the Lyndsay letters: "Could the Rev. Marcus Dods" in the Lyndsay letters also be the "Doddy" in the Douglas letters?[1]

Dods was not an uncommon name—I had earlier tracked down a certainly wrong Dods who appeared in Redding's memoirs of parties at the Robinsons. Nevertheless, the question sent my mind spinning. In her letters, Mary Shelley referred to Isabella Douglas's husband as "D" or "Doddy." From context, it appeared that Doddy was a nickname for Walter Sholto Douglas. But if Doddy was Dods, and Dods was the Reverend Marcus Dods, this meant that the respectable Reverend Marcus Dods had abandoned flock and family to elope with Isabella Robinson. This kind of behavior was not so unusual in Mary Shelley's circle. Among the Shelleys' friends were not only Jane Williams Hogg but Margaret King Moore, Lady Mount Cashell, who in 1805 left the second earl of Mount Cashell and their eight children to live with George William Tighe in Italy as Mr. and Mrs. Mason.[2] And Mary Shelley herself had eloped with the married Shelley thirteen years earlier. To hide his true identity, the Reverend Mr. Dods called himself Walter Sholto Douglas and Mary Shelley assisted the lovers in their passionate and defiant act. Their handwritings proved that Dods was Lyndsay. Was the Reverend Marcus Dods both David Lyndsay *and* Walter Sholto Douglas?

All this would explain why I had not been able to trace the roots of either Lyndsay or Douglas. I knew that the Douglases had dropped out of Mary Shelley's life. Probably their affair didn't last. I tried to think through what might have happened. Dods returned to Belford. Contrite, he was welcomed home and proceeded to do good deeds for the rest of his life. Historical records buried his temporary fall from grace, and his family forgave—if they knew. But this dazzling scenario left a still-unanswered critical question: Why would the *fifteenth* earl of Morton leave an annuity to the Reverend Marcus Dods?

With this new puzzle in mind, I worked through to the end of the manuscript, and came to the second extraordinary question, a simple query about a pronoun in Mary Shelley's July 28, 1827, letter.[3] Mary Shelley, just arrived at Arundel, wrote to Jane Hogg:

> I am happy to find sweet Isabel well—she is anxious about D—from whom we had a most melancholy letter this morning—poor pet—she is very dreary & alone— She cannot visit you till she has *quatrini* & they arrive far slower than the snail of the story—still though circumstances must make her . . . gloomy—good will come soon—Lord M. is to be buried on Monday—the will will be read—& certainty will come.

The *she.* Could the second *she*—"she is very dreary & alone"—refer to *D,* meaning that sometimes D was Mr. Douglas, who was in fact the Reverend Mr. Dods; other times, a third person who should be identified? Of course not. I had been aware that as written, "she" might have referred to D. The structure of the phrases certainly allowed for ambiguity. But the facts argued against this reading. Walter Sholto Douglas and Isabella Robinson Douglas were husband and wife, the parents of Adeline, later the wife of Sir Henry Drummond Wolff. The *Dictionary of National Biography* said so. Isabella was unquestionably the first "she." And, lonely for D, her husband, surely Isabella must be the second "she" as well. I had read the passage to mean that Isabella, who regularly sent kindest regards and thoughts to Jane Hogg via Mary Shelley's letters, wanted to visit Jane Hogg in London but, ever short of money as the letters confirmed, she couldn't. Once the will was read, hopefully all would change. The Douglases would be reunited. Isabella could call on friends. To read the second "she" as a reference to "D" meant that D was a woman! Bizarre. Illogical.

But suddenly, the illogical became the logical. I made a list: David Lyndsay, Walter Sholto Douglas, M. D. Dods, Marcus Dods, and a "Doddy," who was a female. Then I reread Mary Shelley's eleven Douglas letters to find the clues that would confirm this unthinkable new theory—or blow it apart. Beginning with the "she" letter of July 28, 1827, I looked for every reference to the names on the list, testing if the figure named could be a woman.

As I read I saw, for the first time, what was there all along. Hidden, disguised, but there. That first letter said Doddy and Isabella hadn't objected to Mary Shelley bringing Mary Hunt with them. Could "Doddy" be a woman? Why not. The next paragraph, the "she" paragraph, "D" could be Doddy or Douglas. But that second *she* referred to "D." This meant that "D" was a woman. The letter makes no direct mention of the Douglases until the postscript, when Mary Shelley told Jane that "Isabel pictures your fairy home & its presiding Grace & wishes all good to it. . . ." And then, on page four, written sideways on the page: "I have opened my letter to say that Isabel is M$^{rs}$ Douglas here—LHunt does not know my friend's name—but Mary's report will be of M$^{rs}$ D." I had assumed this announcement meant that the Douglases were newlyweds. Or that they were common-law husband and wife. Jane Williams was called

Mrs. Williams, then Mrs. Hogg; Lady Mount Cashell, Mrs. Mason. Not unusual for common-law wives to take their husband's names. But if Douglas was in fact a "she," the logic of this letter meant that Isabella Robinson was married to a woman named Doddy!

The next letter, August 7, reported that Isabella's health did not permit her to enjoy the beauties of the countryside. "She is afflicted with violent headachs [*sic*] & is frequently quite oppressed by fever—D's letters do not medecine [sic] her ills, and her extreme anxiety concerning the future makes her restless." Could "D" be a woman? Again, why not? The last paragraph appears confirmation. Mary Shelley asks Jane to "pray console dear Doddy for"—and here follows a one-and-a-half-inch blank space where Mary Shelley would place her wax seal after folding the letter. When the blank ends, Mary Shelley picks up "she is very sorrowful—& has reason to be so—or has had, I trust I may say—for I hope by this time the contents of the will have been communicated to her & are favourable—but we have not heard as we expected this Morning." I had assumed Mary Shelley had lost track of her sentence, and that the "she" and "her" meant Isabella. Now I saw they referred to Doddy.

The third letter—August 15—brought news that a small annuity was given, but the phrasing is cryptic. "Small indeed is the thing done" and then the full line of writing irretrievably scratched out by Mary Shelley. Mary Shelley is afraid someone other than Jane might read this letter, and learn the Douglases' story. Thomas Jefferson Hogg? Me? I imagined Mary Shelley's hard look of disapproval, but continued on. Whatever the relationship between Doddy and Isabella, clearly their lives were intertwined. Mary Shelley still didn't exactly know their future course of action, but she believed that "the plan of going abroad" will be executed. "When or how must be decided when D. & Isabel meet."

The next letter veered off the Doddy as female trail. Mary Shelley's August 20 letter to Teresa Guiccioli says she is in Sompting with a friend of hers whom she dearly loves and who feels the deepest affection for her. "God grant" they might stay together always, for in her company Mary Shelley feels she might find some remedy for her own many sorrows. "But within a few weeks her husband is coming—they are leaving for Paris—at which time I will very sorrowfully return to London."

Two days later, a worried Mary Shelley informed Jane that Isabella is very ill with maladies Mary Shelley does not understand. What cures her one day seems to "create evil" the next. Happily, Doddy talks of visiting them soon. Isabella is delighted with her promises of going abroad. The "her" I previously thought meant the promises Isabella received from her husband; but "her promises" could simply be "Doddy's" promises.

On the twenty-sixth, the cozy world of Sompting is disrupted. They have been evicted by their money-grasping landlords. Tomorrow they look for lodgings and must remove "*without milk* . . . poor Isabel . . . Pity the poor girl, who for the life of her, ca[nnot] get dry land for the sole of her foot— nor quiet for the soul of her body. The diavolo take these money loving Burrys." Does "without milk" refer to Adeline? Is Isabella Douglas nursing an infant? Just born? But if "D" is Isabella's "partner," and D is Doddy who is a she, then who is Adeline's father? Can D and Doddy and Dods and Douglas actually refer sometimes to a man and other times to a woman?

Two days later, Mary Shelley thanked Jane Hogg for sending half of the ten pounds she asked to borrow and is grateful that Jane will send another five pounds quickly for their move to Arundel. Isabella also thanked Jane for her suggestions of cures, but it is not only diet. She also "suffers extremely from Asthma." Near the close of the letter, Mary Shelley announces: "I am glad for pretty Isabel's sake that D. now seriously thinks of les culottes—I do not expect this person—as Isa names D— for two or three weeks." *Les culottes.* My guess that this implied Isabella's husband was promising they would go to France gave way to a new premise: "D" would wear *culottes*. Nothing extraordinary if D were a man. But if D were a woman, this would certainly warrant an announcement.

Next came the August 30 letter in which Mary Shelley informed John Howard Payne that the charming woman with her is not Jane Hogg, but a "sweet little girl" who is married. The last letter of the volume, August 31, thanked Jane for the second five-pound loan in assistance of the "half-wrecked." Isabella, in better health, sends Jane, through Mary Shelley's letter, thoughts of how undeserving she is of Jane's support and aid. With the postscript acknowledging her thirtieth birthday the day before, written in Italian as a remembrance of happier times—"Oime i venti son omai passato sono gia vecchia!" [*sic*]—Volume 1 ends. But not the Douglas story. I turn to my Mary Shelley files. Each of the some 1,260 letters and any pertinent material are in separate, chronologically dated folders. From these, I assemble the Isabella and Walter Sholto Douglas letters that will be included in later volumes.

Mary Shelley's letter to Jane Hogg of September 7 is routine. She returned the borrowed ten pounds, hoped Jane (who is having a difficult pregnancy) is recovered, and reports that Isabella is "quite an invalid." The symptoms of asthma are confirmed, but asthma is a long-lived disease and the air of France should help. Ten days later, September 17, another letter about Isabella's now-acute attack of intense pain and fever. Mary Shelley constantly nurses and protects her, as "the dropping of a pin was agony" to her poor patient. Routine enough, until the subject of Doddy is brought up. They don't know yet when to expect Doddy. But Mary Shelley, seeing how pale and ill Isabel is, hopes "Isabel will be a little in good looks for the Sposo." Before it seemed simple. Mary Shelley hoped Isabella would look better for her "husband." But that husband—or at least Doddy—might be a woman.

In the September 23 letter to Jane Hogg, Mary Shelley announces, "D. is come & sends ten thousand kind & admiring messages to you—M^rs Carter is at Little Hampton." Mrs. Carter! A very common name. Now it took on new meaning. And shades of David Lyndsay appeared in the Douglas-Robinson letters. The Lyndsay letters from William Blackwood were often sent to the care of a Mrs. Carter. The Douglases and Mrs. Carter—going to France together, as soon as money arrives. D delays, Isabella and Mrs. Carter "are burning with eagerness. They will proceed to Paris, & then pause & reflect." Again, routine, but now, one of those phrases I earlier didn't understand: "Nothing can be better than the arrangements here. Our friend is absolutely fascinating . . . Percy entertains great respect & great wish to please his new friend." Why did she underline *arrangements*? Why is their friend so fascinating? And why does the eight-year-old Percy Florence see D as a "new friend?" I had assumed that the boy had never before met Isabella's husband. *Arrangements*? Absolutely fascinating? Now I assumed nothing.

Here followed the passport letters in which Mary Shelley arranged with John Howard Payne to get Douglas stand-ins for the required appearance at the passport office. On September 23, the first request. If she sent up their names, could Payne get the passports? She has heard "they wont give passports in London except to the persons themselves" and getting them at the port of exit means paying for them. Will one passport serve a party traveling together? she asked.

On September 25, a letter to the publisher Alaric A. Watts: She regrets that delays will prevent her work from inclusion in his publication that year. Is he still interested in her two mythological dramas? She sends with this note a "packet from Mrs Douglas" who transmitted to her the print Watts had sent, asking that she write a story about the events it depicts. Mrs. Douglas transmitted? But Mrs. Douglas was with her, and if Watts knew the one address, he knew the other and could write directly. Unless Watts sent his packet to the Douglas residence in London, and it was forwarded. Or there was someone else in this scenario passing as Mrs. Douglas.

On the same day, another passport letter to Payne. Mary Shelley, now planning to go with her friends as far as Dieppe, described their party so Payne could impersonate them at the passport office. The description took on new importance:

> Mrs Shelley & child—which fair person I need not de-
> scribe to you & whose signature will accompany this
> letter but lest you should beleive [*sic*] that so divine a
> being could not be personated by another I subjoin two
> other signatures for your choice Mrs Douglas is short,
> i.e. an atom shorter than I—dark, pretty with large
> dark eyes & hair curled in the neck—Mr Douglas is my
> height—slim—dark with curly black hair—the pass-

port must be drawn out for M$^r$ & M$^{rs}$ Sholto Douglas—M$^{rs}$ Carter & her two children—boys one ten the
other nine—M$^{rs}$ Percy Shelley and boy—

Clearly, Payne, playing Mr. Douglas, intended to be accompanied to the passport office by a female, playing either
Mrs. Douglas or possibly Mrs. Shelley.

Like Payne, I had believed Mary Shelley's explanation for
asking him to get these passports was monetary. It would save
the expense of returning to London or the expense of a passport
at the port of departure. But now, another reason loomed. If
Douglas was Doddy, who was a woman dressed as a man, better
not to take the chance of her-him being recognized in London.
Instead, Payne, equipped with a "Mrs. Douglas" and samples of
the "Douglases'" signatures, could save both money and the
risk of exposure. As for the signatures, Mr. Douglas's was in
the same handwriting as David Lyndsay and the letters from the
Reverend Marcus Dods.

On October 1, the third passport letter to thank Payne.
"All seems admirably managed—and the double of my pretty
friend deserves infinite praise—the signature alone is a miracle." Though they now had passports, Percy Florence had been
ill and their voyage was deferred. The letter concluded with
what I before thought to be a humorous passage referring to
Mary Shelley's anticipated habitual seasickness on crossing the
Channel. She reminded Payne that once he called her "an heroine in friendship," referring to her relationship with Jane Hogg.
But Mary Shelley told Payne that now she is one indeed:

[T]o cross the odious sea for the sake of my pretty Isabel—sacrifices have been made—as for instance by
Damon & Pythias—but this in my tablets will stand
above all the rest—a matchless example of fortitude,
generosity—friendship and undaunted courage—pray
praise me for I deserve it.

Playful bantering with Payne? Perhaps. But that matchless
"fortitude, generosity—friendship and undaunted courage"

takes on new meaning. If D is Doddy, is a woman, is Mr. Walter Sholto Douglas, Mary Shelley's ironic self-praise has within it genuine self-satisfaction for her part in the "marriage" of Mr. and Mrs. Walter Sholto Douglas. If D is Doddy, is a woman, is. . . .

By October 13, some of the party have left; the others sail the next week. It was well that Payne had gotten separate passports. Mary Shelley may not go at all. On the same day, she sent a letter to Jane Hogg. Their friends were still with her at Arundel. Percy Florence has been ill—Isabella, much better.

Then a gap of six months before Mary Shelley again refers to the Douglases. On April 8, 1828, she explains to her father-in-law's attorney-intermediary that she plans a three-week trip to Paris to see a friend who had arrived there from the south and intended almost immediately to go to Germany. The letters that follow refer to her Paris visit to the Douglases, whom she refers to in two letters to Jane Hogg as "our friends." On June 5, just returned to England and still recovering from smallpox, Mary Shelley wrote to Jane Hogg about Isabella. Jane, angry with Isabella Douglas for being the informer who told Mary Shelley of Jane's duplicitous gossip about the Shelleys' relationship, wants revenge. Mary Shelley tells her not to "talk of anger & revenge" but rather to pity "the poor child! her sufferings transcend all that imagination can pourtray [sic]—they may satisfy your bitterest feelings—as I consider myself as in some sort the cause, so I devote myself to extricate her we shall see whether I shall succeed." How was Mary Shelley in "some sort the cause"? Was the "marriage" her idea?

But despite Isabella's suffering because of Doddy, as the next letter makes clear, Mary Shelley continued to assist David Lyndsay. On June 22, 1828, she forwarded some of his works to an editor, describing him as a gentleman now in Paris, the successful author of *Dramas of the Ancient World,* and a contributor to *Blackwood's* and other annuals.

On June 27, Mary Shelley refers to Mrs. Douglas in a letter to Victor Jacquemont, a friend of Mérimée's who carries some letters between her and both Mérimée and Mrs. Douglas. Obviously, Jacquemont knows Isabella as Mrs. Douglas. Mérimée's letters to Mary Shelley also refer to her as Mrs. Douglas. This suggests that the entire Paris circle knew her as Mrs. Douglas—and Doddy as Mr. Douglas.

June 28–29, 1828, and the last of Mary Shelley's letters that refer to the Douglases—a strange letter. She writes to Jane Hogg:

> You speak of beings to whom I link myself—speak, I pray you, in the singular number—if Isabel has not answered your letter, she will—but the misery to which she is a victim is so dreadful and merciless, that she shrinks like a wounded person from every pang—and you must excuse her on the score of her matchless sufferings. What D. now is, I will not describe in a letter—one only trusts that the diseased body acts on the diseased mind, & that both may be at rest ere long.

"Matchless suffering?" "What D. now is?" "Diseased body?" "Diseased mind?" It appears the fair Isabella suffers mistreatment from a husband sick in body and mind. In a situation so terrible, why doesn't she leave him? I do not think of divorce, knowing the difficulties of legal divorce in this era. But separation was not uncommon, made easier for women whose families could provide for them. Wouldn't Joshua Robinson, a man of substance, assist his daughter financially? He and another daughter, Julia, had accompanied Mary Shelley when she went to visit the Douglases in Paris. Why didn't Isabella reveal her situation to him? Why didn't he observe it? What was keeping Isabella Douglas bound to a husband who inflicted on her "matchless suffering"? And what had happened to "dear" Doddy?

Whatever had happened to him, he was obviously no longer "dear Doddy" to Mary Shelley or to his wife. Only Isabella, in June 1828, remained dear, a fragile victim deserving of pity. Not so by December 1, 1830, when Mary Shelley wrote in her *Journal:*

Good heavens—is this the being I adored—she was ever false yet enchanting—now she has lost her fascinations—probably, because I can no longer serve her she take[s] no more trouble to please me—but also she surely is not the being she once was.

All of these questions about the relationship of the couple turned topsy-turvy when I considered Doddy as a woman. Did Joshua Robinson know his daughter was "married" to a woman? If he didn't know, and if Doddy *was* a woman, it could explain why Isabella didn't tell her father about her suffering. But if Doddy was a woman, why didn't Isabella simply separate herself from "this person," as she called Doddy? And what occurred between 1828 and 1830 to turn Mary Shelley's adored, enchanting Isabella into a being "ever false"?

Endless questions and no clear answers. But reviewing the Mary Shelley letters convinced me that D or Doddy or Douglas or Dods or Lyndsay *could* be a woman and that cryptic phrases I didn't before understand, I wasn't meant to. Obviously, whatever was going on, Jane Hogg knew all about it. No one else who might accidentally read Mary Shelley's letters was meant to. Not even someone who read the letters 152 years later.

I felt more a voyeur than ever, as I put the letters aside. Once I accepted the possibility that D, in all of *his* manifestations, could be a woman, the earl of Morton's will suddenly made sense. I turned back to the file of correspondence with the Scottish Record Office—to their letters about a codicil to the earl's will that provided for two married daughters. They hadn't sent it—I hadn't requested it—because I was searching the will for a son, a male heir, legitimate or otherwise. But was Walter Sholto Douglas a he? Or a she? The son or the daughter of the fifteenth earl? Or both? Legitimate daughters were frequently omitted from the peerage lists. Illegitimate children were almost always omitted.

On April 3 I wrote to Scotland explaining I was still involved in sorting out the question of Mary Shelley's friend who was a legatee of the fifteenth earl of Morton—clue may be in annuity to the two daughters, which they note appears in a codicil on p. 416—would they send a copy of the annuity page or pages and any other information they may have about the two daughters, their spouses, etc. My book will be in the final stages of printing in the next two weeks—most anxious for this information—only today did I realize the answer is possibly to be found in that codicil.

I had reached a new degree of uncertainty about Lyndsay and Douglas. At the beginning, I was searching for biographical information about one writer and one husband. Now there were at least four men, David Lyndsay, Walter Sholto Douglas, M. D. Dods, and Marcus Dods, plus one woman, Doddy. They could all be the same man—or woman. At this point, after fourteen months of hunting, reading, reviewing; after dozens of letters and countless books, I didn't know either the name, the origins, or even the sex of David Lyndsay or Walter Sholto Douglas.

And what about Adeline, the Douglases' daughter? I telephoned Emily Sunstein; the Douglas story was important for her research. I told her what I knew about the man named Lyndsay who wasn't Lyndsay and M. D. Dods and Marcus Dods and Douglas. In this context, the name Dods didn't ring a bell for her. Then I turned to the latest twist, and asked if she had ever come across a *woman* named Doddy? Sure, she said. Doddy. Miss Dods! Doddy is that odd character in Eliza Rennie's book *Traits of Character*—the book she had cited in her information about the Robinsons. She hadn't mentioned that the book also included information about a number of other people in Mary Shelley's circle or that Rennie described Doddy, at some length, as a good friend of Mary Shelley's. Doddy. I would locate a copy of *Traits of Character* and meet this Doddy for myself.

## CHAPTER 8

# "AN ALIAS FOR MR. . . ."

IT TURNED OUT that the Pforzheimer Library held a copy of *Traits*[1] and within twenty-four hours, the two 1860 volumes that may reveal the secret of Doddy were before me. The edges of their purple paper bindings have faded into blue, their spines darkened to black. But nothing has tarnished the gilt that announces *Traits of Character; Being Twenty-Five Years' Literary and Personal Recollections*. The table of contents in Volume 1 lists fifteen chapters, fifteen names of prominent figures—no mention of Doddy. But there is a chapter on Mrs. Percy Bysshe Shelley, and chapters on two members of her circle: Thomas Moore and Dr. Kitchener; in Volume 2, again, no Doddy, but other friends of Mary Shelley: Viscount Dillon and Mrs. Norton. Doddy must be referred to in the memoir of Mary Shelley or one of her circle. I read the three-page introduction, looking for more about Rennie that will connect her to the Shelley circle. It reveals little. Rennie's father's position put her early in life in contact with many eminent persons. Circumstances afterward did the same. It has been suggested her personal reminiscences might be of public interest. But she warns the reader that her portraits are neither biographies nor critical disquisitions. Instead, each person is "represented with all the lights and shades of their character" in order to bring their individualities to "the mental vision of the reader." Hopefully, pages 101–116 will offer a mental vision of Mary Shelley—and Doddy.

But Doddy does not appear. Instead, I find Mary Shelley described as an intimate friend in Rennie's early life. The degree of intimacy is surprising because I hadn't yet come across Rennie's name among Mary Shelley's papers. Later, I would find that her only link outside of her own book appeared to be Lord Dillon's June 13, 1828, letter to Mary Shelley in which he mentions that Miss Rennie admires his newly published book. I read on, looking for new information about Mary Shelley as well as clues to Doddy and Rennie herself. There is no question that Rennie greatly admired Mary Shelley, and appears to know about her life. But occasionally, her statements seem remarkably inaccurate. Admittedly, Rennie writes from memory. She destroyed all letters having "seen most miserable, almost fatal consequences result from keeping letters." Memory, especially with the lapse of many years between the events and her memoir, often reshapes. Or perhaps she was a fringe acquaintance, someone who knew enough about Mary Shelley to now claim intimacy with a famous figure no longer alive to affirm or deny.

From Rennie's perspective, the author of *Frankenstein, Perkin Warbeck,* etc., has not been given the portion of celebrity and appreciation due her. The reason may be in part because of the "colossal genius" of her husband, in part because Mary Shelley was "shrinking and sensitive" in nature. Rennie records that she met Mary Shelley at Dr. Kitchener's a few years after Shelley's death—in the company of "one whose romantic history, were it written, would transcend all of English or even French fiction." Also present, a man who died before the "mystery which shadowed and surrounded him was elucidated." Could these two romantic and mysterious companions be Mr. and Mrs. Douglas? Rennie moves on, keeping her secrets to herself. Mary Shelley, with her "settled sadness, a grave, gentle melancholy, in face, voice and gait" is her subject. Certainly, the detailed description of Mary Shelley's melodic voice, exquisitely fair skin, expressive gray eyes, silky hair of light but bright brown, open forehead, white and well-molded arms and hands, mesh with other descriptions. To accusations of Mary Shelley being cold, Rennie argues she was warm and affectionate to her family and faithful and unswerving as a friend. She was devotedly attached to the memory of her husband, and "represented him as all but perfection," telling Rennie "I know not what temptation could make me change the name of Shelley." This statement echoes at least one of Mary Shelley's letters and her *Journal*.

As for her own writing, Mary Shelley is described as "morbidly averse" to the least allusion to herself as a writer. Rennie says she was told Mary Shelley had given daily lessons to earn income, but she now supports herself and her son from her pen and a slender allowance from Shelley's family. She goes on to state her belief that Mary Shelley thought it unwomanly to print and publish, writing only for hard cash. Clearly, Rennie is not privy to Mary Shelley's aspiration to be a writer from childhood almost to the end of her life. Perhaps Rennie's statement about financial motivation reflects her own feelings about a woman's writing. Nor is there any independent evidence that Mary Shelley ever gave lessons. Rennie also appears not to know other private details of Mary Shelley's life—or, in true Victorian style, seeks to hide them. Mary Shelley's conduct is given as "all correctness." But like "all raised in supremacy above their fellows, either physically or mentally, Mrs. Shelley had her enemies and detractors." "All correctness?" An angelized Mary Shelley, an 1860 Mary Shelley who never eloped with Shelley in 1814 or had anything to do with a Douglas or Lyndsay or Doddy or Dods.

But Rennie's portrait places her interaction with Mary Shelley in the very years of her friendship with Isabella Douglas and her "husband." She even refers to Mary Shelley's 1828 trip to Paris to visit the Douglases, though she doesn't name them. Rather, she points out that Paris is a city where literary talent and feminine charms are celebrated, and many there eagerly awaited Mary Shelley. But, disappointingly, instead of describing the visit, Rennie focuses on the fact that Mary Shelley's complexion lost its brightness as a result of the smallpox that felled her on the trip, details that suggest Rennie did know Mary Shelley well—or she knew someone else who did.

Another factual problem arises when Rennie says she often saw Mary Shelley's father, William Godwin, whom she found to be a disagreeable old man. Something is wrong here. Godwin listed everyone he saw, outside of those in his household, in his daily journal. Rennie's name is absent. I make a note to recheck and, disappointed not to find Doddy in Rennie's Mary Shelley pages, try the chapter on Thomas Moore.

Rennie met Moore at a large evening party at a friend's house in Maida Hill, an obsolete name for London's Paddington section. In her description of the friend's party, I recognize the Robinson's Paddington Cottage home where Mary Shelley so often visited and even resided for short periods. Rennie says she often sees Moore at that cottage-style home of their Maida Hill host and his daughter. As for Moore, his singing and his charm have brought him such popularity that young women wait for him in their carriages outside his rooms in Bury Street, St. James. In a final note that ties the circle together, Rennie mentions a large reception at Mary Shelley's home in Somerset Street, Portman Square, at which Moore sang. I have two records of such a reception. Godwin attended and listed the other guests; Moore, in his journal, confirms his own attendance and notes the liveliness of the gathering. Rennie's name is absent in both records—as is Doddy's in the chapter on Moore.

Next, I turn to Dr. Kitchener, whom David Lyndsay discussed sympathetically in his letters to William Blackwood. Rennie writes at length about the eccentric doctor's fame and fortune as a culinary expert. Kitchener invented epicurean dishes and legislated rules for dining, and sleeping, and dressing, that would lead to general health. Rennie credits him as being, in his way, a philosopher, a wit, a poet, whose interests concentrated on the art and science of cooking and the structure and manufacture of telescopes. She describes Kitchener's small luncheons, to which he invited a few chosen guests to sample his latest experiments in cooking. At one she attended, she is served oysters, toasted cheese, and a new dish. Afterward, the guests are shown Kitchener's monster telescope, his "gigantic pet."

In contrast, Kitchener's famous evening soirees are attended by some sixty guests. She describes one such soiree in some detail, beginning with Kitchener's extraordinary appearance and clothing. The tall, bony, angular host, between fifty

and sixty, comes to life, his body disproportionate and unnaturally tall, with halting walk that resulted from an attack of
paralysis that also cost him the sight of one eye; the unstylishly
dressed doctor in black, shiny material. The good doctor, the
wealthy doctor, who only gives medical advice gratuitously to
friends. Rennie repeats the stories of Kitchener's insistence on
punctuality, stories repeated in other memoirs: "Come at seven
and depart at eleven." And, despite the fact that he was a weari-
some egotist, chiefly in his glory when he could relate what *he*
had seen, discovered, and practiced; despite his request that
women wear "no finery," his evening parties were always
crowded with eminent figures from the worlds of literature and
music.

On the particular evening she describes, the house on Warren Street is filled with sixty guests, almost all authors, publishers, editors of or contributors to public journals, plus two or
three first-rate professional singers. Among the famous, Rennie
lists the handsome, urbane Viscount Dillon, recently returned to
England after a lengthy sojourn in Italy in which he knew Byron, Madame de Staël, Canova, and Lady Blessington; and Mrs.
Shelley, with a girl of the greatest beauty she ever saw. She con-
nects the latter two with the story of an unnamed girl whose *real*
vivid and startling romance would prove Byron's words: "Truth
is strange—stranger than fiction." The girl, a great coquette,
that evening flirts outrageously with Graham, the editor of a
weekly journal who is young, handsome, and very attractive to
women. Only a few months after that particular evening, the
coquette and Graham enacted an "*all* but *fatal* tragedy," which
led to his departure from England to America, and shortly afterward his death in a duel.

Mary Shelley and a beautiful, flirtatious girl whose life is
stranger than fiction. Mary Shelley's companion at the party was
almost certainly Isabella Robinson, the only person among her
friends who fit the description! Mary Shelley and others confirm
Isabella's beauty and youth; Mérimée's letters maintained she
was a flirt. And Rennie, who often visited the Robinson home,
might know enough about Isabella's life as Mrs. Douglas that
would make it stranger than fiction. All this appeared to tie to-

gether Mary Shelley, Isabella Robinson, Kitchener, and Rennie. But where was Doddy?

Apparently not at this particular party, though David Lyndsay clearly indicates he is a member of Kitchener's circle. Instead, in attendance are other writers as well as musicians. I can picture the guests divided into small circles of talkers and listeners, enjoying "genuine rational" and "mental recreation," because Kitchener knew how to "amalgamate his guests." Midstream, Rennie inserts a rare reference by Mary Shelley to *Frankenstein*. Among the guests was one of the lesser poets of the day, an "ill-tempered, disagreeable man." When he was introduced to Mary Shelley, she is reported as whispering to Rennie: "Is he not like my monster in Frankenstein"? Again, Rennie's accuracy is called into question because Mary Shelley's novel is deeply sympathetic to her creature. But I follow on as refreshments are served, and the "feast of reason and flow of soul" concludes with a small concert. At five minutes to eleven Kitchener, as expected, points to a clock and smiles. Obediently, his guests leave. Kitchener, alone, retires to his telescope to view the skies. As I finish the chapter, I feel like one of the departing guests, thanking my host for his gracious hospitality. But it is near eleven in a different century and a different country. I have found a great deal, but not Doddy. More intrigued than ever, I turn to Volume 2.

Viscount Dillon, Lord Henry Augustus Dillon, born 1777, died 1832, author of two romances, a book of poetry, and miscellaneous military and political commentaries, came into Mary Shelley's life in 1827. According to Rennie, it was Dillon who first fostered Rennie's own writing. As a young woman, her days were "all brightness and sunshine," "high-flown" thoughts, plighted vows never spoken, and "maudlin sentimentality." In short, she was a part of the "*spasmodic* school of poetry" whose works frequently appeared in magazines of limited circulation. A friend had shown Lord Dillon some of Rennie's poems and stories. He praised them, and offered hints regarding future compositions. She, an "idle girl," at first felt Dillon's suggested readings a "punishment." But slowly, she became a reader, and she blesses his memory for the joy derived.

Then Rennie turns from herself to Dillon, "every inch" an author vain about his writing, though his books have now "passed into oblivion." Except for this shortcoming, Dillon is described as a man of many gifts, both natural and acquired. Above all, Dillon is entirely honest, not even given to "equivocation." For herself, Rennie finds uttering "myths" a fault. Though she grieves to admit it, "her own sex" is more often guilty of this failing. She then offers an aside that echoes Mary Shelley's mother's *Vindication of the Rights of Woman:* Perhaps the reason for the "myths" is the inadequate education given women. "In youth they are so taught to conceal and mask their feelings" that in later years they do not look upon "an infringement" of truth as base. To illustrate both Dillon's honesty and the tendency of many women to "myth," Rennie tells a story of a conversation that took place at Mary Shelley's house among Dillon, Mary Shelley, a "remarkably pretty girl," and the author:

"Would you fight a duel for me, Lord Dillon, if you saw me insulted?" Mary Shelley playfully asked.

"Yes, I would—or for her," meaning Eliza Rennie.

"And would you for me, too?" simpered out a remarkably pretty girl who was present.

"Certainly not" was Dillon's sharp reply, for "you tell so many stories. . . ."[2]

That remarkably pretty girl *could* be Isabella, her story telling consistent with Mérimée's portrayal of Mrs. Douglas as unworthy of Mary Shelley's friendship. Mary Shelley and the girl are dropped for a number of pages, while Rennie celebrates Dillon's exceptional handsomeness, his six-foot height, his blue eyes, aquiline nose, forehead, and beautiful mouth. Handsome is as handsome does. He is a prince of a man, a "model patrician." Finally, a chink in the armor. It appears Dillon has a taste for people who are "odd." One day, he called on Rennie in great joy, having discovered a "new oddity." He had just been to Mrs. Shelley's, who sends her love and invites her to visit the next day. Dillon says Rennie must go, for Mrs. Shelley has an "extraordinary person staying with her—a 'Miss Dods . . . so wonderfully clever and so queer-looking.'"

A Miss Dods. A woman. This fits with the earl of Morton's codicil to his will. But the will, according to the record office, refers to two *married* daughters. And if Dods is M.D. Dods is Lyndsay is Douglas, this means that the beautiful young Isabella Robinson was married to Miss Mary Diana Dods. And Miss Dods was Adeline's father. Happily, Rennie this time does not veer from her subject. For two and a half pages, she gives her reader Miss Dods.

For Rennie, "Nature, in any of its wildest vagaries, never fashioned anything more grotesque-looking than was this Miss Dods." So grotesque, that the closest Rennie can estimate this woman's age is somewhere between thirty and forty. She describes Dods's hair as cropped, curly, short, and thick, "more resembling that of a man than of a woman." If this is not confusing enough, Rennie goes on to state that at first glance, Dods looked like "some one of the masculine gender" who had "indulged in the masquerade freak of feminine habiliments, and that 'Miss Dods' was an *alias* for Mr. ———."

For the story of the Douglases, it would make sense if Miss Dods *was* an alias for Mr. Douglas or Lyndsay or Dods. The beautiful, young Isabella Robinson *would* have a husband. Isabella's daughter Adeline *would* have a father. The husband and wife Mary Shelley mentions in her letters *would* be husband and wife. The couple Prosper Mérimée met in Paris and spoke of in his letters to Mary Shelley would *be* a couple. But Rennie drops this idea and goes on to describe *Miss* Dods:

> She had small *petite* features, very sharp and piercing black eyes, a complexion extremely pale and unhealthy, with that worn and suffering look in her face which so often and so truly—as it did, poor thing, in hers—tells of habitual pain and confirmed ill-health; her figure was short, and, instead of being in proportion, was entirely out of all proportion—the existence of some organic disease aiding this materially.

Short, curly hair; dark eyes. Both matched Mary Shelley's passport description of Mr. Douglas. But these are too common to be clues in themselves. Dods's pale, unhealthy complexion, her confirmed ill health, fits Lyndsay's descriptions of himself in his letters to Blackwood. It also echoes Mary Shelley's 1828 words about D's diseased body. Again, clues that in themselves are too ordinary. But Rennie's paragraph adds a new fact to the composite picture: Dods's body is entirely out of proportion. Eventually, this fact becomes a major key to the story of the Douglases.

Rennie, always one to describe the clothes as well as the person, turns to Miss Dods's singular dress, which matched Dods's: ". . . physical peculiarities and disqualifications, and only tended to heighten and exasperate, so to speak, the oddity of her *tout ensemble.*" She wears a white cambric dress so close-fitting, and so lean in cut, as to resemble a pillowcase. From shoulder to knee, the dress had a row of little tucks, "as if to have body and skirt of one material was of too ordinary a character for *her* toilette." Over her dress, she wore a tight green jacket. Rennie confesses she had to work hard to control her laughter.

But humor is swept away, and bizarre appearance reconciled, by Dods's "extraordinary talent" exhibited without affectation in her conversation. Charmed and fascinated by her manner, Rennie admits she "quickly ceased to wonder at 'Doddy,' as she was familiarly termed by Mrs. Shelley and her intimate friends, being so especial a favourite." Doddy. Miss Dods. Doddy. Mr. Douglas. Doddy, who is a "great linguist, thoroughly versed in almost every European language." Doddy. David Lyndsay, who translates works from German, Italian, Latin, French, Spanish. Doddy, who "taken altogether" has "remarkable mental endowments." Doddy who was a contributor to *Blackwood's Magazine* and the author of a book called *Tales of the Wild and the Wonderful.* Doddy. David Lyndsay.

And two last sentences about Dods before Rennie returns to the handsome Lord Dillon—two tantalizing sentences. Rennie states she will not "enter upon or touch" the events of Dods's "own 'wild and wonderful' subsequent career," saying only that Dods "resided many years at Paris, where 'she died and was buried.'" Did Rennie know the truth about Dods, Doddy, Douglas, Lyndsay? Why the quotation marks around "she died and was buried"? Were the concluding comments secondhand information? How reliable was this Rennie, who seemed to know and not know at the same time? And how much of the Doddy, Douglas, Lyndsay secret did Mary Shelley know?

Reading and rereading these passages, skimming the remainder of the two volumes for any other references to Doddy, trying to match this story with the material about the Douglases, Lyndsay, and Dods that I have accumulated, I am more confused than ever. Rennie describes Doddy as a woman, but as a woman who appears to be in masquerade; a woman with the knowledge then usually attributed only to men; a woman with a "wild and wonderful" subsequent career; a woman who might actually be "Mr. ———." Was Miss Dods a transvestite?[3] A man who in 1827 left his pillowcase dress behind, donned "culottes," and accompanied by his wife and daughter, resumed his male identity? Or was Miss Dods a female transvestite who in 1827 left her pillowcase dress behind, donned "culottes," and accompanied by her purported wife and daughter, assumed a male identity?

The story of Mr. and Mrs. Douglas and their daughter argued for a man, but what I knew of Mary Shelley argued for a woman. Would Mary Shelley participate in a charade that involved a male transvestite? If Dods was a male transvestite, why was he? And why would he drop his female guise to become a family man? If Dods was a female transvestite, was she readily accepted as a man? Was the pose discovered? And who was Adeline's father? Was Dods, either as man or woman, a transvestite or merely someone in costume? A game? A daring game, played for calculated rewards? Would the will hold the answer? Or, like Rennie, who gave so much but held back so much, would the will simply add to the confusion?

# CHAPTER 9

# THE CODICIL

On April 17 the codicil to the will finally arrived: Record Office pages 416–422, dated August 11, 1827. To double-check that this is the right earl of Morton's will, I turn to page 422, then back to 421 where it states that the earl added this codicil on August 14, 1824. Satisfied this is Mary Shelley's earl, I read. And there, in the very first paragraph, the earl of Morton unlocks the mystery of Mr. Douglas, Mr. Lyndsay, M. D. Dods, Miss Dods, and Doddy. "For the love favor and affection which I have and bear to my reputed Daughters Mary Diana Dods and Georgiana Carter (formerly Georgiana Dods) widow of Captain John Carter. . . ." Mary Diana Dods. M. D. Dods. Doddy. A woman. *And* the husband of Isabella Robinson Douglas.

The will also brings into focus the previously obscure Mrs. Carter, the widow of a Captain John Carter, late of the Bombay Native Infantry. Mrs. Carter, whose addresses were used by the author David Lyndsay for much of his correspondence with William Blackwood. Mrs. Carter, who when the codicil was written in 1824 lived in Duke Street, Manchester Square, London—Lyndsay's 1824 return address. Mrs. Carter, who with two sons, was included in Mary Shelley's passport request to John Howard Payne. Georgiana Dods Carter, Mary Diana Dods's sister.

And the reason neither of the earl of Morton's daughters is listed in *Burke's* or any other family genealogy: The Dods sisters are the earl's "reputed" daughters, a polite way of saying illegitimate. True to David Lyndsay's self-description to William

Blackwood, the very finest of Scottish blood did run through his/her veins. The earls of Morton boasted an ancestry of nobility and power going back to the early fourteenth century.

Then, at last, came the annuity that Mary Shelley wrote about on August 15, 1827, the "small . . . thing done." The Earl instructs his heirs, executors, and successors to pay to the Honorable Alexander Maconachie of Meadowbank, one of the senators of the College of Justice and Lords Commissioners of Justiciary, and Sir William Rae of St. Catherine's, Baronet, His Majesty's advocate for Scotland, "for behoof of the said Mary Diana Dods and Georgiana Carter equally between them and for behoof of the survivor of the two," a clear yearly annuity of two hundred pounds sterling free from all deductions whatever. Two hundred pounds. Portioned out each year on Whitsunday and Martinmas, the first portion to be given upon the day of the earl's death or within ten days. For a man of the earl's seeming wealth, small indeed.

Should Georgiana Carter die before Mary Diana Dods, the annuity is to be reduced to one hundred pounds, free from all deductions. If, on the other hand, Georgiana Carter should outlive her sister, the entire two-hundred-pound annuity will continue to be payable during Georgiana's life. Furthermore, the annuity is to be paid directly to the sister or sisters, whether married or single, and shall not be subject or liable directly or indirectly to the debts, deeds, control, or administration of any husband or husbands with whom the said Mary Diana Dods or Georgiana Carter may hereafter marry.

I had found "my two men." Lyndsay was a pseudonym. And, more amazing, Walter Sholto Douglas's existence meant that Doddy was a female transvestite; that Isabella was "married" to a woman. And Mary Shelley had stood up for the bride and the groom. And this story had been a secret for some one hundred and fifty years.[1] But even with all the evidence, it was hard to believe.

I carefully reviewed again all of Mary Shelley's letters referring to the Douglases, to prove to myself that the logic of Mary Diana Dods as Douglas really worked. As the pieces came together, it became apparent that Dods was in fact the *Sposo*.

Still, it was one thing to plan to pass as man and wife, another for the charade to be accepted. But there was some confirmation it was accepted in Paris. There was the one letter to the Parisian Jacquemont in which Mary Shelley referred to Mrs. Douglas after her Paris visit, as well as Prosper Mérimée's letters that not only refer to the Douglases, but place them in the center of an extensive Parisian Anglo-French social circle.

Mérimée's references to the Douglases make clear that he and his set regarded them as man and wife. They are so married that Mérimée underscored his own contempt for the problems marriage brings by citing the Douglases as an example. The Douglases were also married as far as the *Dictionary of National Biography* is concerned: Isabella Robinson Douglas married the Reverend Mr. Falconer as the widow of Walter Sholto Douglas. Adeline Douglas married Henry Drummond Wolff as the daughter of the late Walter Sholto Douglas.

My first search was set in motion by a fairly simple question: Who were the two men? The answer I expected was straightforward biographical data about Douglas and Lyndsay. Mary Shelley's friendship with Douglas posed no problem; he was the husband of her beloved friend Isabella Robinson. As for Lyndsay, I had hoped to find out how Mary Shelley and he had become acquainted and perhaps why their friendship was so brief. Originally, I assumed simple footnotes would answer. As I probed deeper, I knew I had more: the Lyndsay pseudonym, the already married Reverend Marcus Dods. All this called for more investigation and lengthier explanations. Again, I realized that many writers used pseudonyms and many people eloped. The two notes would be all the more interesting. But Lyndsay and Douglas, author, husband, father, offspring of nobility, were one person, and the will proved that person was a woman.

Hunt concluded, answer in hand, I felt more caught up than ever before in the Douglas/Lyndsay story. Even if I were right about what Mary Diana Dods and Isabella Robinson Douglas and Mary Shelley did, I didn't know why they did it. I needed to find out more about Dods and Robinson to fill in the narrative of Mary Shelley's life. Besides, I simply wanted to know. They—she—had broken out of the framework of a footnote in

Mary Shelley's letters. Mary Diana Dods became the center of her own story. What was to be an end became a new beginning. A new search opened. Not, this time, for two men, but for one woman: Mary Diana Dods, a medium-height, curly-haired, highly cultured author and family man, with her lovely girl-bride Isabella and "their" infant daughter at her side.

## CHAPTER 10

# A NEW TRAIL

WITH THE SECOND SEARCH, I stepped into a house of mirrors. Inside, moving ahead in the half-light, leading me on, were the three women, their long skirts and petticoats rustling as they hurried along. At times, they paused, one, two, or three together, seeing themselves stretched out in one mirror, reduced in another. As I came up behind, trying to put myself in the same frame, to see what they saw, they slipped away. Isabella, the lovely Isabella, impatiently looked for a mirror that truly reflected, even enhanced her noted beauty. But what else might it show? Doddy, dressed now as a man, now as a woman, jotting notes for her next story, called after her wife in French, Italian, and German to wait, wait up. Mary Shelley, golden hair covered by a black lace veil, stared at herself in one, then another mirror. She is thirty years old, five years a widow. Will she ever again find an outside reflection in which she feels safe, loved? I step toward one woman, then the other. They disappear in the shadowy maze, looking, I think, for each other. When I turn around, the three are again together, whispering. But then, of their own accord, they move apart in three different directions. For the first time, I fully understood that Mary Shelley assisting the Douglases to create themselves was larger than the act itself. Each of the three women was drawn to their daring conspiracy by her own inner search, which had as much to do with character and situation as with social mores. And both individual lives and institutions were gambled with in the metaphor of the Douglas marriage.

Legally, of course, it wasn't a marriage. It was a mock-marriage between two women. But, to use a modern term, was it a marriage between homosexuals?[1] I knew generally that male homosexuality in that era in England carried the severest penalties—pillory, public stoning, jail, death by mutilation. Did the same punishments apply to women? I had come across material that considered—or diligently tried to avoid—the question of homosexuality in the life of the very bisexual Lord Byron. As recently as 1979, however, there was relatively little research available about nineteenth-century male homosexuality, and even less about female.[2]

Of course, there were the Honorable Sarah Ponsonby (?1755–1831) and Lady Eleanor Butler (?1745–1829), her companion of fifty-three years. The celebrated "Ladies of Llangollen" are not only included in the *Dictionary of National Biography;* they are listed as famous married couples often are—together. According to the *DNB,* these ladies of Dublin ran away from their homes planning to live together in complete seclusion. Their families, strongly objecting, forced them—like eloping lovers—to return home. But they made good their next escape, living happily ever after in a cottage at Plasnewydd in the Vale of Llangollen, Wales, which neither ever left for a single night, until death parted them. "Their devotion to each other and their eccentric manners gave them wide notoriety," drawing streams of visitors, among them well-known writers and distinguished foreigners. These "two most celebrated virgins," renowned in their time as paragons of sisterly love, were held up as examples of good taste and moral behavior; their accustomed "semi-masculine" costume, merely eccentric. No one in that era, at least openly, raised the question of sexual love between the fair virgins.

In our era, it would be myopic not to raise the question. And if one raises it for the ladies of Llangollen, one must as well for Mary Diana Dods and Isabella Robinson. When Thomas Moore wrote in his diary that he witnessed an "extraordinary scene" at the Robinsons' home in 1824, he gave no details. Possibly revelations of Isabella's homosexual behavior had been revealed, and the outraged Joshua Robinson and his defiant daughter had openly fought. But it was also possible they fought because Isabella, though a girl, was a precocious flirt who worried and embarrassed her father. For a moment it seemed possible they fought because Isabella was already pregnant with Adeline, but the date was too early for the time sequence to work.

In any case, Adeline's existence is a strong reminder that Isabella showed definite symptoms of heterosexuality. But Byron had had male and female lovers. Why not Isabella? Her inclinations might have been heterosexual, bisexual, or homosexual; so, too, her partner, Mary Diana Dods. Dods looked like a man in woman's clothing. She wrote under a man's name. She became a "husband." Still, all this might have had other than sexual motivations. Her feelings for Isabella Robinson could have been those of a loving friend without being sexual. This was, after all, the beginning of an era that placed special value on friendships between women. Mary Shelley herself said that during these years she went through a phase in which she could be "spell bound" over a woman.[3] Was there some question of homosexuality for Mary Shelley at this time? Or, had she, as so many other women, sought affection and companionship within her own sex when she didn't find it in the other?

To understand the Douglases, I would have to explore the possibility of a lesbian[4] arrangement as well as other causes. In every explanation, their "marriage" seriously violated accepted social mores. As Mr. and Mrs. Douglas, they mocked the ordained concept of proper female roles and proper male/female relationships. They also mocked the middle-class concept of marriage itself, in an era when it was coming to new vigor. Did they also mock the law?

The earl of Morton's codicil opened the question of another infraction of social mores. Mary Diana Dods and her sister were illegitimate. English aristocracy had a long history of such children. Born of this class, they were commonly acknowledged and provided for. The ten illegitimate children of the duke of Clarence, later King William IV, and Dorothea Jordon, actress, were named FitzClarence, were openly raised and married among the aristocracy. George Richard St. John, third viscount Bolingbroke and fourth viscount St. John, had at least fifteen children, only the first and last three of whom were legitimate. The eleven illegitimate children, born of two wives and a liaison with his half sister, were also openly raised and married within their father's class. But the earl of Morton was Scottish and Lord Commissioner to the General Assembly of the Church of Scotland. The Church of Scotland was not so accommodating as its English neighbors to the wild-oatsian inclinations of their flock.

As Lyndsay, Dods told Blackwood of a demanding father. But Dods apparently did not live with her father during this period. Had the Dods sisters been raised in their father's estates, south of Edinburgh at Dalmahoy? Or north of Edinburgh, in the shadow of the ruins of the Douglas ancestral castle at Aberdour? Or had they been kept in London, neatly out of sight of Scottish church and nobility?

In late May 1979 I wrote to the India Office Records Office for information about Georgiana Carter and her husband. Their response revealed that Captain John Carter was born on May 2, 1786, at Alderton in Suffolk, the son of John Carter, gentleman, and his wife Ann. On May 22, 1801, just after his fifteenth birthday, Carter was appointed a second lieutenant in the third regiment of Bombay Native Infantry, with which he served for the rest of his career, being promoted to lieutenant February 7, 1803, and captain on January 8, 1816. He was absent from Bombay from late 1808 to early 1810 on furlough in England, and again was on leave in late 1818, but died on December 7 of that year, possibly on board ship on the passage home. Carter probably married in England in 1809, as the India Office has no record of the marriage. They do, however, have records of a daughter Georgiana Isabella Douglas, born June 7, 1811, baptized November 5, 1812, buried April 6, 1815, and an infant son, buried April 4, 1815. Carter's wife's name was Georgiana.

Another source of information might relate to Doddy's apparent language skills and breadth of learning. Might "Sholto Douglas" or "David Lyndsay" have attended Edinburgh University? Could Mary Diana Dods have been admitted? The answer was negative on all accounts. Edinburgh University had no trace of Douglas or Lyndsay—women, at this period, could not have attended classes there—some women attended lectures in 1867—only after 1889 could women enroll at the University—women learned foreign languages at the beginning of the nineteenth century through private instruction by governesses.

A relatively small number of books discuss women's education in the late eighteenth and early nineteenth centuries in England or Scotland. The picture in England was simple and bleak. Women were almost universally regarded as intellectually inferior. Wealthy upper- and middle-class families employed governesses, brought instructors to the home for individual lessons, or sent their daughters to boarding schools, which grew in popularity after the middle of the eighteenth century. Education for woman generally meant—in addition to basic reading—etiquette, dancing, deportment, needlework, music, and French. The objective, depending on class, was to provide only those skills necessary to prepare a girl for the accepted dependency and restrictions of marriage. In Scotland, education for women was better. Parish schools provided universal education for both girls and boys; and attendance, though not mandatory, was viewed as a parental obligation. But, as Edinburgh University had informed me, even in the more progressive Scotland, women could not during Doddy's day attend a university. In both England and Scotland, a relatively few women had and took the opportunity to acquire advanced learning. These women were generally those in families of rank or the exceptions in the middle class, including both Mary Wollstonecraft and Mary Shelley.[5] If David Lyndsay told Blackwood the truth on this point, "he" had learned French and Italian with the "best Masters." Since the "best Masters" were not found in girls' boarding schools, it appears that the earl of Morton provided his daughters with good educations at home.

How well did those educations serve them abroad? I reread the story of the Douglases' remaining days in England—passports, signatures, plans made and remade—to try to work out what happened when they arrived in Paris. The outline of the events emerges from Mary Shelley's cryptic letters that inform Jane Hogg of their progress interwoven with her dissembling letters to Payne about the lovely bride and her husband, both series linked to Mary Shelley's 1828 letters to Jane Hogg about her Paris visit, her smallpox, Prosper Mérimée and her rejection of his "offer," her return home and, within the next two years, the disappearance of the Douglases from her life.

Then another piece of the story fell into place: a newly located 1830 Mary Shelley letter to another Parisian—the famous General Lafayette, hero of the American and French revolutions. As head of the reform movement, he played a leading role in France's July 1830 revolution. Congratulating the "Hero on his final triumph" for his part in "bidding the world be free," she reminds him they had met when she came to Paris and fell ill with smallpox. From all evidence, Mary Shelley's time in Paris was spent mostly in a sickbed or with the Douglases. The Lafayette letter raised two possibilities: Mary Shelley, through a third party, had introduced herself and the Douglases to Lafayette, Mérimée, and others; or Mary Shelley met Lafayette and the others through the Douglases, who somehow had made their way into very elite company.

Mary Shelley provided some additional clues in a red leather volume of *The Literary Pocket-Book* for 1821.[6] Except for a few scattered notes, the diary pages in the volume are blank. But on pages 27 and 28, there was an address list written by Mary Shelley of an impressive Paris circle. On page 27, G. W. Hallam, 8 Rue Neuve de la Jeunes des Maturins [*sic*]; on page 28 and facing, General Lafayette, 6 Rue d'Anjou; Benjamin Constant, 15 Rue d'Anjou; Miss Clarke, 24 Rue des Petits Augustins; Fauriel, 47 Rue de Verneuil; P. M., 16 Faubourg St. Germain; Garnett, 14 Rue de Faux (which later I learned was actually 14 Rue Duphot—had Mary Shelley simply misheard the name as she wrote it down or was she making a joke on "false"?). The undated list could now be placed in 1828. Mary Shelley must have carried the *Pocket-Book* to Paris with her, but it was still unclear who introduced who to whom.

Some names I recognized from general knowledge of the era: Lafayette and Benjamin Constant, the Franco-Swiss politician and author. Their being on a list doesn't mean Mary Shelley met them, but other evidence proved she had. "P. M." is Prosper Mérimée, and Mérimée's 1828–29 letters sent news to

Mary Shelley of her friends Miss Clarke and the Misses Garnett. As for Fauriel, a November 1840 unpublished letter from Mary Shelley to this French critic and historian invites him to call on her, and reminds him since their first meeting "It is now twelve years (Good heavens, how life is once long and short)."

A number of these names are also tied together in A. W. Raitt's[7] biography of Prosper Mérimée. The Misses Julia and Fanny Garnett are daughters of an English family who lived for a time in America but then settled in Paris after their father's death. Miss Mary Clarke for many years was linked with Fauriel and following his death married the German scholar Julius Mohl. Among the international celebrities attracted to the Garnett home, Raitt lists Mérimée, Stendhal, Lafayette—and Mary Shelley. Raitt says Mary Shelley came to Paris to see her friend Julia Robinson, and was taken to the Garnett salon by her friend Frances Wright. Impossible on two accounts: Julia went *with* Mary Shelley to Paris to see Isabella Robinson Douglas; and the antislave activist Frances Wright was in America at the time, as a series of letters she wrote to Mary Shelley between August 1827 and March 1828 proves.[8] No mention of the name Douglas in Wright's letters, but there are occasional references to Mary Shelley's "dear friend," whom I now understand to be Isabella Douglas, and in one letter Wright sends "My love to Isabel."

Wright's letters begin to tie the circle even closer together with two other references to names on Mary Shelley's Paris list. In her first letter dated Paris, August 22, 1827, introducing herself to Mary Shelley, Wright gave her return address in France as c/o General Lafayette, Rue d'Anjou, and 7, St. Honoré, Paris. And her letters explain that she remains in Paris because of the impending marriage of her dear friend Julia Garnett. A number of questions arise. When Frances Wright visited Mary Shelley at Arundel in 1827, did she meet Isabella? Was it Isabella Robinson or Isabella Douglas? Did she also meet "Mr. Douglas"? Was it Frances Wright who introduced the Douglases to the Paris circle? And, if so, to whom? Lafayette? Mérimée? The Garnetts? Someone whose name has not yet come up? Were the names in the *Pocket-Book* given to Mary Shelley by

Wright in 1827? Or written in while Mary Shelley was actually in Paris? If the Douglases were the means of introducing Mary Shelley to the stellar company she met in 1828, it meant that not only Mérimée but the entire Paris circle accepted "Mr. and Mrs. Douglas."

I could picture Mary Diana Dods and Isabella Robinson—Mr. and Mrs. Douglas—entering a Paris apartment. "He" assists "his" wife to remove her wrap, handing it along with his top hat, coat, and gloves to a servant. Offering Mrs. Douglas "his" arm, the couple together enter the parlor. Their hostess crosses the room to greet them. Mr. Douglas kisses her hand. Mrs. Douglas and she embrace. Mr. Douglas then greets several others in the room, shaking hands in the English fashion with the men, kissing the hands of several of the women. The charming Mrs. Douglas lightly embraces the women of her acquaintance. She gives more attention and time to a number of the men in the room, as they rush forward to kiss her hand in greeting. Her gay laugh, her flirtatious remarks light up the room while her husband retreats into a corner, scowling in disapproval.

## CHAPTER 11

# FANNY WRIGHT, PHILANTHROPIST AND AGITATOR

WITH LITTLE TO GO ON, I decided to see where Frances Wright might take me. Her letters to Mary Shelley more than suggested she was the link between Mary Shelley, the Douglases, and the Paris circle. The *Dictionary of National Biography* (*DNB*) provided a thumbnail biography under Frances Darusmont, "better known by her maiden name as Frances Wright (1795–1852), philanthropist and agitator."

Born in Scotland to a father of independent means and strong liberal convictions, she and her younger sister Camilla were orphaned in early childhood and raised by relatives in England. Through study on her own, Fanny Wright came to support the same beliefs espoused by her father. She, accompanied by Camilla, made the first of many trips to America in 1818, remaining there for two years. During this part of her life, she wrote several books and produced a play,[1] all expressive of her liberal philosophy. From 1821 to 1824, she lived in Paris, where she enjoyed the company of Lafayette and other liberal French leaders. In 1824, she returned to America. With her own money she established at Nashoba, Tennessee, a colony in which slaves could work and earn sufficient funds to buy their own freedom.

Nashoba was to be a model that southern planters would follow and thereby set free their slaves. Fanny Wright, overworked and seriously ill, again returned to Europe in 1827.

Once restored to health, she went back to the United States, where she published a socialistic journal and gave public lectures, many antireligious in nature. She made a number of trips between the United States and Europe during the 1830s, finally marrying M. Phiquepal-Darusmont in 1838. The marriage failed in the 1840s, and she ended her days in the United States.

While in Europe, on August 22, 1827, Fanny Wright wrote to Mary Shelley introducing herself as one who devoted her time and fortune to "laying the foundations of an establishment where affection shall form the only marriage, kind feeling and kind action the only religion, respect for the feelings and liberties of others the only restraint and union of interest the bond of peace and security." The *DNB* confirmed that Wright was a friend of Lafayette and Mary Shelley, but gave no additional details.

I had a copy of Wright's letter, with its words of reverence for Mary Shelley's parents.[2] Wright intended not only to befriend the famous daughter, and wife, of radicals, but to persuade her to return to the Nashoba colony with her. On September 12, 1827, Mary Shelley responded to the radical philanthropist, author, and social reformer with a self-revealing letter that mixed high praise of Wright with pride in her parents and Shelley. Though Mary Shelley enthusiastically welcomed Wright's friendship, she declined to join her. So much could be put together from Wright's and Mary Shelley's letters. But to understand what, if any, role Wright played in the Douglas story, I needed more details about the willful six-foot-tall pioneer of personal freedom; this social reformer who drew attention to herself as much for her unconventional female behavior and height as for the audacity of her antiestablishment views.

Frances Wright biographies further suggested that she may well have been the link to the 1828 Anglo-French Parisian circle. According to Perkins and Wolfson's *Frances Wright: Free Enquirer,*[3] Wright became close friends with John Garnett, his wife, son, and two daughters, Julia and Harriet, in 1819 in their country home near New Brunswick, New Jersey. When Garnett died in May 1820, his wife and daughters moved to Paris. Four years later, Wright visited Paris and reestablished her intimate friendship with the Garnetts. During that same visit, Wright, through Benjamin Constant, met General Lafayette. The young radical and the old became companions, close enough to worry Lafayette's family that their elderly, widowed father might marry Wright. If his family was relieved when Lafayette sailed alone to America in August 1824, that relief must have been short-lived: Frances and Camilla Wright sailed a few days later. Once abroad, the three openly traveled together. The plentiful Lafayette biographies I searched refer to his friendship with Wright, but not a word about Mary Shelley or the Garnetts.

Two other names in the Wright-Shelley letters were possible sources of information about the Paris circle, both of them English. Frances Wright met Frances Trollope[4] in England in 1822, probably through Trollope's lawyer husband. The independent pioneer and the seemingly thoroughly domesticated wife, a mother of six, became fast friends. To the surprise of their circle, Frances Trollope became Wright's new recruit for Nashoba in 1827. Later, Trollope wrote about that United States experience, launching her own notable writing career with her scathing *Domestic Manners of the Americans*. On the other hand, Robert Dale Owen's association with Wright was no surprise to anyone. Namesake of his father, the famous Manchester industrialist and social reformer, Owen met Wright in 1826 at his father's experimental utopian colony in New Harmony, Indiana. When New Harmony failed in the spring of 1827, Owen went to Nashoba and joined forces with Frances Wright for the next several years. It was Owen, who had met William Godwin through his father, who suggested that Fanny Wright contact Mary Shelley that August of 1827. From these bits of information, it appeared that it was Wright who probably introduced Mary Shelley and possibly the Douglases to the Paris circle.

I returned to the *DNB* to find Robert Dale Owen (1801–1877), publicist and author, born in Glasgow to Robert Dale Owen (1771–1858), socialist and industrialist, famous for turning his New Lanark mills into an experiment to educate and improve the lives of his workers. The son followed his father's liberal precepts. He dedicated himself to public life in the United States, serving three terms in the House of Representatives, and as Minister at Naples. Throughout his life, he staunchly fought slavery and supported women's rights. As for his relationship with Wright, the *DNB* only confirmed what Wright's biographers had said about their friendship.

Owen's autobiography, *Threading My Way*,[5] provides more details about Wright and Mary Shelley, but only a passing remark about the 1827 summer visit to Paris. He comments on Wright's character, describing her as an ardent advocate of universal suffrage, with no regard for either color or sex; a radical in politics, morals, and religion whose strong, logical mind was both independent and zealous. For all his admiration, he goes on to criticize her vigorously for lacking discipline, for over-enthusiasm in aiding others without sufficient information, and stubborn adherence to her own opinions. Despite these shortcomings, he regards her as an exceptionally talented lecturer and writer, committed to carrying out her beliefs, whatever the sacrifice.

Owen's criticism of his longtime associate Wright is striking in comparison with his undiluted praise for Mary Shelley, with whom he spent relatively little time in that fall of 1827. To him, she was "genial, gentle, sympathetic, thoughtful, and matured in opinion" beyond her twenty-nine years, a person "essentially liberal in politics, ethics, and theology" but lacking prejudice against either the old or the new. Above all, he valued Mary Shelley as "womanly." In retrospect, he wished that he had been under her influence rather than Fanny Wright's, because he would have accepted from her the "guiding-rein" he required. Owen was with Wright in the heady years of the late 1820s, when she and his own father both founded experimental villages to demonstrate to the world the dream of social organization based on egalitarian principles; Owen's autobiography was written some fifty years later—time enough for him to take a more pious view of his own young years.

Owen proved to be a dead end in the search for Doddy. I returned to Frances Wright. An introduction to an article in a

*Harvard Library Bulletin*[6] by Cecilia Payne-Gaposchkin provided the most informative material yet about the Garnetts. John Garnett (1750–1820) came from a Bristol family of well-to-do importers in the China trade. He and his wife, Mary Gordon (1762–1848), had seven children, five of whom survived: Anna Maria, Henry, Frances, Julia, and Harriet.[7] It appears that toward the end of the eighteenth century, John Garnett, a man of liberal beliefs, decided to leave England. In 1797, the year of Mary Shelley's birth, the Garnetts established themselves at the Whitehouse estate in New Brunswick, New Jersey. In 1819 and 1820, the Garnetts were hosts to Frances and Camilla Wright. The Wright sisters and Julia and Harriet Garnett became affectionate friends. After John Garnett's death in 1820, when Mary Garnett and her daughters returned to Europe and made their home in Paris, the Garnetts and Wrights began their correspondence. Julia Garnett also corresponded with many other friends and kept most of her letters. Among Julia's letters were those written to her by her mother and sisters after she married and moved to Hanover in 1827.

Predictably, the bulk of the letters have nothing to do with Doddy. Their focal point is the Wright sisters and in their interaction, the Garnetts. Frances Wright, circa October 1820, tells the sisters that "the bent of my heart" is to become an American citizen. She has an aversion for England, because of its climate, its government, its society and:

> . . . the recollections w^ch make all these doubly offensive to me . . . this island, I know it contains much of good & something yet of happiness, but vice & misery are heavier in the scale . . . I cannot see begging in our town & villages, & read of injustice in every paper I cast my eye upon, & <witness> /meet/ political & religious hypocrisy where I turn without feeling pain, indignation or disgust.

Of America, there is much to celebrate of its prosperity and freedom, but:

. . . the crying sin of her slavery weighs upon my heart; there are moments when this foul blot so defaces to my mind's eye all the beauty of her character that I turn with disgust from her . . . my heart is at war with man, I loathe his nature & his name & attribute his <being> /creation/ to a malignant demon, rather than /to/ a beneficient God.

These views, expressed to her "loved Harriet," sum up the guiding philosophy that pervades Frances Wright's letters—and her life. The segments of the letters published discuss historical and political institutions, social mores, books, politicians, economics, law, and industry. They are informed and urbane, sometimes cynical. Certainly, most of her contemporaries would have been surprised that a twenty-five-year-old woman had written them.

The next letter was written in 1824. Four years had passed. The Garnetts were in Paris. The Wrights were in America with "the loved Genl." The geography has changed, but not Wright's politics. The letters are filled with fascinating details about people and places. Year after year, Wright grows increasingly tormented by the plague of slavery. With each letter, she feels compelled to some action against the depraved system, and the plan of Nashoba is born. Nashoba will prove to southern slave owners the morality and economic benefits of freeing their slaves.

In July 1827, Fanny Wright, ill, is en route to Europe accompanied by Robert Dale Owen. In August, Frances Wright sends a letter to Harriet Garnett from Lafayette's country home, La Grange, near Rosnay, Seine-et-Marne, talking about Nashoba. That same month, another such letter, this time referring to Julia Garnett's imminent marriage. Wright is still ill, and her hair, though she is only thirty-two, is "turning white again." The next letter is written from Harrow on October 7, 1827, several weeks after the new friends had met at Arundel. All this wonderful material, but nothing about the days spent together by Wright and Mary Shelley and, perhaps, the Douglases.

On December 26, Frances Wright, accompanied by Frances

Trollope and Owen, writes to Julia Garnett, now Pertz, from on board the *Edward* as they enter the Mississippi; another letter in March 1828, a very long account to Harriet Garnett, sending news of Nashoba, and of many friends. Toward the end of this letter is one paragraph, the only paragraph in the entire sixty-three-page article, in which Wright refers to Mary Shelley and the Douglases. And it is extraordinary in what it reveals about Frances Wright, the Garnetts, the Douglases, and their various friendships with Mary Shelley:

> The D's account of Mary does not surprise me she did not strike me as a person of sensibility & my first impression was decided disappointment I resisted & lost this, & became interested in /&/ for herself tho the interest excited by her parentage & history has always held a large share in the interest I feel in her. The D's account may be all true (& my own recalled impressions w$^d$ rather go to confirm it) but it makes much against *them*. Not only have I seen them evince the fondest kindness for Mary, but Isabel's letters, w$^{ch}$ I have seen, are in a strain of the fondest & most dependent friendship. Deficient sensibility is a negative quality but hypocrisy is <an> /a/ positive one of the worst char$^r$ [character] 'Tis a bad & hollow world my Harriet as it is now whatever /it/ <I> may be hereafter, & <every> all I hear of or from it makes me rejoice in the breadth of the wilderness that separates Nashoba from it.

And an explanatory footnote that would shift the focus of my search:

> Mary is Mary Wollstonecraft (Godwin) Shelley (1797–1851). Among the Garnett letters are copies (in Julia's handwriting) of a letter from Mary Shelley to Fanny Wright (12 September 1827) and of one from Fanny Wright to Mary Shelley (15 September 1827). The "D's" are the Douglases; Isabel (mentioned subse-

quently in this paragraph) was Mrs. Sholto Douglas
(née Isabella Robinson). They were neighbors of the
Garnetts in Paris and are frequently mentioned in the
correspondence.

The "D's." Mrs. Sholto Douglas. Neighbors of the Garnetts. The "D's" who have discussed Mary Shelley with Harriet
Garnett, and have not drawn a very pretty picture. Nor is Frances Wright the loving friend to Mary Shelley that she appeared
to be in their correspondence. Wright had first found Mary
Shelley wanting in what she called "sensibility." The unabridged
*Oxford English Dictionary* has seven definitions, with several
subsets, and examples of the use by famous writers, of "sensibility." I would guess Number 5, "Quickness and acuteness of
apprehension or feeling; the quality of being easily and strongly
affected by emotional influences," meets Wright's use of the
word. But Number 6, used rarely after the eighteenth and early
nineteenth centuries: "Capacity for refined emotion; delicate
sensitiveness of taste; also, readiness to feel compassion for suffering, and to be moved by the pathetic in literature or art"
might also be what Wright had in mind.

Why did Wright feel Mary Shelley was deficient in sensibility? It is difficult to know because in fact Mary Shelley was
remarkably sensitive to the needs of others all her life, very
often to her own emotional and financial cost. Her very relationship with the Douglases is an illustration, however ironic.
Perhaps it had to do with Mary Shelley's reticence in social set-
tings. In any case, Wright apparently overcame her initial feeling and did become interested in Mary Shelley, because Frances
Wright's letters to Mary Shelley certainly sound caring and affectionate. But Doddy? And, more important, the dear, loving,
angelic Isabella on whom Mary Shelley heaped such love and
attention. Isabella, who, according to Wright, wrote fond and
dependent letters to Mary Shelley. Isabella, to whom Mary
Shelley gave, and for whom she risked, so much.

Here was the first clue to understanding why the friendship
of Mary Shelley and the Douglases ended. I disagreed with
Wright's idea that Mary Shelley lacked compassion for others. I

agreed that a lack of sensibility is a negative quality. And I certainly agreed that "hypocrisy is a positive one of the worst character!" The word *hypocrisy* brought to mind Mary Shelley's December 1830 *Journal* entry about Isabella, the being she adored, who she now realizes was "ever false yet enchanting—now she has lost her fascinations—probably, because I can no longer serve her she take[s] no more trouble to please me."

The passage in Wright's letter also suggested that the Douglases were not simply neighbors of the Garnetts in Paris. They seemed to be intimate friends at least of Harriet Garnett—perhaps of all the Garnetts. Equally revealing, Frances Wright indicated that she had personally seen the "D's" interact with Mary Shelley. The only time Wright could have seen them together was in the south of England, when she visited Mary Shelley in early October 1827. Wright's reference in this letter makes it clear that she is not talking about a Miss Mary Diana Dods and a Miss Isabella Robinson. By the time Wright visited, Mary Diana Dods had become their "strange friend" Mr. Walter Sholto Douglas. And it was to Mr. and Mrs. Walter Sholto Douglas that Mary Shelley introduced Frances Wright, who obviously accepted the couple at face value and liked them. And probably wrote a letter introducing the Douglases to the Garnett family in Paris. Passports in hand; letter of introduction to good society in hand; the Douglases were en route to their new life, thanks to Mary Shelley who, according to the D's, was wanting in sensibility.

I combed the remainder of the article, hoping for more about the Douglases and Mary Shelley. Political concerns continued. Testimony of loving friendship between the Wrights and Garnetts continued, offering clear evidence that the Wrights are the nucleus of a larger network of women whose friendship and affection are sources of lifelong support. The Wrights' story spins itself out. Camilla Wright formed a union with another member of Nashoba in 1828; gave birth to a son, who died in 1829; she herself died in 1831. In 1828, Nashoba failed and was abandoned. In January 1830, Frances Wright accompanied the slaves she had intended to earn their freedom at Nashoba to Haiti, where they were "advantageously and happily settled." In

July 1831, Frances Wright married Darusmont, their first child already a year old. A second child was born in 1832, but died two months later. As the *DNB* indicated, the Darusmonts lived first in Paris, returned to the United States, and later were divorced. Frances Wright died in Cincinnati on December 13, 1852. There were no other references to the Douglases or Mary Shelley.

But the footnotes and the brief patches of narrative in the article made it plain that these were excerpts. Payne-Gaposchkin was concentrating on the remarkable Frances Wright and her politics. Probably the only reason the Douglas paragraph was included was because it illustrated an aspect of Wright's moral character at the same time that it called attention to Wright's friendship with the author of *Frankenstein*. It seemed possible that the omitted sections of these letters could contain further references to the Douglases and Mary Shelley. The Garnett letters, mentioned but not quoted, could as well. Frances Wright had led me to the Garnett circle; now I would go looking for the Garnetts. Somehow, somewhere in that mass of Payne-Gaposchkin letters, I expected the Garnetts to lead to Mr. and Mrs. Sholto Douglas, who arrived among them in October 1827.

The letters were in the Manuscript Division of the Houghton Library at Harvard—in all, 430 letters.[8] I had visions of finding wonderful information about the Douglases and the Garnetts in Paris in 1827–1828, and perhaps afterward. Would the Garnetts' handwritings be difficult to read? Requesting microfilm or photocopying was out of the question because of the size of the collection. It required going in person to Harvard and combing through. I was back on Doddy's trail. How well did the Garnetts know the Douglases? Did they have the same negative opinions of Isabella as Mérimée? What did they think of Mary Shelley in light of the Douglases' accusations of want of sensibility? Was there more about the D's in Wright's and the Garnett's exchanges? Did they suspect that the charming, flirtatious Mrs. Douglas was married to a woman?

## CHAPTER 12

# A POEM OF SECRET SORROW

MISTAKEN IDENTITY involving Mary Diana Dods was not only a thing of the past. Witness the 1977 *Keats-Shelley Review*[1] publication of an article suggesting that a poem, a sad lament about the death of a beloved, "drafted on one of the endpapers of a book entitled *Dramas of the Ancient World* by David Lyndsay" seemed to be by Mary Shelley. The poem was first written in pencil, then traced over in ink. Because Mary Shelley's signature appeared on the title page of the book, and her *Journal* entry indicated she read *Dramas* in March 1822, the author asserts it is "evident" that she owned this copy in 1822. There were also notes in the text in two or three different handwritings, "one of them almost certainly Mary's and another possibly Shelley's." The author believes that the poem was written by Mary Shelley after Shelley died.

Except that the poem is dated "Feby—1822"—and Shelley died on July 8, 1822. Based on handwriting, expert testimony, resemblances to other things she wrote, and the suggestion that Mary Shelley "had a strange psychological blockage which made her unwilling to write '1823,'" the author believes there is enough evidence to justify attributing the poem to Mary Shelley. The article ends with a photocopy of the poem. It was the photocopy that announced the major problem with all this evidence and conjecture. Having then spent four years reading Mary

Shelley's letters and manuscripts, I had no doubt that the poem was *not* in her handwriting. Also, I knew from a published Mary Shelley letter that the copy of *Dramas* the Shelleys and Byron read in 1822 belonged to Byron.[2] I didn't send a correction in 1977 because I didn't know whose handwriting it was.

That was before Lyndsay-Douglas-Doddy. Since April of 1979, I knew precisely who had written the poem on the end-paper of that copy of *Dramas* in February 1822. The countless hours reading David Lyndsay's and M. D. Dods's letters made me quite familiar with that distinctive script. It belonged to Mary Diana Dods. But to unravel the puzzle of the poem it was necessary to determine if that signature said to be Mary Shelley's was indeed hers; to compare the pencil against the ink copy; to see if those notes in the text were written by Mary Shelley or possibly Shelley. Most of all, I wanted to know if this book would tell more about the friendship of Mary Diana Dods and Mary Shelley.

I saw the volume in the James Buchanan Duke Library at Furman University, Greenville, South Carolina, in March 1980.[3] There, at the top of the title page, was Mary Shelley's signature. On the back endpaper was the sad poem about a dead lover and a bereaved mourner, written and dated by Doddy. I leafed through the volume, page by page, to inspect the thirty notations in the text. They were written in two different handwritings. Mostly, they are by Doddy. The other, which appears less than a handful of times, belongs to neither Mary Shelley nor Shelley.

Some of the comments by Doddy are corrections or revisions. On page 4, "to night" has written above it "last." On page 270, at the word "Flora," she writes: "an error. Flora is a roman Goddess. D—." On the facing page, at the word "twilights:" "There are no twilights in Greece D." Other notes are reflections on the text. Next to a passage on a call for celebration, Doddy wrote that Schiller has a passage resembling this in *Die Räuber*. On one page she comments that a "fine wild" Turner drawing exists on the subject; on another, that *Sardanapalus* was misprinted throughout the text—"for the proper accentuation see Juvenal." On page 192, in her drama

*Cain,* she places an "X"-mark at Cain's speech made when he is cast out after he has killed Abel. At the bottom of the page, a matching "X" followed by a quotation from Byron's *Cain:*

> After the fall too soon was I begotten
> Ere yet my Mother's mind subsided from
> The Serpent and my Sire still mourn'd for Eden—
> That which I am, I am. I did not seek
> For life, nor did I make myself—
>
> Lord Byron

Did she copy these lines here because she felt Byron's words were better than her own? Or perhaps because she found an echo of her own life in Cain's arrogant assertion, "That which I am, I am."

After completing the book, I felt convinced by the commentary that this was a copy of *Dramas* that first belonged to Doddy herself. She used it to make revisions, probably for the second edition she had so hopefully written to Blackwood about. It was in her possession when she used the endleaf to write in that lover's lament in pencil in February 1822. I would imagine it was hers until sometime after she met Mary Shelley in 1825, when Mary Shelley's assistance in her personal life and her—Lyndsay's—writing career prompted Dods to give the volume to her friend as a gift. And Mary Shelley signed the book as she did with the other books she owned. This scenario logically explained both Mary Shelley's and Doddy's handwritings. But what would explain the poem itself?

> There is an anguish in my Breast
> A sorrow all undreamed, unguessed—
> A war that I must ever feel—
> A secret I must still conceal—
> I stand upon the Earth alone
> To none my secret spirit known
> With none to sooth[e] the speechless stings
> Of my wild heart's imaginings
> With none to glory in my fame
> Or halo with sweet joy my name—

The Star of Love for me hath set
And I must live yet not forget
How once it shone upon my Brow
Though I am lorn and lonely now
A blighted Herb a blasted Tree
A living lie, a mockery—
A Lump of Earth that still, still glows
With so much perfume of the Rose
As will not let it meanly mete
With aught less lovely or less sweet—
Yes—thou art gone! O what to me
Can others admiration be
Then silent—sacred—on thy Bier
I place the strain thou canst not hear
To none I give the hallowed line
It shall, Beloved, be only thine—
From none the smile thou canst not give
My buried Love will I receive—
Genius and Taste, if such there be,
Too late, I consecrate to thee.
O what have I to do with pride
It withered when mine Angel died
And but one thought remains to me
My heart's lone deep dull agony—

                         Feby—1822—

Anguish. Secret sorrow. Alone on earth. None to glory in
the author's fame. Genius and taste consecrated to a buried
Love. A war she always feels. A secret she must conceal. A
living lie. I played with a biographical reading of the poem, always potentially misleading unless one really knows about the
life of an author. Still, apart from the information about a lost
lover, the remainder sounded like Doddy. And perhaps it wasn't
accidental that the sex of neither poet nor lover is made clear.
Was this simply a stylized piece of the period? Or was this
Doddy? I compared it to copies of the two letters Doddy had
sent Mary Shelley, the letters I originally thought were playful
courting letters from a man. "Something approaching to pain"

when she thought it would be five days before they would meet again—"miene Liebling"—"mine eye delights in retracing thy character. . . ." Nor would she "by an unnecessary delay lose one half hour of your Company . . . ever my dear Pretty's Admiring Friend MD Dods."

If Doddy gave this volume of *Dramas* to Mary Shelley, surely she recognized that the poem on the endpaper also reflected the continued sorrow of the grieving young widow. And perhaps it was then that she retraced the light pencil in ink, so the widow would clearly see Doddy's own aloneness, her sorrow, her "wild heart's" secrets. Though it claims the mourner would refuse a smile—or any joy—from someone other than her "buried Love," I wondered if this poem, this gift, was not an invitation to Mary Shelley to try.

It seemed more and more likely that Mary Diana Dods was a lesbian. Her poem, her letters, her attitude toward Isabella Robinson Douglas, her pseudonym, her transvestism. Behind everything she did I could see that secret sexuality, a torturous burden in an era that condemned male homosexuals to death. But then I thought about letters Mary Shelley, Fanny Wright, and other women of the nineteenth century wrote to their women friends. They were heavy with endearments, pledges of affection, promises of lifelong devotion. Was Mary Shelley a secret lesbian? Fanny Wright? All the women who wrote those earnest caring letters? Lesbians? I thought there was sufficient evidence to argue that neither Mary Shelley nor Fanny Wright was a lesbian. So I put on hold the idea that Mary Diana Dods was a lesbian. I simply didn't know enough about her yet for any conclusions.

## CHAPTER 13

# THE LADIES OF 14 RUE DUPHOT

NOTHING EXTRAORDINARY HAPPENED on the Douglas search until just weeks before I visited Harvard in early December 1980. In one of our exchanges of Mary Shelley information, Emily Sunstein loaned me brief, typed excerpts, provided by the Fanny Wright biographer Celia Morris, of Garnett letters from the Payne-Gaposchkin Collection; also, through Morris, a copy of Payne-Gaposchkin's privately printed volume of selections from the Garnett letters.[1]

The typescript excerpts were from letters written by Maria Garnett and her daughters, Harriet and Frances Garnett, in Paris, to Julia Pertz in Hanover. Dated November 13, 1827, to circa July 8, 1828, there were seventeen quotations, some from the same letter. On these pages, each quotation began with points of ellipsis—". . ."—and ended ". . ." with many a ". . ." sprinkled in the texts. There was no way to know if the omissions ellipses indicated the handwriting couldn't be read or if Morris left out everything she considered irrelevant to Mary Shelley. But even with their omissions, these seventeen snippets seemed to outline the story of Mr. and Mrs. Walter Sholto Douglas in the Garnetts' lives in 1827–1828.

I hoped the Payne-Gaposchkin book would fill in the omissions in the typescript. But in the introduction, Payne-Gaposchkin explained that from the correspondence of Julia

Garnett Pertz, her great-grandmother, written between 1820 and 1852, only letters relating to the Wright sisters and Frances Trollope were reproduced in full; the remaining "other subjects" were excerpts. The volume is broken into topic sections, and then arranged by date within each section. Headings on the pages identified their topics: Fanny and Camilla Wright, Julia Pertz, Frances Trollope; "Public Affairs"; writers, including Mérimée, Stendhal, Harriet Martineau; personal friends. But the Douglases and Mary Shelley fell into Payne-Gaposchkin's category of "other subjects," referred to only through selected comments. Without an index or table of contents, the only way to find references to them was to read through page by page.

By matching the dates on Morris's sheets with the dates in the book, I located the Douglas material. Happily, more was included there about the Douglases than on the sheets. Comparing the two, it appeared that the three pages of quotations had been taken from this volume. But, like the sheets, the Garnett volume fascinated as much through omission as through what was revealed. Payne-Gaposchkin, in concentrating on the Wright sisters, left out anything that referred only to the Douglases. Even mid-sentence, phrases about them were shortened by the ubiquitous ellipses ". . . ," and there was no way to judge if whole paragraphs about the Douglases were missing. This tantalizing puzzle could only be pieced together by working with the manuscripts.

At the Houghton, what struck me more than ever was the affectionate language the women used to and about each other. Frances Wright's October 7, 1827, letter to Julia Pertz refers to her as "my Julia," wishing "thee, my sweet love" happiness in her new life as a married woman in Hanover. Harriet Garnett is *Harry,* from whom Wright received a "sweet letter." Fanny Trollope is "our dear." Comparing another woman to Julia Pertz, Wright says the other woman "was hardly tried, my sweet love, seeing that I looked at her when I had just withdrawn my eyes from Julia. Farewell fondly. Nay every joy be with thee. Adieu, my own lamb." On October 8 she addressed "my sweet Harry," thanking "my love" for her "sweet letters." Amid her news of other friends, she sends "my affectionate love" to a

Madame Dupont. Trollope, in the same letter, refers to Wright as "this 'angel' (yes, Harriet, you are right—she is an angel . . . 'where her country is there shall be my country.'" These endearments brought to mind how quickly the stranger Mary Shelley became in Fanny Wright's letters "dear friend" and "dear love."[2]

The many expressions of deep love strewn through the letters were startling. By today's standards, we would assume these were love letters; their writers, homosexual. But the more I read the letters, the more I became convinced that these women did not fit that mold. Pertz was newly and happily married. Trollope was married and the caring mother of six. Fanny Wright would have one child before marriage, marry the father, and have another child. Camilla Wright formed a common-law marriage and had a child.

At the same time, it was apparent that the women *did* love each other. Profoundly. They depended on each other, and openly declared, one to the other, how they felt and what they thought. These relationships could be understood only by not insisting they conform to modern categorization. Perhaps, on some unconscious level, sexuality was involved. And perhaps Freud is right: Sexuality is involved in all human activity, calibrated to the individual. What remains true here, however, is that these women spoke with each other in a highly stylized language, a language that was conventional among cherished women friends of the middle class. That language reveals another example of how they, in their world, were different from us, in ours. As I turned to the letters in which Mr. and Mrs. Douglas made their appearance, I realized that the commonality and language of affection between the women added considerably to the complexity of understanding Mary Diana Dods.

Or Walter Sholto Douglas. Or Mrs. Walter Sholto Douglas. In the next folder of letters, dated October 31, 1827, through July 8, 1828, the Garnetts, amid other chatty news they send in their jointly written letters to Julia Pertz, trace the rise and fall of the Douglases in the Garnett circle. The story begins with Harriet Garnett passing along news to Julia Pertz from Fanny Wright on October 31. Fanny Wright had finally met Mary

Shelley and "was delighted with her, but her boy prevents her going to Nashoba." Whether Mary Shelley had actually indicated an interest in going to Nashoba is unknown. But certainly she could not join this utopian settlement, even if she wanted to, without leaving Percy Florence behind. According to Shelley's father's decree, his grandson had to remain in England.

The November 13 letter from the Garnetts to Julia announces wonderful new friends. A letter from Fanny Wright introduced them to

> . . . a Mr. and Mrs. Douglas, friends of Mrs. Shelley, and with whom she passed a week at Arundel—I am delighted with them. He is very clever, agreeable and amiable, and she beautiful, interesting and likewise very clever—both are warm admirers of Fanny, indeed both love her. What a claim to our affection! they pass the winter here, and in Dec$^r$ Mrs. Shelley comes to pay them a visit. They talk often of Julia, & say they know & love you—you w$^d$ love them.

So Mary Shelley *did* introduce Mary Diana Dods and Isabella Robinson as Mr. and Mrs. Douglas to Fanny Wright. Mary Shelley, Fanny Wright, and the Douglases had spent an entire week together in Arundel. It is likely that Mary Shelley continued to share quarters with the Douglases, while Fanny Wright lodged nearby. It is easy to imagine how they spent their days. Brief notes carried by servants back and forth. What time will you be free to dine? Tea? The air is fine today—shall we have a walk? No doubt this party of women, with one "man" among them, spoke about their usual subjects: friends, economics, slavery, women's rights; about politics and the ideas of Godwin, Wollstonecraft, Shelley; about how Nashoba's success would set the example for the entire United States to abolish slavery. No doubt they shared stories of the past and visions of the future.

But the future had already arrived for the Douglases. Fanny Wright provided the opportunity for a dress rehearsal for their first adult audience. Mary Shelley's September 23, 1827, letter made clear that Percy Florence, then nine, had accepted the transformed Mary Diana Dods as Mr. Douglas, a "new friend," though he had known her before. But he was a child. How would the game play with a full-time adult spectator in an era of strictly defined gender roles? They would spend hours, almost whole days with Wright. There was no question of pretending to be awkward in their interaction because they were newlyweds. "Their" baby Adeline was about a year old then. To be accepted as a conventional couple in respectable society, they had to behave as if they had been married for at least two years.

But Dods had become a man only four weeks earlier. Would "he" have difficulty remembering to offer "his" arm to "his" wife as they walked? To stand behind her chair when they went to dine, gently moving "his" spouse to a comfortable position at the table? And to assist the other ladies in the same way? Did Dods struggle to control the impulse to pour tea, waiting instead for "his" wife or Mary Shelley to conduct the ceremony? When the time came for Wright to take her leave, did the middle-height Mr. Dods assist the six-foot Miss Wright into her carriage?

When Dods joined the women at Arundel, she arrived dressed as a man. The fashion of the day permitted a relatively easy disguise: a large top hat, worn low on the head; trousers somewhat tight but jackets with tails that easily might hide a woman's figure; full shirts with elaborately tied cravats; full overcoats or capes. Doddy would require special tailoring because of her irregular shape, but that would not be a problem because in this era preceding mass-manufactured clothing, gentlemen's attire was still custom-made. And if necessary, Mr. Douglas could join other modish men of the era by wearing a corset.[3] What did she tell the gentlemen's tailor she called on for this unusual purchase? Perhaps that she required it for a costume party. Or perhaps she selected one of the very best tailors, and being gentlemen's tailors, they would by habit ask no questions. Innkeepers and servants would accept Mr. Douglas at face value. For four weeks, she had random opportunities to practice with outsiders. And she had to maintain male manners sufficiently to convince Percy Florence and Mary Hunt, the thirteen-year-old daughter of her friends that Mary Shelley had brought along. But the children would not have paid attention to social customs; and others Mr. Douglas came into superficial contact with would have done what most people do—assign gender according to clothing.

Wright's visit also called for Isabella Robinson to become a full-time wife for the first time. At teatime, did she remember to serve her husband first? To ask Mr. Douglas if "he" would like some biscuits? If an outing was suggested, did she defer to "him" about whether or not to go? Did she wait for "him" to drape her wrap over her shoulders? If a possible expense arose, did she get "his" permission? And, perhaps most trying of all, how well did she cope with the problem of "his" name? As customary, the Douglases in public would be expected to address each other with the formal Mr. or Mrs. It was one thing for Mr. Douglas to look at "his" wife and call her Mrs. Douglas. At least the Mrs. and the gender went together, even if the name was fictitious. But Isabella had to look at Mary Diana Dods and call her Mr. Douglas. How many times during the week of Wright's visit did she slip? And how did she cover her mistake?

If they were nervous at first, Mary Diana Dods and Isabella Robinson must have gained confidence as day after day they continued their public debut. Apparently, they played their roles well. Fanny Wright, never doubting they were a married couple, sent a letter of introduction to the Garnetts, her dear friends who lived at 14 Rue Duphot. And the Douglases, again through Mary Shelley, were provided with a second counterfeit passport to their new lives.

Harriet Garnett's November 13 letter is the first of a series of firsthand descriptions of Mr. and Mrs. Douglas in action. On November 20, Frances Garnett takes up the same letter, to add news of Fanny Wright and Fanny Trollope, received from Mrs. Douglas. Both Douglases speak of Wright with great enthusiasm, though they fear her plans will fail and she will die of a broken heart. As for the Douglases, Frances Garnett describes Mrs. Douglas as a very pretty, interesting young woman. Mr. Douglas, however, "is a little deformed but clever." *A little deformed but clever.* Her words echo Rennie's description of the masculine-looking Mary Diana Dods in her odd white dress.

Maria Garnett adds even more assurance. Continuing the family letter, she tells Julia that Harriet is indeed charmed by the pair, and for good reason. They are both very interesting. To Frances Garnett's description, she adds: "Mrs. D. beautiful but so artless and simple. He is clever, a little dwarfish and crooked, yet I am sure it was a love match, he worships his little wife."

"A little dwarfish and crooked." Furthermore, Maria Garnett believes the marriage was a "love match" because she can see that Mr. D worships "his little wife." Her first observation of Mr. D is accurate. What of her second?

Did Dods worship his little wife? Had Mr. D fallen in love with Mrs. D? Not unheard of in marriages of convenience. Or perhaps Dods was in love with *her* little wife to begin with, making the charade even more appealing for Dods. But what of Isabella? Her youthful motherhood suggested a heterosexual inclination. Was her precocious sexual activity an unhappy experiment, resulting in a baby *and* a change of sexual preference? After all, she was exceedingly young. Or perhaps the answer was simply that both Douglases, in their family finery, were heterosexual consummate actors.

Harriet Garnett picks up the letter where her mother and sister left off. In her portion, she refers to the Douglases as "my dear friends" who have taken a great deal of her time:

> I do love them & you wd love them also. We are every morning & every evening together—she is an angel— as amiable as she is lovely & I love him also—Isabel I shall call her, & love her as if I had long known her— she often talks too of dear Julia & says she will go to Hanover to see you. & so does Douglas her excellent amiable husband.

Not only is Harriet Garnett's "heart warm towards" the angel and her amiable husband, she assures Julia she must already feel affection toward them even before she knows them. She knows Julia will feel the same because they have always loved the same persons. As for the Douglases' friend Mrs. Shelley, they expect her to come to Paris in December. In the meanwhile, Harriet Garnett will try to get the Douglases to move from the Rue Richepance to quarters close to their own.

While all three Garnetts adore the Douglases, apparently Harriet is most enamored. On November 27 her mother reports that Harriet is as fond of them as "she ever was of Miss Wright, but that is entre nous." The Douglases will move nearby and they all plan to "pass every disengaged evening together" as they "deserve the fullest affection." Either Harriet's ardor for the Douglases speaks to the fragility of her affection for Fanny Wright, whom she has known and loved for some nine years, or to the remarkable impression the Douglases have made. In any case, in the space of little more than one month, the Douglases had certainly arrived as far as the Garnetts were concerned. And with them, "Mrs. Carter the sister of Mr. Douglas"—who occasionally sleeps in the Garnett's dining parlor. The widow lost her husband in the East Indies and has put her two little boys in school in Paris. They expect her to remain in Paris at a pension. At the moment she writes, Frances Garnett and Mrs. Carter were out together. Then Harriet Garnett picks up the same letter. She has more to tell Julia about the Douglases. The next evening they will go with the dear Douglases to their friend Mary Clarke's first soiree.

This was no ordinary soiree. It was a preamble to what became one of the most famous salons of Paris, where for sixty years Mary Clarke, later Mrs. Mohl, gathered around her writers, artists, scholars, journalists, as well as pioneers of women's rights. The purpose of salons in general was to create an atmosphere conducive to the exchange of ideas about art, religion, politics, and philanthropy.[4] Young authors brought their manuscripts for judgment, their disappointments for consolation; established celebrities might try out new theories.

In Clarke's time, salons also functioned as a kind of refuge for struggling literary men, usually bachelors. The salon welcomed them after a day's work, providing them with the comforts of a home they couldn't afford. For women, the salon, in an era that predated women's colleges, provided a rare opportunity for intellectual education and stimulation.[5] Clarke's mother, recognized for her forceful character and cultivated mind, had associated with intellectual circles in her native Edinburgh. When, because of her poor health, she went to France with her two young daughters, Mrs. Clarke continued to seek comparable company. Eventually, the Clarkes befriended Mme. Jeanne Récamier, who gathered to her famous salon many of the great figures of literature and politics. Mary Clarke became Mme. Récamier's apprentice *salonnière*.

Under Récamier's tutelage, Clarke learned the art of stimulating the kind of lively conversation that was at the heart of the successful salon. In the early 1830s, Clarke became the main convener of the Récamier-Clarke salon. Her mother's favorite subjects were religion and politics, but her daughter was not political. Her abiding interest was society itself.[6] Unconventional, quite intelligent, extremely well-read, she made the salon her career. By the 1830s, it was well established, eventually attracting acclaimed celebrities of France, Britain, and America, including Florence Nightingale, Elizabeth Gaskell, George Eliot, Thackeray, the Brownings, and Trollope. Even in the early years, besides her beloved Claude Fauriel, Clarke's evenings were already attended by Stendhal, Mérimée, Hugo, Tocqueville, Benjamin Constant, and other lights of France. And it was to such a soiree, at Rue des Petits Augustins, that the Garnetts brought the Douglases in November of 1827. As a result of this introduction, Mary Clarke would eventually play her own major role in the unraveling of the Douglas story.

Perhaps inspired by Clarke's example, the Garnetts decided to hold soirees of their own. On December 12 Harriet Garnett reported to Julia that they began what would become a regular Monday soiree. Their guests included Benjamin Constant, Miss Clarke, some Americans, and some French. The Douglases were absent because of illness, but present was their sister Mrs. Carter, who for a fortnight had been staying with the Garnetts in their little alcove. On the twelfth all the Douglases would dine with the Garnetts and then sleep in their new apartment close to them—Number 4, in the passage. Harriet explains that she has been much occupied assisting them to get moved and settled. In closing, she mentions that General Lafayette is shortly expected in town. From the context it is clear that Mr.

and Mrs. Douglas are about to be introduced to one of the towering figures of French and American history.

By this time, the Douglases have been in Paris some two
months. They passed the test of Fanny Wright at Arundel. In
Paris, they were accepted wholeheartedly into the Garnett
household. Mrs. Carter even slept in their dining alcove. Almost
inseparable, the Douglases and the Garnetts went together to
Mary Clarke's soiree. There, besides their hostess and her
mother, Mr. and Mrs. Douglas met Mme. Récamier, Stendhal,
Fauriel, Mérimée, and Hugo. Apparently this highly sophisticated assembly readily accepted Mr. and Mrs. Douglas. The
beautiful, clever wife; the articulate, learned husband. There
was no question of male or female, only the question of how
intelligent, how interesting, how liberal in politics these new-
comers were, as conversational partners moved around the
room, speaking now French, now English. Within days,
Lafayette would arrive in Paris. Were the Douglases unnerved at
the prospect, each introduction a new hurdle, a new fear? Might
some English guest recognize Mr. Douglas as the odd Miss Dods
they had seen at Dr. Kitchener's or other fashionable gatherings
in London? Were they constantly haunted by the notoriety, perhaps legal prosecution, that discovery could bring? Newspaper
headlines. Social ostracism. Family disgrace. Or had Mr. and
Mrs. Douglas settled quite comfortably into their singular marriage?

No letter goes to Julia without mention of these loved
Douglases. On December 18 Frances Garnett reports that Mrs.
Douglas does not go out at all being ill with the tic douloureux
and, "Poor creature, she suffers in all ways dreadfully." With
the New Year letter of January 3, 1828, Mrs. Douglas is quite
recovered from her "painful complaint—& she & her little husband always desire their best love to dear Julia." The previous
evening the Garnetts and Douglases spent together. But on another occasion, the Douglases did not join the Garnetts "owing
to his being ill; he has wretched health poor man—& I fear will
never be well."

David Lyndsay informed Blackwood that his chronic poor
health—a liver ailment—forced him to retire to the country for

rest. That was in 1824. In about 1826, Rennie said Dods was in "habitual pain and confirmed ill-health; her figure was short, and, instead of being in proportion, was entirely out of all proportion—the existence of some organic disease aiding this materially."[7] In 1828 Mary Shelley spoke of D's "diseased body" that she trusts "acts on the diseased mind" expecting "that both may be at rest ere long."[8] Perhaps illness was one of Dods's motives for making a life for "himself" on the Continent. In that era, British doctors commonly recommended the seaside or the Continent to the extremely ill. The change of air, the gentler climate particularly of Italy, the waters at Baden-Baden, might bring recovery. Shelley, Keats, Mary Shelley, Mary Clarke's mother, all journeyed abroad with this goal in mind. But Mary Shelley's letter makes clear that the prescription had failed Dods. On the contrary, both Dods's physical health and mental health apparently deteriorated during her first year of "marriage."

On January 9, Harriet Garnett sends news of Constant, Miss Clarke, and their friends the Neuvilles. There was another Garnett soiree, and the three Douglases and others "filled our little room." She omits the others' names, leaving unknown who else the Douglases may have met that evening. But on the day she wrote this letter, she extended the Douglases' circle even further by introducing them to the Neuvilles. On January 16 Harriet adds a guest list attending Monday's soiree: Mme. Paul and Mary, Mr. and Mrs. D, Miss Clarke, Mrs. Smith, Fauriel, and others. Mérimée didn't attend. He had fallen from his cabriolet and was confined to his room with a bruised arm.

Harriet Garnett's January 23 report to Julia Pertz sympathetically continues the story of Mérimée's health. The poet attended last Monday's soiree, but looked very pale and thin, his arm in a sling. He has suffered a great deal from the fall. But sympathy is limited when Harriet turns to the Douglases. She confides to her sister that now she likes Douglas better than his wife:

Dear Julia, she is beautiful & clever & amiable I think, but a little vain & affected. He is very clever certainly

& very kind. He has hopes of obtaining a place in the diplomatic line and said he hopes it may be at Hanover & that he will [? us] there—He is a good soul, but very much out of health.

It has taken three months of close interaction, but Harriet Garnett now believes Mrs. Douglas "a little vain & affected." This moves in the direction of Mérimée's disapproving words about Mrs. Douglas in his letters to Mary Shelley, though Harriet is not as severe in her judgment. Then again, perhaps Mérimée wasn't either, in these early stages of their acquaintance. Given his own flirtatious disposition, perhaps his roving eye was at first charmed by this clever, beautiful newcomer.

Harriet Garnett's February 8 letter suggests otherwise. She reports to Julia that the Garnetts had been to the Italian opera with their friend Mr. Hallam and the Douglases. In the middle of this news, she says she has been interrupted by a note from Mérimée. He is bringing Stendhal to Monday's soiree "to introduce him to Madame Douglas 'car ils sont faits l'un pour l'autre' and a rare flirtation shall we have." Stendhal's reputation was already established as a great writer and a great Don Juan. In saying Madame Douglas and Stendhal were made for each other, Mérimée makes his opinion of her quite clear. As for Harriet, she is quite upset because she finds Stendhal most disagreeable—she will report the event the following week.

Mérimée's sport at the expense of his friend Stendhal seems incongruous given his own hyperactive love life. In fact, this letter informs Julia that Miss Clarke told her the real story of Mérimée's injured arm. He had not fallen from a cabriolet.

It was a duel—on account of a lady in whose house he was staying & who has a brutal husband who beats her. I suppose she flirted a little with Mérimée—for while he was playing at words the husband insulted & challenged him.—they fought the husband grazed his shoulder—M—fired in the air—the other was not satisfied but again fired & wounded him in the arm.

Before this letter ends, there is another comment about the Douglases, this by Harriet's mother. If Harriet's feelings toward the once-dear Douglases express the beginning of a changed attitude, her mother's comments are even more altered. Maria Garnett says simply that she does not like the Douglases "nor does Harriet, as she did." On February 15 Maria Garnett explains her reasons. Mrs. Douglas is always pretty but she is also always full of conceit. "A professed beauty is seldom agreeable. She is a great coquette." As for Mr. Hallam, he is a great favorite of Mrs. Douglas. And he is pleased with her "fine eyes and civil manners." To this, Harriet merely adds that last Monday's soiree was fuller than usual—that Stendhal did attend—that he asked after Julia. No mention of the expected show of flirtation.

On February 21 the Garnetts report the Douglases intend to spend the summer at Mannheim, and from there they hope to go in season to Baden. This neutral commentary gives way to decided hostility in the February 27 letter. In mid-April, the Douglases will give up their nearby apartment. Harriet sends news that Mrs. Douglas told her that Mrs. Shelley had received a letter from Fanny Wright written two hundred miles from New Orleans. What follows is an onslaught not only on the Douglases but on Mary Shelley: "Dear Fanny has I fear bestowed more affection on her new friend Mrs S than she merits & on the Ds also. It is painful to change our opinion of those we have liked."

How could Harriet Garnett think poorly of Mary Shelley when they had never met? Under the circumstances, the answer was obvious: Mr. or Mrs. Douglas or both had spoken ill of their supposed friend. And Harriet, in the blush of her early love for the Douglases, not only believed them, but wrote about their unkind feelings to Fanny Wright. And Fanny Wright responded with that March 20 letter in which she agreed that "deficient sensibility is a negative quality, but hypocrisy is a positive one of the worst character." In the many weeks it took for Harriet Garnett to send and receive these judgments, she had come to the same opinion.

On March 5 and 14 the usual family letters go from Paris to Hanover, but with no mention of the Douglases. On March 30 Maria Garnett tells Julia that the Douglases are "less and less amiable." Mr. Hallam, now Mrs. Douglas's "decided beau," is very dull, very reserved, and proud. It appears he had earlier been Julia's suitor and her mother tells her Hallam declares his attachment to Julia would have been very great. This, she reports, Mr. Douglas himself told her. So by the end of March, not only is Mrs. Douglas a recognized coquette in the eyes of the Garnetts, but Mr. Douglas is well aware of his wife's behavior.

The letter of April 7 sends news of many of their friends, but nothing of the Douglases. In mid-April, Harriet Garnett makes clear the reason for the omission: "We seldom see the Douglases—Mr. Hallam is devoted to Madame D." On April 22 Harriet Garnett again tells her sister they see little of the Douglases. At the same time, she announces a new link to those once-dear friends. "Mrs. Shelley is arrived but ill & I have not yet seen her." She goes on to say that she does not expect to like her, since Mrs. Douglas has "described her character to me & I have seen her letters to her most intimate friends." Strangely, Harriet Garnett's opinion continues to rely on the word of the now-disdained Mrs. Douglas.

On April 28 no word of the Douglases, but a health bulletin on Mrs. Shelley. Apparently Mary Shelley nevertheless interests Harriet Garnett. She has not yet seen her. Her illness turned out to be smallpox, but she is recovered "& has had it very favorably," meaning it has not badly scarred her. On April 27 Mary Shelley described her illness to Jane Hogg. She had traveled with a high fever, arrived in Paris, and took immediately to bed. She thought she had a virulent strain of chicken pox—her friends kept the true illness from her. She writes now that she has passed the crisis and is convalescent. Her great regret is that she endangered Julia Robinson, who had traveled with her, and had put their friends, i.e., Mr. and Mrs. Douglas, under interdict because Parisians are so afraid of infection. She has made a "sick house" of their friends' home. And though the doctors say she will "not be in the least marked," she appears such a fright then that it will be a long time before she can show herself.

On May 8, no word of the Douglases or their recuperating friend. But on May 12 there is word of both, and another shift in

the wind. The Garnetts have at last met Mary Shelley. To their
surprise, and despite the Douglases' reports, they are rather
taken with her. Maria Garnett tells Julia that the night before,
Mrs. Shelley and the Douglases drank tea with them. "She is
gentle & pleasing, recovered [from] the small pox she was seized
with on her arrival in Paris, which has taken her beauty if she
ever had any." With the first part of this report, Mary Shelley
would have been pleased. With the second, she undoubtedly
would have agreed. A full month later, she wrote to a friend
about her "hateful illness and its odious results" from her hiding
place on the English coast. Her doctor had said "sea bathing will
assist materially the disappearance of the marks" on her face.
As for her experience in Paris, she emerged after three weeks of
illness, "brilliant" in health "but ugly as the——— I went into
society—I was well repaid for my fortitude, for I am delighted
with the people I saw. . . . It was rather droll to play the part of
an ugly person for the first time in my life."[9] In August, still in
the south of England, she reported she had been "obliged to
sacrifice the few remnants of my hair & am cropt—so my fright-
fulness is complete—Oh this odious illness!—"[10] Into September, the reports continue of disfigurement, though with hope
that by winter she will be "more visible—& myself—"[11] Her
complexion had before been remarked on as clear, even lumi-
nous. It would never be again.

Harriet Garnett also found Mary Shelley "pleasing in
her manners" though "rather fond of admiration but not dis-
agreeably so." Certainly her response was unanticipated, given
her correspondence with Fanny Wright. And Mary Shelley
added to the Garnetts' interest by bringing word of Wright.
Nashoba was falling apart. The legal trust on which it was
founded was already dissolved; the project failed and ended.
This, the Garnetts had anticipated. Certainly their abiding lack
of confidence in the plan must have influenced Harriet Garnett
not to fulfill her early intention of going to Nashoba herself. Nor
were they at all surprised when they learned earlier that Fanny
Trollope remained only ten days at Nashoba. On arrival, Trollope realized Wright's idyllic descriptions of the colony were of
the future; the present offered leaky hovels and swampland. Her

quick response was to pick up herself and her two daughters, bid Wright farewell, and return to what she hoped would be civilization in Cincinnati. Her best-selling report of this misadventure, *Domestic Manners of the Americans,* left little doubt that as far as she was concerned, nowhere in the United States was civilization to be found.

Between May 12, the Garnetts' first report of Mary Shelley, and May 25, their second and last, some of her activities as well as the Douglases' and the Garnetts' can be pieced together through Mary Shelley's letters. During that fourteen-day period, Mary Shelley, through the Garnetts, was introduced to General Lafayette, Stendhal, Benjamin Constant and his wife; Claude Fauriel, G. W. Hallam, and most important to her for a period, "one of the cleverest men in France, young and a poet," Prosper Mérimée.[12] The Douglases and Mary Shelley appear to have spent a great deal of time with the Garnett's who, on May 24, held a farewell soiree in Mary Shelley's honor.

Two letters speak of this special evening. The first, Mary Shelley's to Mérimée, written that same evening, in which she returned Mérimée's letter because she is "not a coquette" and would not "like to keep the expression of sentiments which you will probably repent of later," offering friendship instead of love.[13] Drawn throughout her life to struggling writers, she offers to share his aspirations, success, happiness, or unhappiness. On Monday, she leaves; tomorrow she will spend the day with her friend, no doubt meaning Mrs. Douglas. She regrets Mérimée cannot spend the whole evening at Madame Garnett's but "I shall see you there and again I shall assure you of my Friendship."

According to Harriet Garnett, assure him she did. On May 25 Harriet Garnett told Julia that the previous night the Garnetts drank tea with the Douglases to take leave of Mary Shelley. Mérimée arrived with a copy of a book he had just published.[14] The evening, in Harriet Garnett's eyes, was a "flirting party." Mary Shelley flirted with Mérimée. Mrs. Douglas "flirted with both Hallam and Fauriel, and all others." As for Mr. Douglas, he "looks sick and disconsolate."

Here is a picture to pause at. Mary Shelley, recovering from smallpox, her lovely complexion marred, her once-opulent golden hair grown thin. Still, she is *the* Mary Shelley, author of *Frankenstein* and two other novels; editor of Shelley's *Posthumous Poems.* A woman of remarkable learning and personal grace, fluent in French and Italian. A woman often described as charming though at times somewhat reserved. And perhaps it is as much her reserve as everything else about her that attracts the young Mérimée. He is only twenty-five and conscious that he is not a handsome man. Two of his books have been published and well received. He brings his third, *La Jaquerie,* to the party with him. It is as much a gift for the Garnetts as a calling card on the young widow. She is ever attracted to people of talent and those who are, or see themselves as, sufferers. In Mérimée, she found both. If Mérimée appeared to suffer, there was no question that she certainly had. At thirty years old, her life was a blend of romance, artistry, tragedy. One could see beneath the smallpox-marked face a lovely appearance, if one looked carefully. In the same way one could see, beneath the articulate manners, the sadness of her widowhood and struggle and loneliness. The two writers had much common ground. He had been rejected as her lover, but welcomed as a friend. Perhaps they were flirting on this last evening together in Paris.

But from his letters to her that followed during the next fourteen months, we can assume that they were also discussing their latest works and agreeing to assist each other's careers. She will help bring attention to him in England by writing a review of his three books for the *Westminster Review.* He will offer to send her information for *Perkin Warbeck,* the novel she is now writing, and other material for other projects. In their letters they exchange opinions and confidences about their professional and personal lives, now pleasant, now pointed. They encourage each other not to be sad. They discuss "crystallization," Stendhal's theory of a cycle of imagination that transforms a beloved into a being apart from all others in the same way that salt crystallizes around a branch of a tree turning it into a multitude of brilliant diamonds.[15] They exchange copies of their works. She sends him a small money pouch she crocheted for him. He sends reports of the circle of friends she met in Paris that spring—the Garnetts, Mary Clarke, Stendhal—and those sharp, disapproving words that try to warn Mary Shelley about the true character of her beloved Mrs. Douglas.

In the beginning of their correspondence, Mérimée is still the suitor. He is anxious for her return to Paris. He sends close friends who are in England to visit her and they carry letters and messages back to Paris. At one point, he appears considerably disturbed at the rumor that she has married the adventurous Edward John Trelawny, the Shelleys' old friend. But as the months go on, Mérimée becomes uncrystallized as far as Mary Shelley is concerned, only to be recrystallized by first one, then another woman, and writes to Mary Shelley about his amorous wanderings. At the end of his March 1829 letter to a mutual friend, Mérimée asks that he tell Mrs. Shelley that he thinks of her every day but he is too horribly lazy to write.[16] Mary Shelley, perhaps sensing this would be the case, insisted their correspondence be kept secret. Her letters to him have not been found. But his to her trace a remarkably open, even bantering, friendship between the two before he apparently became distracted by new interests and new loves, and their correspondence ended.

But what of the others on that May evening at the Garnetts? Mrs. Garnett, Harriet, Fanny, Hallam, Fauriel, Mr. and Mrs. Douglas. Probably Mrs. Carter, possibly a few others; not a crowded affair. The Garnetts serve tea, and Harriet Garnett has time and room to observe her guests. With more than a note of disapproval, she writes to Julia of a "flirting party." She could not know that Mérimée had sent a love letter to Mary Shelley. Or that Mary Shelley, telling Mérimée she is not a coquette, returned his letter and offered friendship instead. Perhaps Mary Shelley was not flirting with Mérimée that last evening, but only trying to comfort him for the rejection already sent. Whatever the case, Harriet Garnett hardly knew Mary Shelley. Nor could she guess that Mérimée, after only two weeks, had declared his ardor for the young widow. A misreading of the two by Harriet Garnett is quite understandable.

But there is no misreading about Mrs. Douglas. Here is the married woman, again a guest in their home, again brazenly flirting with Hallam and Fauriel. With every man present? Is it a game for her, her promising glances briefly satisfied with the knowledge that her beauty has again triumphed? Does she move about the room, in the wake of each victory passing on to the next, purposely pitting the feelings of the man left behind against the one newly engaged? Is she, as the Garnetts and Mérimée agree, nothing more than a coquette, the end of her game never-sated conquest? To the onlooker, this may be so. But other games may be afoot. She may be tired of her "love-match" with her "little husband," tired of pretending to be the wife of Mary Diana Dods. Isabella Douglas is young, clever, beautiful. Her name and her child's name are temporarily protected by the elaborate charade the Douglases and Mary Shelley have spun. She can be confident that Mary Shelley, ever afraid of any new scandal that might harm her child's life, would never reveal their secret. Nor could Dods expose her without exposing herself. And it was the woman dressed as a man, the transvestite, who would surely attract the most gossip—and the most harsh legal penalties. Robinson had a child; she could demonstrate she was not homosexual. Still, it could be a nasty business. But she had encouraged, if not persuaded, Dods to come to Europe, to become a man. Perhaps now, if she found a real husband, she could convince Dods to let her go. And perhaps that was what all her flirting was about. Nervously, anxiously, she may have been casting about for a real marriage, a real lover.

But what of her husband, who "sick and disconsolate" looked on? What role did Dods play as she watched her "wife" move from man to man like an explorer on a fresh wind? Is she, Mr. Douglas, the husband, embarrassed because she feels the agony of a man being made a fool of by his wife? Does she avert her eyes and bury herself in conversation, gradually losing awareness of her seductive "wife," as she drifts away from the salon into the larger world of politics or literature? Or is the matter worse for Mary Diana Dods? Perhaps Mr. Douglas is not the tortured man, but the tortured woman. Was Dods, far more than any of the men she dallied with, Robinson's prey? Isabella Robinson sparked Mary Shelley's love, but Mary Shelley loved her as a friend. Had Robinson promised more to Mary Diana Dods, because she knew that Dods belonged to the unmentionable caste of female homosexual? Had Dods told Robinson her secret, her words becoming her own shackles? Was Dods in love with Robinson, each new flirtation a new torture? Or by that May, perhaps Dods had come to realize that Robinson had merely used her and now, safely established as Mrs. Douglas, was preparing for the next scene of her adventures on her own. Mary Diana Dods and Mr. Walter Sholto Douglas were both unceremoniously to be abandoned. Did she realize all this, standing in the corner of the Garnett salon, watching the beguiling Isabella, forgiving all deceit in the solitary wish that her "wife" once again love her?

Eventually the evening would end, as it has for many an unhappy husband before. The closing moments could be imagined: Mérimée, as he indicated to Mary Shelley, left earlier. Then perhaps Fauriel. Now Mary Shelley, still recovering from smallpox, begins to tire. Is Mr. Douglas ready to leave? "He" is. The two cross the room to Mrs. Douglas, in gay conversation with Hallam. Their dear friend Mrs. Shelley has grown tired. Mrs. Douglas has little choice: She must publicly obey her husband. They thank their kind hostesses, and promise shortly to call. The Garnetts wish Mrs. Shelley a safe journey home to England and promise to call on her should they come over. Mrs. Shelley waits at the door, with Mrs. Carter. Mr. Douglas offers "his" arm to Mrs. Douglas. She will, for appearance's sake, accept it. Out of sight, they will separate. There are words, sharp, recriminative. Or silence, which for the wordsmith Doddy, in love or hate, was probably worst of all.

Mary Shelley left Paris on May 26. Her name disappears from the Garnett letters. But there is another trace of the Douglases. On July 8 Harriet Garnett reports to Julia Pertz that last night's party included Mérimée, Fauriel, Mary Clarke, and the Douglases. It appears Fauriel, rather than Hallam, now "seems to be the favorite beau of Mrs. Douglas." To add to the situation, Miss Clarke "does not seem to dislike it. How odd it is after the mother's confidence of his engagement to her daughter." Odd, because it was well known and accepted that Mary

Clarke was in love with Fauriel, her senior by twenty-one years. And it was supposed he returned her affection. Perhaps she actually did mind Fauriel's attentions to Mrs. Douglas, but out of pride and hurt pretended not to. After all, she waited until his death in 1847 before she married the scholarly Mr. Mohl. Who is next in line after Fauriel with Mrs. Douglas?

The Garnett letters don't say. Hundreds of pages of letters between Paris and Hanover indicate that the party with Mrs. Douglas and her new favorite beau was the last mention of the Douglases in the Garnett letters. They drop from their place in the correspondence as surely as they must have dropped—or been dropped—from the Garnetts' inner circle. Occasionally, these former dearest friends must still meet. The Douglases are still in Paris. Mérimée's reports to Mary Shelley confirm that. But then the Douglases disappear from Mérimée's letters as well. Perhaps they have left Paris for Hanover, as planned. If they did, they never made contact with Julia Pertz, who surely would have reported seeing them to her mother and sisters.

But there is another possible scenario: Perhaps they never went to Germany. Perhaps they have separated. Mrs. Douglas has taken her daughter and gone south, to show up again in England in 1830. Mrs. Carter remains in Paris, to be near her sons who are in school there. And Mr. Douglas, transmuted, is again Mary Diana Dods. She and her sister take an apartment a good distance from the Garnetts, Mérimée, Stendhal. Partially out of fear of being recognized by any of the dozens of Paris friends they knew, partially as a result of the illness that is claiming her body and mind, Mary Diana Dods never leaves home. The neighbors see the *"anglaise"* Mrs. Carter, but not the invalid sister. Sick, despairing over her lost Isabella, she still writes, as much from habit as for money. In 1829 she makes her last attempt with Blackwood, signed "X," offering him the 171-page poem. Blackwood rejects "X's" poem, prompting Lyndsay to confess it was he who sent it. No further explanation; no further letters. Blackwood never discovers David Lyndsay's actual identity.

The Douglas trail comes to an abrupt end. Though so much has been revealed, I am left feeling sad and abandoned. For three days, I was almost in the world of the Douglases and Mary Shelley. Almost Paris. Almost 1827–1828. Now the Garnetts, Mérimée, Stendhal, Lafayette, and Mary Clarke have faded into the shadows of their own world. I knew where to find Mary Shelley, but the Douglases had disappeared; escaped around unseen corners, into new mirrors. I had no idea where they had gone or whether I would ever again find them. The place I looked was Paris.

A miniature by Reginald Easton, courtesy of the Bodleian Library, Oxford

Portrait by Amelia Curran, 1819, courtesy of the National Portrait Gallery, London

ary Shelley

Percy Bysshe Shelley

Adeline Wolff,
daughter of Isabella
and "Sholto Douglas"

Portrait by Simon Jacques Rochart, courtesy of the Bibliotheque Nationale, Paris

Prosper Mérimée

Frances Wright

Engraving by H. B. Hall and Sons, courtesy of the National Portrait Gallery, Smithsonian Institution, Washington, D.C.

John Howard Payne, the American actor who impersonated "Sholto Douglas" at the passport office

Mary Clarke (Madame Mohl)

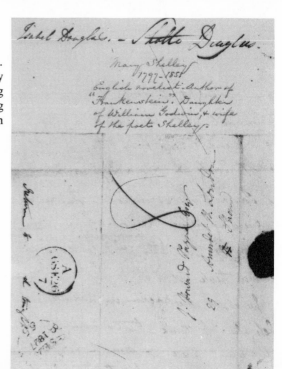

Signatures of "Mr. and Mrs. Douglas" at the end of Mary Shelley's letter to Payne describing the Douglases and requesting passports for them

James Douglas, thirteenth earl of Morton, and his family

Courtesy of the Scottish National Portrait Gallery

The fourteenth earl of Morton

Ratho Church, the traditional burial place of the Douglases before 1850

Courtesy of Braemar Films, Ltd.

Dalmahoy House, an ancestral Douglas home

Aberdour Castle, an ancestral home of the earls of Morton

Courtesy of Historic Buildings and Monuments, Scotland

CERTIFIED COPY OF AN ENTRY OF DEATH

GIVEN AT THE GENERAL REGISTER OFFICE, LONDON

Application Number Y77150

REGISTRATION DISTRICT Kingston

1916. DEATH in the Sub-district of Hampton in the County of Middlesex

| No. | When and Where died | Name and surname | Sex | Age | Occupation | Cause of death | Signature, description and residence of informant | When registered | Signature of registrar |
|---|---|---|---|---|---|---|---|---|---|
| 292 | Thirty first March 1916 Hampton Court Palace Hampton W.D. | Adeline Drummond Wolff | Female | 89 Years | Widow of the Right Honble Sir Henry Drummond Wolff | Infirmity of age Passic Congestion of Lungs few days Cardiac failure Certified by G.C. Digle M.R.C. Henry N. Fotherton | Yseulda Drummond Wolff Daughter in Law Present at the death Hampton Court Palace Hampton Court | First April 1916 | Walter Henry Fry Registrar |

CERTIFIED to be a true copy of an entry in the certified copy of a Register of Deaths in the District above mentioned.
Given at the GENERAL REGISTER OFFICE, LONDON, under the Seal of the said Office, the 5th day of June 19 89

This certificate is issued in pursuance of the Births and Deaths Registration Act 1953. Section 34 provides that any certified copy of an entry purporting to be sealed or stamped with the seal of the General Register Office shall be received as evidence of the birth or death to which it relates without any further or other proof of the entry, and no certified copy purporting to have been given in the said Office shall be of any force or effect unless it is sealed or stamped as aforesaid.

DX 451973

CAUTION:—It is an offence to falsify a certificate or to make or knowingly use a false certificate or a copy of a false certificate intending it to be accepted as genuine to the prejudice of any person, or to possess a certificate knowing it to be false without lawful authority.

Adeline "Douglas"'s death certificate

CERTIFIED COPY of an within the District of

ENTRY OF MARRIAGE

British Consul Leghorn

Application Number PSR 77130

District of British Consul at Leghorn

1853. MARRIAGE solemnized at Leghorn in the Consuls Office

| No. | When married | Name and surname | Condition | Rank or profession | Residence at the time of marriage | Father's name and surname | Rank or profession of father |
|---|---|---|---|---|---|---|---|
| 11 | January 22nd 1853 | Henry Drummond Charles WOLFF | Full age | Bachelor | Attaché to H M's Legation | Via Larga Florence | Joseph Wolff | Clerk D.D. L.L.D. |
| | | Adeline DOUGLAS | Minor | Spinster | | Villino Gasperini Florence | Walter Shatto Douglas | Officer in H M's Service |

Married in the Consuls Office according to the Rites and Ceremonies of the Church of England by Licence by me, Theo Sleeman British Chaplain

This marriage was solemnized between us, Henry Drummond Charles Wolff Adeline Douglas in the presence of us, Leontine Gordigiani — Dorothy Walpole, Alex Mackean Her Majesty Henry L. Bulwer Harriet Anne de Bonlay H.P. Fenton Consul

CERTIFIED to be a true copy of the certified copy of an entry in a Register of Marriages in the Consulate above mentioned.
Given at the GENERAL REGISTER OFFICE, LONDON, under the Seal of the said Office, the 5th day of June 1989.

This certificate is issued in pursuance of the Marriage Act 1949.
Section 65 (3) provides that any certified copy of an entry purporting to be sealed or stamped with the seal of the General Register Office shall be received as evidence of the marriage to which it relates without any further or other proof of the entry, and no certified copy purporting to have been given in the said Office shall be of any force or effect unless it is sealed or stamped as aforesaid.

Cons. KA 008335

CAUTION:—It is an offence to falsify a certificate or to make or knowingly use a false certificate or a copy of a false certificate intending it to be accepted as genuine to the prejudice of any person or to possess a certificate knowing it to be false without lawful authority.

The marriage certificate of Adeline "Douglas" and Henry Drummond Wolff

Isabella "Douglas" Falconer's death certificate

CERTIFIED COPY of an within the District of the

ENTRY OF DEATH

British Legation at Florence

Application Number PSR Y 77130

DEATH within the district of the British Legation at Florence

| No. | When and where died (1) | Name and surname (2) | Sex (3) | Age (4) | Rank or profession (5) | Residence at the time of death (6) | Signature, description and residence of informant (7) | When registered (8) | Signature of consular officer (9) |
|---|---|---|---|---|---|---|---|---|---|
| 130 | February 7th 1869 Pistoia | Isabella Falconer Born Robinson | Female | 59 yrs. | Wife of Revd Wm Falconer | Villa Falconer near Pistoia | Minister of Grace & Justice | Feby 10th 1869 | Robt Loftus Tottenham Chaplain |

CERTIFIED to be a true copy of the certified copy of an entry in a Register of Deaths in the district above mentioned.
Given at the GENERAL REGISTER OFFICE, LONDON, under the seal of the said Office, the 5th day of June 19 89.

This certificate is issued in pursuance of the Births and Deaths Registration Act 1953 (as applied). Section 34 provides that any certified copy of an entry purporting to be sealed or stamped with the seal of the General Register Office shall be received as evidence of the birth or death to which it relates without any further or other proof of the entry, and no certified copy purporting to have been given in the said Office shall be of any force or effect unless it is sealed or stamped as aforesaid.

Cons FA 2443

CAUTION:—It is an offence to falsify a certificate or to make or knowingly use a false certificate or a copy of a false certificate intending it to be accepted as genuine to the prejudice of any person, or to possess a certificate knowing it to be false without lawful authority.

of your Company – with me therefore
of how the case stands –

Thanks for Shelleys beautiful Letters. why
do you not publish them?. they would
do more good to his memory than
all that Friends can say. they
contain in themselves such perfect
and decided
refutation of many of the silly
columnies floating abroad. it is to
be wish'd for his own sake and yours.
it is necessary for your Son's –

Plato's Banquet – but that shall
be talk for us anon – it is charming.

– Ever my dear Pretty's
Affectionate Friend
M D Dods –

Thursday M.S.

Courtesy of the Abinger Collection, Bodleian Library, Oxford

Letter from Mary Diana Dods to Mary Shelley

Courtesy of the Trustees of the National Library of Scotland

Letter from "David Lyndsay" to
Blackwood, 1825

Letter from Mary Diana Dods to
her father, the fifteenth earl of
Morton

From the Morton muniments in the Scottish Record
office, with the approval of the Keeper of the
Records of Scotland (G.180/1 Part 8 and T/107)

## CHAPTER 14

# TRANSMOGRI-FICATIONS

ON SUNDAY, January 11, 1981, I arrived in Paris, where the Douglases' play ran for some fourteen months, perhaps longer. Perhaps after it closed here, it was picked up again in some other city on the Continent. One hundred and fifty years later, I think of Doddy in Paris. After February 1829, what happened to the couple? Did they stay together? If Dods and her "wife" separated, what did Dods's mirrors tell her?

She may have remained in Paris with her sister. But whom did Mrs. Carter see when she looked at the person who had been her sister and her brother? Was Georgiana a partner in her sister's deeper secrets? Did she know what I wanted to learn: why Doddy became a man? Did she consider the possibility that her sister was homosexual? If so, was she embarrassed? Ashamed? Understanding? Supportive? As a member of the 1827 party in the south of England, Georgiana Carter played her own role. She openly traveled, with her sons, in the company of Mr. and Mrs. Douglas to Paris and was introduced to the Garnetts as the sister of *Mr.* Douglas. As a man, Dods could provide social protection beyond *her* own "wife and child" to *her* widowed sister as well. Or did Georgiana Carter believe her sister was only in costume to gain the career and social privileges her own gender denied her?

As Douglas, Dods gained both freedom of movement and

freedom of speech. With all this to gain, perhaps Dods had remained, for the rest of her life, Douglas; or perhaps the fantasy had begun to crumble, turning her again into the very odd-looking Miss Dods, sad, sick, disconsolate. Did Georgiana Carter mourn for her sister, the sadness in her sister's eyes the only mirror left for Doddy?

The search resumed at the Archive Nationale, where I found the death certificate of Georgiana Douglas Carter. The "Acte de Décès" states that in the year one thousand eight hundred forty-two, on the nineteenth of August, there died in Paris, at rue d'angouleme 14, first arrondissement, Georgiana Douglas, renter, forty years old, born in England, the widow of Jean Carter. It is signed by a member of the commission. Unquestionably, it is Georgiana Dods, though her maiden name is now given not as Dods, which was probably her mother's name, but as her rightful Douglas name. As for her age, the India Office Records and the ages of her children indicate that she was beyond forty in 1842. If Mary Diana Dods had been there, she could have told them her sister's correct age. Carter's children should have known. But perhaps they didn't; perhaps that was Carter's own little masquerade. Or the children were away from home when the death certificate was filled out, and a friend or the concierge gave the year.

The Garnetts had indicated Carter was going to remain in Paris to be near her sons, who were in school there. She may have remained there for a while, then returned to England and come back again to Paris many times during the years between 1828 and her death. But the certificate suggests at least the possibility that Carter, renter, had made a home for herself in Paris. And where the widowed Carter lived, there was at least the possibility that her sister—or brother—was with her or nearby. 1842. Could the mentally and physically diseased Doddy have outlived her sister? A few more years into the records, there is an 1845 death certificate for a man named "Douglas." No first name. Only that he died on August 13, 1845, at Rue de Ponthieu, Number 19, first arrondissement. That he was male; born in Scotland; unmarried; around forty-six. No first name, but male. Obviously no one knew him very well, or they would have known his full name. Was it possible that if someone knew him very well, they would also have known he was a she? An interesting speculation, but far from proof.

It is disappointing not to find Doddy, but Carter opened another prospect: Georgiana Dods Douglas Carter died in Paris in 1842. It was possible that her sister was with her part of that time. Until then, I could trace Dods only into early 1829 and that with fairly scanty evidence. The last substantial information about her occurred in June 1828. Lord Dillon's June 13, 1828, letter to Mary Shelley sent his kind regards to Miss Robinson and requested Mary Shelley to send him "Miss Dod's [sic] donation." This surely means a piece of writing for a publication Dillon was involved with. It also surely means Mary Shelley continued to act as Dods's literary go-between.

On June 22, 1828, Mary Shelley sent to the *New Monthly Magazine* "One or two articles—and some verses, the productions of a gentleman now abroad . . . He has as M^r David Lindsay [sic] been the successful author of 'The Dramas of the Ancient World' . . . contributed . . . to Blackwood & for several of the annuals." Mary Shelley informs the editor that her friend wrote his earlier works "as M^r David Lindsay." Might this indicate David Lyndsay was about to drop her pseudonym—only to pretend her real name was Walter Sholto Douglas?

Then there was Mary Shelley's late June letter to Jane Hogg, talking about the misery to which Isabella "is a victim," so dreadful and merciless, making her shrink like a wounded person. The suffering is so severe that even Mary Shelley "trusts" that Doddy's diseased mind and body will both soon be at rest. Beyond these references, Mérimée's letters give some traces of the hapless couple into early February 1829. Then there is a ten-month gap; the last Doddy clue, that November 1829 "David Lindsay" letter to William Blackwood. Lyndsay, "his" return address then 2 South Molton Street, Grosvenor Square, London, asks for a response either to the Molton Street address or in care of Blackwood's London publishing associates. Lyndsay—Doddy—is seemingly alive and back in London, at least temporarily. Except for one considerable problem: The letter to Blackwood is not written in Dods's handwriting. Still, if he were ill, his sister or a friend might have written it. Or Mrs. Walter Sholto Douglas might have. Or Dods might not be in London at all and her sister or her "wife," knowing about Lyndsay's past success with Blackwood, might have tried to earn ten or twelve pounds by selling Lyndsay's lengthy poem to his once-receptive publisher.

The November letter had too little to verify Dods's existence or whereabouts. The last proof placing Dods remained Mérimée's evidence of February 1829 when he speaks of the unhappy marriage of the Douglases. As for Mrs. Douglas, she was certainly back in London in November 1830, when Mary Shelley wrote in her *Journal* about the "false yet enchanting" being she once adored. Ever false, now, because Mary Shelley "can no longer serve her," she takes no more trouble to please. No mention of Dods. And perhaps the reason Mary Shelley can no longer serve Robinson is because the game is over: Dods is dead. Mrs. Douglas, widow, is set free. In ten years, she will shed her mourning to become the wife of the highly respected Reverend William Falconer.

The death certificate is the first certain proof of either of the Dods sisters beyond February 1829. I needed to know much more. What were the real reasons for the Douglas marriage? Who was the father of Adeline? Was there a divorce? What happened to the couple? Was it possible that the certificate of the unnamed male Douglas who died in 1845 was Doddy's?

That following spring, checking through journal publications in the newly published *Wellesley Index,* I found under *Blackwood's* all the David Lyndsay articles I already knew it had published. On a hunch, I also checked under the name "Douglas" to see if Mary Diana Dods had published anything under her other male name. There was a Douglas publication— a story titled "My Transmogrifications" that appeared in *Maga* in August 1826. But to my complete surprise, its author was one Mrs. Sholto Douglas. Proof that she wrote it is cited as a letter from Mrs. Douglas to Blackwood written July 17, 1826.

Once again, this called for sorting through the accumulated Dods papers. Mary Shelley's letters and the Garnett collection led to the conclusion that Mary Diana Dods had made an honest woman of Isabella Robinson in the fall of 1827. Dods became Mr. Douglas, Robinson Mrs. Douglas, and "their" baby Adeline Douglas. But according to her death certificate, when Adeline died in the second quarter of 1916, she was eighty-nine. This could place Adeline's birth anytime between July 1826 and June 1827. And in May 1826, Thomas Moore recorded in his journal that he had received a note from Miss Rennie asking if he knew that "Miss R. (my Paddington Friend) was married—told her I had had a letter from her from Dover since I came to town,—full of romance at the prospect of soon seeing 'the ilex groves of' Spain,"[1] with no name of Robinson's spouse. Certainly the Rennie-Moore notes suggested that Mary Diana Dods had become Isabella Robinson's protector—or lover—as early as May 1826.

But in her August 28, 1827, letter, Mary Shelley wrote she is "glad for pretty Isabel's sake that D. now seriously thinks of les culottes." This and other evidence in Mary Shelley's letters had indicated that Dods took on the full-time guise of Mr. Walter Sholto Douglas just before the trip to Paris. But Dods may have used the name Walter Sholto Douglas earlier, and for more than one reason. She made her entry into *Blackwood's* pages by becoming the man-about-town "David Lyndsay." But by March 1826, David Lyndsay's days as a *Blackwood's* writer had ended. "His" work had been consistently rejected for several years. Why not send *Blackwood's* other works under the name "Douglas"? Nothing in the evidence precluded the idea that the Douglases had already plighted their troth by August 1826.

Dods might even have occasionally dressed as a man earlier, but this seemed highly unlikely. She was apparently well known in London. Fear of recognition—the same fear that caused Mary Shelley to ask John Payne to act the part of Douglas to get passports—almost certainly prevented Dods's transmogrification into Douglas while she was in England. Perhaps she never originally planned such a total change, content simply to write using a male name. Perhaps she was convinced to take this further step by Isabella, who would gain much benefit from it. The tone and wording of Mary Shelley's August 1827 letter certainly suggests that Doddy's serious consideration of "les culottes" is itself a daring new step.

Back to the *Wellesley Index* citation of *Mrs.* Douglas as the author of the August 1826 story: Was the very young Isabella Robinson also an aspiring author? Did Mary Diana Dods take on the name Mrs. Sholto Douglas to reopen the pages of *Blackwood's* to her own writing? Or was the couple "married," with Mrs. Douglas serving as the conduit for Mr. Douglas's writing? It turned out that "My Transmogrifications" was a three-page, first-person, autobiographical story—of a boy growing into manhood.

It opens with a compliment and a complaint. Miss Mitford, an important author of the era, had written an amusing story of the "transmigrations of the female part of humanity in its progress through childhood, girlhood, and womanhood, to marriage and old age," but Mitford denied to those of "the more lordly sex" a parallel mutability she has not recognized—"solely because she is not one of us." The author goes on to give details of the "history of my own Transmogrifications." The character begins with a portrait of himself, painted for his dear, tender mother, when he was a two-year-old. At the time he was "fat, roguish, black-eyed, curly-headed . . . happiness, round, rich, luscious, rosy happiness, in every feature." Three years later, the fat little boy was replaced by a youngster growing tall, slender, impudent, self-willed—the "delight of his father, the torment of his sister, and the curse of servants." Wild, though he still showed signs of a better nature, he became friends with a band of gypsies, and often slipped away from home to be with them, at times moved to tears by their melancholy songs. Their wild spirits and freedom—they had no elder sister to keep them in order, or elder brother to thump them—more than tempted him to want to join them. But at seven he was put in trousers and told that he "was a man" and should behave in a more "grave and gentlemanlike" manner. He studied. He realized he liked girls, his sister best of all. It was she who comforted him when his father took out his brother Henry and left him at home, or threatened to sell his pony to his playmate Richard Howard. To his sister he "deposited" his tutor's severities, his brother's wrongs. He was then, "in truth, a most pathetical nit."

At ten he metamorphosed into a lad who was impudent to his sister, contradicted his father, fought his own battles with his brother, played truant to his tutor. He constantly wandered the countryside, returning home "defaced by mud or dust." His mother wept; his father swore. He was up to all sorts of villainy, including stuffing a goose with gunpowder, which blew up into ten thousand pieces when cook took a lighted paper to it to singe it. His nickname became "Gallows." And off he was sent to private school more to learn decorum and obedience than to acquire knowledge. Four years later, he turned melancholy instead of mischievous. His love of the beautiful, undirected by reason, lead him to read novels and pathetic magazine stories. He fell in love with the moon, wrote "verses to every little star that twinkled."

At that time, he was thin, with long arms and legs. Though active, his health was fragile. His face was pale, dark, surrounded by masses of black curling hair. Seeing himself in the mirror, he "concluded that I should be a tall, thin, pale, pensive-looking young man, and acted up the character accordingly." In short, he loved to be thought of as an invalid, and developed a cough that he pretended was a warning to his mother of an early death. To carry off the picture further, he wrote lengthy verses called the "Dying Boy," lamenting his early doom, and taking a sad farewell of nature. It brought tears even to his own eyes to read it. Later, he learned it had the same effect on others, but from "a very opposite emotion." He sent the verses to magazines. They were published. And he became a very proud "Scholar and a Poet!"

All that he lacked at fourteen was to fall in love, a condition he rectified by falling in love with a beautiful, accomplished young woman of twenty-two. He spent his time staring at her, listening to her, reading to her, gathering flowers for her hair, weeping over her. He dreamed of becoming a king so he might place her on the throne beside him. One night, he fell on his knees, took her hand, and vehemently declared his eternal passion. He spoke to her of the "delights of married life" and "promised to make the best of husbands, the tenderest of fathers." He wept at the thought of anything that should separate them. And finally, he told her he had ten pounds saved up, and they could elope that very night. She laughed. Boundlessly. And darted from the bower in which they sat. First his brother came to the bower, with an "unspeakable grin"; then came his father, whistling. The story spread. He became a laughingstock for friends and family. She, a week later, became the wife of a man of thirty.

This, for a while, ended his courting days. At seventeen he was a dandy, who detested poetry, the moon, children. Then, at last, came "whiskers, mustachios, love, real love, marriage, business, bustle, and twenty-nine." Here he ends the story of his transmogrification. It is up to his friends to decide whether the boy is anything like the man. He thinks not. He takes his leave, then, with "all the usual cares of life, and some, perhaps that are not usual."

Here was a pretty story. Perhaps parts of the story were true. After all, Doddy had a sister. But a brother? His first trousers at seven? And attending private school? Hardly likely. And all the other forms of boyish villainy confessed? Possible. Falling in love with an older woman? Quite possible. Dark eyes and dark curly hair? True. Tall and thin, decidedly untrue. Whiskers, no; but "love, real love, marriage, business, bustle" at the time Dods wrote this? Very likely. And the last words about the usual cares of life and "some, perhaps that are not usual" probably most true of all. It is another Doddy joke, like the joke about being "a short-lived man" in the introduction of *Tales of the Wild and the Wonderful.*

In mid-May, the National Library of Scotland indicated they had only one letter from Mrs. Sholto Douglas; a microfilm copy was en route and with it two letters from Blackwood to Mrs. Douglas located in *Blackwood's* letter books.[2] Unfortunately, they were so faint that it would be pointless to photograph them. Instead, they sent typed transcriptions, uncertain words preceded by question marks. What an extraordinary packet the three letters made.

On March 22, 1826, William Blackwood writes to Mrs. Douglas, thanking her for her confidence in sending him a tale she had written, with an apology for not responding sooner. With even more regret, he returns the tale because his editor did not agree it should be published. He hastens to tell her, however, that it does possess "very considerable merit"; had it not, it would have been returned sooner. In encouragement, he invites her to try *Blackwood's* again. Her planned trip to the Continent will surely lead her to find interesting subjects. And a hint: "you should not be over ambitious" in style; the more natural and simple, the better the expression. In closing, he says he can neither suggest future topics nor assure publication. But he does say that he has "every desire to avail myself of your talents."

This indicates that by March 1826 there was a Mrs. Sholto Douglas. Isabella Robinson? Mary Diana Dods? Someone else? Whoever she was, she was shortly to visit the Continent. This checked with Moore's *Journal* note about his Paddington friend's imminent departure on a honeymoon trip to Spain. Whether the information in Moore's note or in Blackwood's letter is accurate is uncertain.

Three months later, Blackwood again writes to Mrs. Douglas, which suggests that as of June 23, 1826, she is still in England. But if her travel plans have been delayed, her publishing plans have moved forward impressively. Blackwood indicates he received a May letter three weeks earlier when he was in London. He is flattered and hopes eventually to have the honor of knowing who it is that Mrs. Douglas knows who says "she knows me and my friends." As for her works sent, it is with great satisfaction that he informs her "The Owl" is in the present issue of *Blackwood's* and "My Transmogrifications" will appear in the next—both these little pieces are "very creditable whomsoever may be their author." And he invites her to send more.

Back to the library for *Blackwood's Magazine,* July 1826, Volume XX, pages 13–16, "The Owl." A three-page poem, written in rhymed couplets, about an owl, his wife, and their baby owls. So much a gentleman was this owl, that not to intrude on his wife while she nursed her three young, he slept outside the hollow that held their nest. One day, a young boy came and took mother owl and children. The father helplessly followed the boy, who took them home, and then, for the sport of it, with a hot steel pin, blinded them. Each died. The boy said only, "Lo! The little birds are dead," while the father owl, "tore his breast in his despair; And flew he knew not, recked not, where!" But everywhere he went, he thought he saw them, "And he scream'd as they scream'd when he saw them fall/ Dead on the floor of the marble hall." Years passed, the father owl ever haunted by the horror of the scene. One night, a stranger and a beautiful woman come to hide in the forest, pursued by the woman's husband. The husband passed the lovers' hiding place, but the owl shrieked out, attracting the lovers' attention to himself. The husband's foe was the owl's own: "in the man" he recognized "the lad who had destroyed him." The owl's eyes haunt the man, who the next day, "haggard, wild, and bad," kills the lovely lady. Before he can bury her, the owl's shrieks frighten him away. The body is found; the murderer caught and hanged. No one mourns him. And the owl, with a "staring eye, and a dismal scowl" shrieks aloud that revenge is sweet.

A gothic morality poem, everything spelled out. Murderers, destroyers of family units, be warned. Not a bad story. A little sentimental, a little predictable; the section about the murder of the woman not altogether clear. The section about the pin, more than a little gory. Still, Blackwood and his editors thought his readers up to it. After all, the purpose of this poem about loss and horror and revenge was to teach children and adults what they shall not do.

From Blackwood's letter, it appears that Mrs. Douglas, in sending the manuscripts, indicated she was not their author. I turn to the one Douglas letter in the *Blackwood's* collection. Dated Dover, July 17, signed "Isabel Douglas," it is a lengthy, chatty letter about Mr. and Mrs. Sholto Douglas, as nervy and fraudulent a letter as those written by David Lyndsay to Blackwood. And possibly, despite its signature, handwriting, and protestations, it is actually another piece of biographical fiction from the hand of Mary Diana Dods.

To begin with, Isabella Douglas thanks Blackwood for his kind reception of the work sent. But immediately she protests, telling him he is quite mistaken if he thinks—as his letters insinuate—that she is the author of the pieces he has done her the honor of publishing. Though she is aware that "all sorts of fictions are usual, and permitted in this kind of correspondence," she insists she has told him her real name and situation. She promises to "hold to the simple truth" in all her correspondence with him. Having taken this solemn oath, she then goes on to tell him she is very young and married just over six months to a Scotsman named Sholto Douglas. They have "little more than pride, and talent, and love to live on." Still, they do not quote Moore's verses "Long of Love and Poverty" and to her every melancholy foreboding, Mr. Douglas answers, *"A bon temps viendra,"* bringing her a smile of comfort.

Page two opens with an assurance of the truth of the "domestic picture" she just described, revealing this story with "faith in your promise" not to let the information go further. On this basis, she corresponds "frankly and fearlessly." As for her own writing, last May she had spent some time in Kent—long enough to have formed impressions of the place and its inhabitants—and now sends him a piece she has written called "Village Wanderings." She takes to heart Blackwood's hints about simplicity of style. Will this piece suit his "magnificent journal?" If not, please to inform her of her faults of "omission and commission" and though it "shall go hard" she will improve by his instruction.

In this romantic, idyllic storytelling, truth and fantasy are freely interwoven. She is young. The author of the pieces is undoubtedly her "husband." The couple appear to live on his pride and talent—and very possibly, his love. Mr. Douglas is Scottish. And we know from Lyndsay's translations that he is quite capable of speaking in French his comforting prediction that good times will come. But fiction decidedly takes over with Isabella Douglas's claim she is a bride of six months.

Not only is the marriage a hoax, but so too is its purported date. Surely if the marriage "arrangement" had taken place in February as Isabella claims, she would have established it with her friends Thomas Moore and Eliza Rennie at that time rather than in May. But perhaps the midwinter date was the time that Isabella Robinson went to live with Dods. Her reason: to remove her from close observation by her family and acquaintances when she realized she was pregnant. This was not an unusual pattern for those who could afford it. In 1815, the Shelleys hid Mary Shelley's stepsister, Claire Clairmont, at Bath to keep her pregnancy with Byron's child a secret from the Godwins. And Jane Hogg would later hide her own daughter, Dina, in an English country town when Dina was expecting the child of the man she would eventually marry. Were the "Douglases" trying to hide the truth from Isabella Robinson's father and family? And does that explain why Isabella Robinson was apparently dependent on Dods rather than her wealthy father?

From Mr. Robinson's visit to the Douglases in 1828, it appears he was on friendly terms with his "married" daughter. But perhaps that visit was by way of a reconciliation. Perhaps when she realized she was pregnant, she simply told her father that she wished to board with their family friend, Mary Diana Dods. Her father might have refused. Moore's *Journal* records that earlier quarrel between Mr. Robinson and one of his daughters, and it appears to be Isabella Robinson who was Moore's special "Paddington Friend." Perhaps Father and daughter again quarreled when she announced her intention to live with Dods. Without his approval, or his money, she went anyway. Another scenario might be that Mr. Robinson did approve of her living with Dods—and even knew of his daughter's pregnancy; but he provided only the relatively small board and allowance that was needed to maintain this wayward teenager in someone else's home in London. Certainly he did not want to encourage her to new escapades. And if she required additional funds, Isabella, escorted by Miss Dods, could simply take a public tram to the Robinsons' home in Paddington and ask or send a letter by the penny-post that delivered mail within London six times daily.[3]

Possible. So, too, was it possible that sometime in April or May 1826, when Isabella Robinson's condition became more apparent, Dods and Robinson retreated from their London friends to the anonymity of Kent, with or without the knowledge or aid of Robinson's father. There Isabella Robinson took on the name Mrs. Douglas, in anticipation of the birth of her child. And Dods continued her career and added to the family coffers by having *her* wife act as intermediary with Blackwood, who might well recognize David Lyndsay's handwriting from his particularly elaborate capital letters. No need for Dods to dress as a man at that time. A "marriage" in name was sufficient. And it probably took place that spring rather than in the summer of 1827, as I had previously believed. This suggests that perhaps Adeline was born to Walter Sholto Douglas, father, Isabella Robinson Douglas, mother, sometime circa May–June 1826 in Kent. The birth might have been duly recorded in a parish record book. And afterward, Mrs. Sholto Douglas and her newborn daughter, accompanied by her older friend—or perhaps the neighbors were told, by her aunt or cousin—Miss Mary Diana Dods—covered their trail by moving from Kent.

Not home to London, though, where Adeline Douglas's appearance would explain matters that Isabella Robinson did not want explained. Instead they went to Dover, where they probably had no friends to recognize them. Before the baby was born, all was no doubt kept secret. After all, everyone was aware that the incidence of miscarriage and infant mortality were extremely high. But once the child was born, and survived, Isabella Robinson apparently was committed to keeping her daughter: a protective story must be created. Who better than Mary Diana Dods to create a story? At the safe distance of Dover, Mary Diana Dods and Isabella Robinson could begin in the summer of 1826 to build their public fiction of the Douglases' marriage by informing both Moore and Eliza Rennie of the wedding.

All this speculation, woven in with the facts and nonfacts that the Douglases presented, arose just from reading the first page of Mrs. Isabella Douglas's July letter to Blackwood. In the next part of Mrs. Douglas's letter she told him not to think it strange that she always assumes the person of a gentleman in everything she writes, because in truth, she does "not think women gain much by being known as writers even in this age of universal charity." So that Blackwood can tell which pieces are hers, and which the "more spirited and better written" works of her husband, whose works she copies because he writes a "chaotic scrawl," she signs her works *Lilla*. As for her husband, he is not "particularly orthodox in his opinions" but, knowing Blackwood's freedom from bigotry and prejudice, he writes openly. Still, if the editor should find anything not admissible in the works of her husband, Blackwood may erase it. Her own works, Blackwood may change any way he wishes.

There was no way to tell if the two writers involved, the husband and wife, were not both the "husband," that is, Mary Diana Dods. Certainly, Isabella Douglas's excuse for copying her husband's works did not hold: Her handwriting was more difficult to read than Mary Diana Dods's, so familiar to Blackwood as David Lyndsay's. Matters of authorship become even more confusing when Mrs. Douglas goes on to identify a work called "Bridegroom" and a poem about "Charles of Calais" as hers, written in the same meter as Douglas's "Owl," though she fears not as well done. As for her "good man's 'Loose thoughts on the Cardinal Virtue &cc,'" she hopes Blackwood will agree with her that it is a very clever, spirited work. Still, her good man now works on a piece she likes even better, which she will send to Blackwood hereafter.

After asking him to identify the author of a regular *Blackwood's* contributor whose work she particularly liked, not an unusual request given the anonymity of all *Blackwood's Magazine* articles, and wishing him much enjoyment of the delightful season, she signs herself with the conventional "indeed truly Yours &cc Isabel Douglas." Though in fact she is not "indeed truly" his. Nor would a closing note written upside-down on page four, perhaps an afterthought, seem unusual to Blackwood. Mrs. Isabella Douglas tells him that if he *"really"* is sufficiently interested in making their acquaintance, and if he will inform her when he plans to visit London, if they are still in England they will return to the capital for a few days and arrange with him to dine with her papa and her husband: "I think you would like them both, and of vanity! should have no fears for myself."

Either the Douglases did not expect this invitation to be taken up or, for the moment, they had fallen so much in love with their own charade that they didn't worry about the consequences of so cavalier an invitation. If Blackwood said yes, they could always find a way to back out. Or possibly one of them, perhaps Isabella Douglas, planned to actually meet him. At her papa's home in Paddington? A ruse? Or could Mr. Robinson have been a party to the larger ruse of the marriage between Mr. and Mrs. Douglas that protected his beautiful daughter's name?

Following the invitation to dine at papa's was yet another invitation. Written on the top of page one, as afterthoughts to letters often were, Mrs. Douglas assures Mr. Blackwood that if she goes abroad he shall have their address. He would be most welcome to visit them. And any other to whom he chose to give a letter of introduction would also be welcomed, for his sake.

And then a final note: "Pardon me for trespassing so much on your time with this long and irregular letter." Given the era, Blackwood would understand the word "irregular" as a reference to all the openly personal details Mrs. Douglas sent about her life with her "good man." How irregular the letter actually was, he probably never knew.

## CHAPTER 15

# PIECES OF HISTORY

THE NEXT CHAPTER of Doddy's story emerged as a result of an August 1985 research trip in London, where I mainly grappled for facts about Mary Shelley's daughter-in-law, Jane Gibson (widow of the late Charles Robert St. John) who married Percy Florence Shelley in June 1848. When she was born, married, died was apparent; but I couldn't find anything about her family. That search then took me to Edinburgh in March 1986, allowing me at the same time to get my first look at new material about the Douglases at the Scottish Record Office. Among their Morton family papers, tucked away in "Miscellaneous" files of nineteenth-century letters to the earl of Morton, were letters from Mary Dods, Georgiana Carter, and a J. Aubin on personal and family business, particularly about Mary Dods and her sister, Mrs. Georgiana Carter.[1]

Looking through the stacks of files, I didn't recognize the handwritings or signatures until I opened one and found the unmistakable script of David Lyndsay and M. D. Dods. But this time, the letter was not to Blackwood or Mary Shelley. Dated only "saturday Evg," it was written to "My dear Lord," and signed, "Your affectionate Children, G. Carter, MD Dods." Doddy wrote on behalf of herself and her sister, telling "My dear Lord" that they were obliged to him sincerely for the letter he had sent that morning, but they are not "relieved from our apprehensions of Lawyer's Letters &c." Indeed, she assures him that they had no wish whatever to keep him in the dark respecting their debts. They would gladly have paid them long before but couldn't without some encouragement from him. Her sister's debts are not many.

Her own debts are more, because they are of a much older date. She is happy in the hope of getting rid of them and was not anxious to place them before him. Georgiana's debts are mainly for money borrowed from friends to pay bills contracted long ago, when her prospects of repaying them were different—at a time when Georgiana didn't "imagine that she would ever be compelled to trouble you my dear Lord." Those bills were paid through the help of kind friends and now Georgiana is of course most anxious to repay her debts. He shall know the particulars of "*all*" in the handwriting of their creditors themselves, to whom, if he doubts any part of their statement, he may himself inquire. Her own two principal bills are also from borrowed money, though she also has some tradesmen's bills. "We are my dear Lord compell'd even *now* to borrow money, as we have no credit." They also have a friend living with them, who pays them two guineas per week for her board. Of course, however little they care about their own wants, they *must* provide for her. The accounts shall soon be "laid before you my dear Lord and if you will clear us with the World and pay us our allowance *regularly* afterwards" they promise he will never again have reason to complain of them, and he will "confer no triffling [*sic*] blessing upon your affectionate Children, G. Carter MD Dods—"

The handwriting matched. The signature is certain. But what has happened to the self-confidence of Blackwood's correspondent David Lyndsay? And where is the playful, courtly writer of those two letters to Mary Shelley? Both have disappeared, replaced by one of two supplicating daughters, apparently both deeply in debt. Borrowed money from friends. Tradesmen's bills. Creditors. "My dear Lord" repeated like a leit-motif. *My dear Lord.* Was he their *dear Lord*? Were the sisters momentarily in exceptional circumstances? Did Morton pay their debts and start them over with their allowance, regularly paid? I hoped to find, in the remainder of these family letters, the Dods I thought I knew: the learned Doddy, the urbane David Lyndsay, self-confident, independent, daring.

From one folder to the next, there were "MD Dods, Georgiana Carter," and "My dear Lord." Many had partial dates and were in different folders, so there was no way to know immediately the order in which they were written.

By the end of two days, thirty-nine letters were inventoried: from Dods; Carter; Mr. Aubin, who apparently handled the earl's business matters in London; and one from my dear Lord himself. The dated letters ranged from 1818 to 1824, with one as early as 1807; but most had only the day of the week or the day and month, no year. The words *bills, my dear Lord, misfortune, allowance, money, promise, house, children,* were strung throughout.

For the first time, I began to get an idea of what kind of man my dear Lord was. But I came away from the record office seriously questioning whether, after all that time, I knew who his daughter was. In a way, I felt thrown back to 1978, at the beginning of the search for both Lyndsay and Douglas. I had scanned enough of the new letters to know another character had entered the Dods story. And I suspected this character could reveal a great deal about Dods and the Lyndsay pen name and, most important, the Douglas charade. But piecing the story together would have to wait until I received the photocopied documents at home, and could establish dates, and develop a logical sequence. Then, I could meet my dear Lord's affectionate daughters. In the meantime, though I had come so close, Mary Diana Dods had again eluded me.

But despite her lack of cooperation, the next day I paid another call on Miss Mary Diana Dods. Headed north from Edinburgh toward Dundee for research on Mary Shelley, I would be only a few miles from Aberdour, the earl of Morton's ancestral home—and castle.[2] The Douglases, among the most powerful Scottish families in the later Middle Ages, date their rise from the friendship between King Robert the Bruce and Sir James Douglas, who died in 1330 while taking Bruce's heart to the Holy Land. Aberdour Castle is built on lands granted by King Robert the Bruce to his nephew Thomas Randolph, earl of

Moray, about 1325. When the earl of Moray died at Mussel-
burgh in 1332, the lands succeeded to his elder son, who died at
Dupplin that same year. The lands passed to the younger son,
who granted its barony to his friend William Douglas, Knight,
on February 18, 1342. From that time, the property has belonged to the Douglas family, first the Black Douglases, then,
from 1455, the Red Douglases. In the fifteenth century, a Douglas, about to marry Joanna, deaf and speechless daughter of
James I of Scotland, was created earl of Morton. Thus, the
Douglas and Morton names are intertwined.

A guidebook indicated that what remains of Aberdour Castle represents four main building periods: the medieval tower
house was rebuilt in the fifteenth century, extended to the south
in the sixteenth century and then to the east in the seventeenth.
But sometime in the late seventeenth century, less than one
hundred years after it was complete, the castle burned and much
of it was destroyed. The Mortons abandoned the castle, purchased Cuttlehill House, west of the castle, in 1725, renamed it
Aberdour House, and the Morton family subsequently lived
there. The east range of the castle continued to be used as a
barrack, schoolroom, Masonic hall, and dwelling until 1924,
when the castle was placed in the guardianship of His Majesty's
Office of Works. The southeast wing was restored and modernized at that time to be used by the incumbent custodian of the
castle.

Walking among these pieces of history, I wondered if Mary
Diana Dods and her sister had ever played here, climbing the
heaped stones, wandering through the remains of centuries past.
She of the wild imagination had mentioned some castles in her
stories, but nothing specific. Perhaps because it might have been
a clue to her actual identity or perhaps as a child she had rarely
been there. She may have been raised at Dalmahoy, her father's
other home. Or the two "reputed daughters" may have been
kept out of Scotland altogether. Neither Rennie nor the Garnetts described Mr. Walter Sholto Douglas as a Scotsman. Born
in England. Raised in England. Safely far from Scotland, where
the Dods sisters would have cast shadows on their father's reputation as an upstanding member of the church. If on occasion

Dods had been brought to Aberdour when young, it appeared to be hidden in her recorded memories. I couldn't find Mary Diana Dods at Aberdour. Instead, amid those walls, broken and whole, I felt the strong presence of her father and the generations of Mortons before him.

The sometimes brittle, sometimes faded Morton archives, and the stones of Aberdour, together told their larger tale of births, marriages, titles, deaths. The record office kept the records of the everyday business of the fifteenth earl. Ledger books and ribboned documents: deeds, Midlothian rentals, Fife rentals, bonds and assignations, financial statements, cashbooks, drafts of trusts, genealogical records, commissions, gifts, grants, and two Bibles. Among those papers were the stories of many petitions. Would the powerful and rich fifteenth earl adjudicate this difference between parties? Could he assist with a sum of money, often small? Would he intercede to gain advancement in the army for a worthy young man? Would he pay his club dues? Again, a reminder to pay club dues. And again. Other bills as well came to the earl more than once for payment.

The earl himself also petitioned. He had a lengthy correspondence with Lord Melville for the honorific position of Lord Lieutenant—and another honorific title as well. He took obvious pride in his local position and was conspicuously ruffled if he felt himself passed over. Still, his bill-paying habits showed that he easily bypassed those to whom he owed money, including salaries. Even a quick look at the ledger books of Aberdour and Dalmahoy indicated that the earl appeared to reserve his money for building one or another of his several estates. And the purchase of new estates. And the general care of the estates. And for his fashionable residence in London. And for purchasing packs of hounds. And for horse breeding.

Seeing Aberdour, even the ruined Aberdour, I had the image of a man with a fixed sense of a lineage who had consorted with Kings and Queens. They had been to the Crusades and one had been caretaker of a king's heart. They had served as custodian to a queen and one had been regent. They had stood side by side with royalty, fighting, protecting, building not only a nation but their own wealth. They had married, begat, died, passing their nobility from generation to generation. They were consummately busy: not too busy for hounds and horses, nor for the buying and selling of immense estates; not too busy to have illegitimate daughters. But much too busy to be troubled by the petty claims of shopkeepers or farmhands or gentleman's clubs for trifling sums. And, if Dods's letter of her debts and her sister's debts was the rule and not the exception, too busy to send their daughters' allowance on time. Too busy to dig into those seemingly vast stores of money for the relatively small sums requested by their "affectionate daughters."

## CHAPTER 16

# BLACKWOOD TO LYNDSAY

I HAD NOT EXPECTED to meet up with Mary Diana Dods again on that trip. But having completed my other research early enough to return to Edinburgh on the day before the flight home, I headed for the National Library of Scotland. Doddy was never one to do the expected; perhaps more might be uncovered about her in the immense holdings of Blackwood papers. And there it was: a new cache of Mary Diana Dods material, again in the guise of David Lyndsay. She—he—existed in a series of letters William Blackwood wrote in response to David Lyndsay's thirty-two 1821–1829 letters.

William Blackwood was a very busy man and a very orderly one. Like other busy, orderly men of the nineteenth century, he had clerks who copied his correspondence into letter books. Among those letter books were scattered some seventeen letters Blackwood wrote to or about Lyndsay.

I had gone to Edinburgh to find out more about Mary Diana Dods and I had: the daughter of "My dear Lord" as well as the recipient of William Blackwood's letters. But finding out more about a person sometimes means finding a new person. I felt I had found two new Doddys—her father's and her publisher's. Both, or either, could be the mirror image of what I already knew about her. Or they could throw what I earlier knew into the chaos of a new perspective, perhaps drawing me even further away from understanding the Douglases' charade.

Resettled at home, I entered into the world of *Blackwood's Magazine* from its renowned publisher's perspective. In the first letter, dated August 18, 1821 and addressed in care of Mrs. Carter, Blackwood indicates he had received, a week earlier, two "most invaluable packets with your kindly flattering letter to our friend Christopher." Apparently Lyndsay opened his relationship with *Maga* through its editor who then turned the material over to its publisher. Blackwood told Lyndsay "it would be absurd to say anything in the way of praise to the Author of such scenes, for the mind that was capable of conceiving and so admirably executing them, must be conscious of its own powers, and feel that the world must do them justice." He considers himself most fortunate in receiving such a communication that will "add so much lustre" to his magazine and hopes he will have the honor of counting Lyndsay among his regular contributors. In payment, he annexes a small order that will be drawn on the London account of Blackwood's publishing associates Messrs. Cadell and Davies—the article is printed in the current *Maga* with no comments, requiring none—it will bring equal honor to Author and native country. Following this highly flattering paragraph, Blackwood invites Lyndsay to publish a volume with him—he will do it as much justice as his brethren—it will give him great pleasure to have the honor of hearing from Lyndsay with regard to it.

Then Blackwood, to my surprise, opens the subject of assumed names. He tells Lyndsay that he is much accustomed to his magazine correspondents assuming names, so when he hears from a stranger he is always uncertain whether the signature is real or not. He never, however, asks further than what his correspondents choose to communicate. Whether he addresses Lyndsay under his own, or an assumed, name, Blackwood is grateful to have heard from him and hopes to hear from him frequently ". . . Dear Sir Yours Sincerely."

An extraordinary letter for a first-time author to receive from a publisher. Send more. Would you like to do a book? You may be who you say or not; no matter. Send often. No wonder Lyndsay's August 27 response was so self-confident. Blackwood's letter clears up a number of questions that remained from Lyndsay's side of the correspondence. There was no longer a question about how Dods began her relationship with *Maga*. Like many an aspiring author, she wrapped her manuscripts, probably said a prayer or two, and sent them directly to the publisher. And the opening letter wasn't among the author's letters to Blackwood because it was addressed not to him but to *Maga*'s editor. And Dods, no doubt self-conscious about being David Lyndsay, might have said something about his newly acquired name, provoking Blackwood to explain, whether true or no, it didn't matter. Here was another factor that must have added considerably to Dods's self-confidence: Blackwood appeared to grant all the anonymity Dods wanted. Probably more than she actually wanted. Lyndsay's half of the correspondence established that the question of identity became a game between the correspondents. I had assumed Blackwood had pressured Lyndsay to reveal the truth. But these letters indicated it was as likely that it was Dods, secretly wanting recognition, who pressured Lyndsay.

Blackwood's letter book next logs three letters to Lyndsay. Two, written on November 14 and November 16, to "10 Somerset Street, Portman Square London" are listed. Only the November 17 letter is given in full. Blackwood indicates that the day earlier he mailed the two proofs of Lyndsay's book. He hadn't had time to revise them, but hopes they will be "pretty correct" and that from them Lyndsay will be able to judge the appearance of what he expects to be a "very handsome volume." If Lyndsay still wishes to open the volume with *Cain,* it can be done—has not sent the manuscript because he still needs it—supposes Lyndsay has another copy—some capital letters now missing will be inserted by printers when they finally correct. He hopes Lyndsay will receive the packet on Tuesday morning and, like most publishers with a book on track, presses his author to review and send it back by return mail. As for payment for the volume, Blackwood is just then too busy with *Maga* matters and has not yet decided, but assures the author the terms will be liberal. He sends along the first copy he has of that issue of *Maga,* with the hope Lyndsay will like it. Next month, they will publish two issues, and he implores Lyndsay to send material. Will *Foscari* be ready? They could print it first in

*Maga,* then in the volume—don't let this idea interfere with Lyndsay's own views—most desirous of help for *Maga* but understands if he is too busy with *Death of Cain.*

And after all these invitations to Lyndsay, a bit of a disappointment. Lyndsay apparently made an offer to send letters written by a lady to Sir William Draper, a military figure who had died in 1787; these Blackwood rejects. He would, however, accept them if there existed more of Draper's own letters, and Lyndsay would write a short introduction. In the same way, the other part of the correspondence from a Mr. Williams could be used. In the meantime, he returns them along with an order on Mr. Cadell for ten guineas for Lyndsay against *Maga*'s account.

Blackwood continues to flatter his newfound author, making Lyndsay comfortable enough to offer the publisher letters in a friend's possession. Returning to Lyndsay's letters, there is one to Blackwood dated November 17, the day of Blackwood's third letter; but this letter seems to answer some of Blackwood's questions sent that very day. Perhaps a misdate, or one of Blackwood's earlier letters contained some of the same questions. In any case, it is easy to imagine how pleased Dods was, and how easily she slipped into Lyndsay's worldly tone with Blackwood. I also note Dods gave Somerset Street, 10 Portman Square, as her return address.

On November 20, Blackwood answered Lyndsay's of November 17. He is delighted Lyndsay goes on with *Cain*—not the smallest doubt it will be a drama read and admired "let my Lord Byron come out when he may." Still, would like to get it out as soon as possible—they make *Cain* the last piece in volume so he can have more time—will *Destiny* and *Death of Cain* be one drama—he can give no opinion—"your own judgment should entirely guide you" though it ought to be in this volume—he has changed the title to *Dramas* which he thinks Lyndsay will approve . . . hopes he has received the pages and approves . . . return proofs the sooner the better . . . revise *Plague of Darkness* as printed in *Maga* . . . write by return if he has corrections or alterations.

Now Blackwood comes to the subject of payment: A common method is for publisher to take the risk of all expenses and then divide profits with the author—saves trouble when a sum is agreed to for copyright—publisher feels delicacy in naming sum—wishes author to. "My dear Sir," Blackwood proposes —if Lyndsay has proper price in mind tell him so frankly—impossible to predict sale of a book—if this is not successful "I shall be more mistaken than I ever was in my life." Blackwood also is confident in Lyndsay's newly projected work based on Saul, to open the second volume—title should be "Saul, a sacred Drama, with such and such as you may have ready . . . by David Lindsay, author of Dramas of the Ancient World." He goes on to discuss publication of Lyndsay's second volume and other business related to the first volume, imploring him to exert himself to the utmost. "Lord Byron's Cain, whatever may be its other merits, will be very inferior to your's in the tone of hallowed feeling—for I cannot think he can do well with heartfelt interest. But we shall soon see." As for helping with items for *Maga,* do not inconvenience—Lyndsay has enough to occupy at moment in finishing *Cain*—"I am My Dear Sir." And a postscript telling Lyndsay not to pay postage of his letters—it is a bookseller's responsibility to pay postage both to and from authors.

Blackwood confirms that Dods knew Byron was writing on the same subjects as she. She may even have selected those subjects specifically to compete with the great Byron. She was now a man. And "he" would enter the lists with the hero of the day. Glory to the victor. And what more encouragement than to have a renowned publisher as standard-bearer. Blackwood had no doubt—book a success—second volume.

This letter was a set with Lyndsay's December 1 letter, describing his haste, his completion of *Cain,* his news that Byron's *Cain* will be out that next Tuesday. On December 21 Blackwood writes again, this time enclosing copies of *Dramas* and two new issues of *Maga* with a "spirited critique" of *Cain* and a short notice of other pieces. Does Lyndsay like it—is he pleased with appearance of volume?—the drama he sent for *Maga* needed more room—will be in January number. Since *Dramas* was only that day published, has no impression on public—his own friends think very highly of them—will be popular notwithstanding Byron's—in a whirl of bustle—apologies for not sending terms—first moment he can spare to get calculations of expenses, will write—enclosed order for more copies of *Dramas* for friends on Cadell—make free use—copies given this way are no loss but help make book known—"I am My dear Sir."

No wonder Lyndsay's December 26 letter was so confident. Blackwood's high opinion of Lyndsay, even in comparison to Byron, spurred Dods to talk more about herself. But which self? Everything Dods said about Lyndsay may well be true, with the one exception of gender—several years younger than Byron, before lazy, now ambitious to make place in literary world. As for Byron's *Cain,* it is daring to interpret Cain as someone to be admired for questioning his father's ways and setting his own standards. Even the most pious must think this way occasionally. Even—or might one say especially—Mary Diana Dods. In closing, Lyndsay asked to hear quickly from Blackwood, as his friends where he previously received mail (Sloane Street) are moving and he is about to move from his Somerset Street address as well and go to the south of England for some weeks to avoid cold weather.

On January 3, 1822, Blackwood tells Lyndsay he is gratified by the appearance of *Dramas*—sorry the review was not "even more favourable"—nevertheless spirited and will help make book known—publisher should not laud book overly in own magazine—most helpful if Lyndsay's friends can get reviews in London papers—but over-flattery harms reputation of a book. Gossip about a contemporary author—Jeffrey too busy—could he get Gifford to review—*The Monthly Review?—The British Critic?* The sooner the better. Sales of the *Dramas* have not yet been great ". . . but I hope it will go on." Those who have seen it think well—much merit—most favorable.

And finally, terms: Costs for a thousand copies, including printing, advertising, free copies, paper, add up to £332.5. Expected profit, supposing edition entirely sold out, £139.5. Expenses more than originally thought—if agreeable, will pay Lyndsay £75—hopes satisfactory—wishes good health to enjoy many happy years, and a postscript describing praise of *Dramas* just received from a valuable correspondent—production of a man of genius—*Deluge* and *Cain* both display great power—fears *Sardanapalus* will be "cast in shade by Lord Byrons" but *The Nereid's Love* one of the most beautiful classical pieces ever read.

The mutual romance between publisher and author continues. On January 8 Lyndsay responded to Blackwood's offer by saying he would be perfectly satisfied with fifty pounds paid immediately instead of seventy-five pounds when the edition is sold out—he is trying to get friends to exert influence to get *Dramas* noticed in London newspapers—would Blackwood like to publish translations of Raynouard? On January 12 Blackwood is all agreement. Fifty pounds is fine—great happiness that their feelings are in unison—hopes that the more they know of each other the more their mutual confidence and friendship will grow—sends draft of brother's for money rather than usual credit. And the *Dramas* received good notice in *Stoddart's* paper, where they were compared with Lord Byron's. And Raynouard would make an excellent article for *Maga* but perhaps better would be a *Song of Horae Gallicae* like the *Horae Germanicae,* with a spirited analysis with copious extracts—this to avoid the dull parts. The "Ring and the Stream" is in this issue of *Maga* and will be admired by everyone—letter from valued London correspondent—speaks very highly of *Dramas.*

How delighted Doddy must have been. Fifty pounds. The equivalent of half a year's 1827 annuity from her father. "The Ring and the Stream" published, with money to come. Blackwood asking for more works—a series of works—and compliments—and accolades. The publisher's reference to their mutual trust and friendship no doubt made her feel even more confident in her masquerade. Her *Dramas* was a success. Her projected translations were predicted to be a success. Not least of all, her personal drama was a success. If only by correspondence, she established the existence of one David Lyndsay. When she wrote to Blackwood, she became him. And he was a success. The lesson learned was that nothing prevented her from succeeding in a man's world—except appearance. Surely the seeds were planted here, if not earlier, for Dods's transformation into Walter Sholto Douglas.

So Lyndsay wrote again on January 15 thanking Blackwood, discussing the business of selling the *Dramas*, confident it will do well in London, promising to follow Blackwood's suggestions about Raynouard, revealing he learned French and Italian under the best masters, dismissing the idea he knew that the author Proctor had planned to write a *Deluge*, glad of the competition with Byron because curiosity will make his own sell better. And, change of address: send under initials D.L. to James Weale, 19 York Buildings—Baker Street, where Lyndsay will be on his return to town. On February 8, another letter from the author, very businesslike, reporting on his progress with Raynouard. He repeats much of the previous letters about reviews, competition, but adds a complaint about the typesetting of his piece in *Maga*. Here is a confident Dods indeed.

That confidence was no doubt reinforced by the Blackwood–Charles Ollier correspondence of February 1822, when Blackwood asked the London-based publisher about the sale of *Dramas* and also "something" about its author, whom he knew only through their correspondence. When Ollier told him he knew a good deal about *"David Lyndsay's"* dramas and that the gentleman who conducted the business is in their shop every day and is much gratified, he certainly informed Weale of Blackwood's interest. And Weale certainly informed Dods. Blackwood's next letter to Ollier again asked about Lyndsay, hoping one day to meet him, although the *Dramas* have not succeeded as he expected; still, Blackwood had confidence. Ollier's March response indicated he had discussed Lyndsay with Weale, who declared he was not Lyndsay; and "no one will ever know who is." Again, Weale, friend and intermediary, no doubt told Dods.

But for all Blackwood's curiosity about the author, the romance appears to be on the wane. Blackwood doesn't answer Lyndsay's February 8 letter until February 25—ashamed at being so long—delayed because he expected to get Lyndsay's article into that issue, but had so much other material of contemporary nature—hopes it will be in the next—very busy—the Raynouard notices are very striking—hopes he has done article on the tragedy—give most striking passages with spirited prose analysis—extracts being large as in their *Horae Germanicae*—

noticed several errors in Lyndsay's piece—quite vexed—manuscript destroyed—could not give errata—not sure it now worth it as readers make large allowances for hurry of periodical work but if Lyndsay wishes—shall take particular care in future—hope new issue—sent copy of Adam Blair—what is opinion—happy *Dramas* may be reviewed in *Quarterly*—would do a great deal for the book which yet requires to be known—small prospect of a second edition—sales both here and London have not at all come up to my expectations—Cadell sold only about 130—hopes the work will "soon be known as it deserves to be." After these last disappointing and disappointed words, a friendly last line about sending volumes or copies of *Maga* to Lyndsay under his new address in care of "James Weale Esq at The Right Honble William Huskisson, Office of Woods Etc, Whitehall."

The publisher had courted and wooed his new author. He had sincerely praised and confidently invested in *Dramas*. He had gone so far as to put his judgment on the line in his November 20 letter when he wrote that if *Dramas* was not successful, "I shall be more mistaken than I ever was in my life." But his judgment was mistaken. Though some reviewers and readers thought well of *Dramas,* it did not sell. And sales, for a publisher, is the measure of success. Having these two sets of letters side by side, it became evident that the climax of Dods's relationship with Blackwood was spelled out as early as that November 1821 letter. Blackwood remained polite to the author he had once held in such high esteem. He continued to send him free copies of *Maga,* and occasionally books published by his house. And their polite, sporadic correspondence stretched through 1825. But from February 1822 onward, it was Mary Diana Dods who did the courting and wooing. Blackwood published only two other pieces by Lyndsay, in 1822, and after that no more.

Lyndsay's career with Blackwood was closed, but Dods was as yet unaware of its demise. Possibly Blackwood was not quite aware himself. On March 23 Blackwood wrote to Lyndsay, again under care of Weale, indicating he had no response to his last letter. Now he writes to say that Lyndsay's article was again omitted from the latest *Maga* due to space restrictions. He encloses proofs however—please send any corrections—will soon be at press again—any word if Gifford will review *Dramas* in the *Quarterly*—most anxious to hear—wish much your friends would make exertion to get *Dramas* talked about—sent another book—anonymous author is actually Lady Charlotte Campbell, Duke of Argyll's sister—he believes this will be pretty well known.

Estrangement precedes divorce. Blackwood doesn't write again until May 24. His letter confirms my conjecture that Lyndsay's brusque letter docketed by a Blackwood's clerk as written in June was actually written in May, because this Blackwood letter is in reply. Though polite, Blackwood, too, is brusque. He has already explained to Lyndsay's friend Mr. Weale that Lyndsay's projected "Dramatic Critiques" would not be suitable to *Maga* because it is so much overused by the Cockneys (a disparaging reference to the Shelleys' friend Leigh Hunt among other "liberal" competitors) "every one is sick of hearing about the Theatre"—he returns the article—Lyndsay's "States of Blois" is in this issue—the sooner he sends the analysis and extracts the better—not more than six or eight pages—and spirited—so much backlog, will not be able to insert much of his for a month or two—he may perhaps send a critique on some new book or other—write beforehand to see if it is already in other hands.

Surely this searching around for possible work for Lyndsay is in response to Lyndsay's confession in "his" May letter that like others of "his" rank "he" must "make a respectable appearance upon a very moderate allowance from his Father." And then a double-edged close. Blackwood would be glad to recommend Lyndsay's literary labors to others—but send more to him—rest assured any work of his is looked upon with favor. In his letter, Lyndsay expressed regret at the poor sale of *Dramas,* hoping the publisher had not lost money. Blackwood appears to make no comment. But both in tone and content, his response is clear.

It was becoming clear to Dods as well. On June 10 Lyndsay again wrote, apologizing for the lateness of his translations—forthcoming—enclosed is a poem—is it acceptable? On June 29, another Lyndsay letter, brief, in shaky handwriting, asking to review Sir Walter Scott's *Halidon Hill*—translations will be sent in a few days. July 13, a third Lyndsay letter, brief, enclosing the review.

Only this last brings a response from Blackwood on July 25—apologies—so busy—correspondents ahead of him—could not insert any of Lyndsay's article—expected "Death of Isaiah" to be in this issue but had too much—returning Lyndsay's critique of *Halidon Hill*—decided not to notice it—very sorry— hope you like this issue of *Maga*—sorry you could not get *Dramas* noticed in the *Quarterly*—"The sale I am sorry to say is in a great measure stopped" but a good review would revive it— quite angry with Lyndsay for paying postage on his critique. Despite the friendly chiding for Lyndsay paying postage after Blackwood told him not to, this letter is all rejection.

Dods responded almost at once with the August 2 letter that revealed that Lyndsay was a pseudonym. Having Blackwood's correspondence gives that central letter new meaning. Lyndsay was not simply offering new projects; "he" was desperately fighting to preserve "his" relationship with Blackwood. My earlier interpretation of Lyndsay's letter changed. "His" news that "he" was to leave for France with a friend, a "clever man but bitter," was possibly true. But chances were Mr. David Lyndsay's bitter traveling companion was another woman. Too early to be Isabella Robinson. Perhaps Dods's sister? And Lyndsay's remarkable confession of an incognito a full year and numerous publications after the beginning of "his" correspondence with Blackwood—that "he" is a countryman; that for strong reasons "he" must keep "his" identity a secret; that "he" is well known to Charles Lamb but not under that name; all this confession was sent not because Lyndsay felt more at ease with Blackwood. On the contrary: It was intended to reinterest the publisher in his author. Dods had gotten Blackwood's message. Anxious for career and income, she tried whatever she could. Lyndsay's polite little reminder in that same letter that Blackwood owed payment for "his" last publication in *Maga* seemed written by a far different person from the jaunty author who initially implied to the publisher that money was no object.

In August 1822 came the long overdue publication of

Lyndsay's "The Death of Isaiah," the last work by David Lyndsay to appear in the pages of *Maga*. Then there was silence between the former steady correspondents until November, when Lyndsay tried again with his offer of adapting tales from childhood reading—"The Yellow Dwarf"—less grave than tragedies, better for *Maga*—encloses sample—*Dramas* much admired in Paris, expects sales—friend assures him Byron much annoyed by *Dramas* but Shelley admired them—then his attack on the Shelley-Byron circle's projected publication, the *Liberal*, and a lengthy passage of literary critical judgment. Here was not the urbane Lyndsay sharing his insights, but Dods, eager to publish: poetry, essays, tragedies, possibly literary critiques—if Blackwood will only notice how clever and insightful Lyndsay is.

Blackwood sends no answer. On February 23, 1823, a disappointed Lyndsay tried again. On March 8 a polite but cool Blackwood finally answers—but to James Weale, who apparently has written on behalf of Lyndsay. With apologies for the delay, Blackwood is of the opinion that the tale sent last November, though quite good, is not suitable for *Maga*. And a collection of such tales is equally not suitable. A London publisher should be found. He returns the manuscript, along with a letter to "our friend David L." and further apologies.

The enclosed letter to Lyndsay also opens with apologies. Blackwood didn't write because he had disagreeable news to send and so found excuses to delay. Now "consciousness of having used a friend ill by this procrastination" causes him to write and ask for forgiveness. Still, he must reject the "Tale of the Orange," which despite the pleasure it gives is not for *Maga*. As for Lyndsay's projected *Tales of the English*, he would need to see more of them but with that title, they should have some "really English stories" rather than the ones Lyndsay referred to. The "Orange Tree" seems more like Grimm. If Lyndsay sends some samples, Blackwood promises to respond at once. Which leads him to the *Dramas*. They "have not been at all successful." Therefore, he "most positively" tells Lyndsay not to attempt to publish more poetry, whether tales or dramas. "The truth is there is no relish for it nowadays and commercially speaking it will not answer." Blackwood says the *Dramas* are only one example among hundreds, but this is not true of getting dramas produced. He therefore congratulates Lyndsay on the news that a play of his will be given in London next year by Kemble, and hopes for its success. In the meanwhile, he encloses a tragedy he, for all his advice, just printed though he doesn't expect it to make a noise.

From this point in Lyndsay and Blackwood's correspondence until its end, the proportion of letters sent tells the story. To Lyndsay's fifteen letters, he receives only five responses. Friendly. Polite. But finally, rejections. The disproportionate series begins with Lyndsay's response of March 23—continues to work on tales, some based on English tales, some German—offers the entire to Blackwood—thanks him for books sent—on April 7 he sent a sheet of varieties for *Maga*—on June 11 proposing returning to German translations he offered on 23 February—goblin tales—will Blackwood publish? On July 2 Lyndsay thanked Blackwood for the good news that he is interested in German tales—Lyndsay thinks they will make three volumes. This welcome communication came through Weale, who met Blackwood in London during this period. On August 3, Lyndsay sent a goblin story for *Maga,* chitchat about the kind words that appeared in *Maga* about his old friend Kitchener whom Blackwood dined with in London, and literary opinions about Byron and others—not as knowledgeable about some aspects as he is new in literary world—sends third story to give Blackwood choice.

Blackwood responds on August 26. The goblin story sent has just appeared in someone else's three-volume collection—he therefore returns it—thinks perhaps that publication appeared before Lyndsay wrote his. A polite, but clear, suspicion that Lyndsay knowingly took the idea for his project from that one—suggests Lyndsay give up plan—glad Kitchener is his friend—surprised Lyndsay thinks well of the *London Magazine,* which Blackwood goes on to attack—and then expresses his "wonder" at Lyndsay's allusion to Patmore, who is a "degraded and contemptible creature" who had the nerve to publish Blackwood's private letters. And about this despised creature, Blackwood goes on at length. By return mail, Lyndsay's deeply apologetic letter—agrees Patmore is a scoundrel—Lyndsay is a young man, but a true Gentleman—noblest blood of Scotland—if this apology not acceptable, he is willing to duel; deserves a bullet for his impertinence. To the implication that Lyndsay was aware that some of the stories he writes have already been translated, he asks if Blackwood would send him a copy of the volume in which the story is printed and wants to know if "Magic Love" is also translated—and as Weale is away, would he address to him at Mrs. Carter's, Duke Street.

Lyndsay had published dramas on the same subjects as Byron. Now, he tries to publish German translations that someone had recently brought out. A second coincidence. Though Blackwood must have known that publications about the same subjects were not uncommon, there is the hint in his letter that if Lyndsay is writing at the inspiration of other people's publications, he may run into difficulties getting into print. As for Lyndsay's offer of a duel, Dods either got carried away in her Lyndsay persona or, far more likely, she knew full well that Blackwood would accept the idea as a gentleman's offer of true remorse rather than take him up on it.

Blackwood, the gentleman, responded at once. On September 5, in a very short letter, he sends his regrets that Lyndsay should have been so upset about his last letter—"God forbid" he should for one moment have thought unkindly of him ". . . unknown as we are personally" always felt fullest confidence "I was writing to a gentleman." His anger was at that scoundrel Patmore—he now owes Lyndsay an apology. As for the German tales, the book's title is *Popular Tales and Romances of the Northern Nation* and he arranges for Lyndsay to get a copy from Cadell.

Blackwood always felt the fullest confidence he was writing to a gentleman. What pleasure that line must have brought Dods. If she was not just then successful in getting her works published by Blackwood, she certainly continued to succeed in her personal fiction. But this was not enough. When Lyndsay replied on September 9 that the tales sent had only one duplicate, and that in all they were inferior, "he" was obviously trying to get Blackwood to change his mind. Two weeks later

Blackwood sent a very brief response, agreeing that Lyndsay should forward the two tales for *Maga* and then Blackwood would decide about possibly publishing a collection. So Lyndsay's October 10 letter enclosing a story, promising to send more, and pressing about publishing the collection for Christmas was not an obstinate shot in the dark: It was in response to Blackwood's invitation. But Blackwood may have opened the door to Lyndsay out of guilt about their misunderstanding regarding Patmore because material in hand, he sends no response. In writing Lyndsay's December 30 letter concluding that Blackwood's nonresponse meant rejection and requesting the return of his three stories, Dods must have been especially disappointed. The door, momentarily reopened, was shut even more firmly.

The publisher continues to supply Lyndsay with some books and copies of *Maga*. But he neither writes to his anxious author nor returns his tales. On February 16, 1824, Lyndsay sent a reminder. No response. On March 17, another reminder, this one asking if *Dramas* gets on, and whether there might be a second edition. No response. In May, some lines of a drama. No response. Whatever Dods felt about Blackwood's apparent neglect, she continued to send him "gentlemanly" letters. But his message of silence she well understood. And being a woman of ambition, she took her wares elsewhere—and sold them. Her *Tales* were to be published by Hurst and Company. No wonder Lyndsay's January 16, 1825, letter was so confident. The great Blackwood, who "had been my first Friend in Literature," had abandoned him. She found a new path. Crediting Blackwood for assisting her through *Maga*'s kind words about Lyndsay in the November issue, Lyndsay asked permission to dedicate his *Tales* to the publisher.

Newly confident, Lyndsay tries to reenter *Maga* with an essay. Should Blackwood not find it suitable, no worry. Some friends are planning a quarterly magazine—Lyndsay will publish it there. "He" also indicates "he" has essays on phrenology, poetry, and a short history of Olney. Any interest? And as much to impress as to interest the publisher, Dods sends gossip about the stir caused by two recent biographies about the late Byron and the London quarrels over the question of Byron's and his biographers' truthfulness. Lyndsay's own station in that literary world has been enhanced; "he" knows Lady Byron slightly, is intimately acquainted with many of her connections and friends, and is also now acquainted with Mrs. Shelley.

Finally, on January 22, 1825, Blackwood sends a letter to David Lyndsay. He writes on receipt of Lyndsay's of January 16, apologizing for allowing the author's earlier letters to go unacknowledged, but quickly moves to the subject of the dedication of *Tales*. He declines, fearing it would appear rather odd and be of no use in promoting the volume. Still, he allows Lyndsay to decide. The essay sent is clever but not suitable to *Maga*. He therefore returns it. As for the other essays offered, they have so much material that though he would of course be happy to see anything sent, they must reject very often papers of great merit. But don't send the Olney essay; it is unsuitable. Blackwood thanks Lyndsay for his literary gossip. It is a great treat to him. Should Lyndsay have leisure, he would happily receive frequent chitchat of that sort. This is Blackwood's last letter to David Lyndsay.

But not Lyndsay's last to Blackwood. Four more follow, two in 1825; one in 1826; the last in 1829. In May, Blackwood is asked to announce in *Maga* that *Tales* will be published in June. In December, perhaps to pick up the thread again, Lyndsay sends the kind of literary gossip Blackwood eagerly invited. This time, it is all about the "fine creature" Mary Shelley and Shelley and the fracas between Byron's friend Hobhouse and Shelley's cousin Medwin about Medwin's biography of Byron and Trelawny and Hunt. In short, it is a letter that could have been written only if Lyndsay—Mary Diana Dods—was indeed an intimate of Mary Shelley's. "He" also sends a story for *Maga*. No response. In March 1826, a brief note, asking for the return of the story. Then, three years later, a letter making clear that Lyndsay—or someone using Lyndsay's work—tried to publish under another pseudonym, only to be rejected in that guise as well.

When I first read Lyndsay's letters, I took them to be written by a man, and was uncertain about how much he wrote was dependable. I had long since learned Doddy's secret, but still struggled to learn her truth. Interweaving Blackwood's letters with Lyndsay's brought the facts closer in focus. It became clear how Blackwood, the critic, had encouraged Lyndsay to write, experiment, translate; then how Blackwood, the publisher, was persuaded by the financial failure of *Dramas* to cut the author off from *Maga* and the house of Blackwood. Blackwood's ever-polite replies drew Dods on. And Dods did not realize Blackwood responded as one gentleman of the era would to another gentleman, and that within each politely worded rejection, each delayed answer, was an invitation to send no more. The house of Blackwood had ended its relationship with the writer David Lyndsay, though its publisher would consider it rude to state this fact flatly. Lyndsay was a gentleman. He would have to work it out for himself.

But of course Lyndsay wasn't a gentleman. The recipient of Blackwood's letters could not recognize the masculine code—and offended, or angrily embarrassed, or both—quickly break off the correspondence. There was no male fight pattern. Instead, letter after letter tried to convince the publisher to change his mind: a female pattern of attempted negotiation. If there was anger, it had been suppressed. Lyndsay was, after all, a nineteenth-century woman. She had broken through the diffidence and public silence her era expected of women, and gained a public place for herself—but it was a largely secret place. She wrote and published stories and poems as David Lyndsay, a creation so successful "he" endured in literary and historical records for some one hundred and fifty years. Lyndsay's letters freely mixed fact and fiction; Blackwood's letters set Lyndsay's in the cold light of Dods's reality. But with all I knew about Mary Diana Dods by this time, I still did not expect the woman I met in the Dods-Carter-Morton letters.

## CHAPTER 17

# MY DEAR LORD AND HIS DAUGHTERS

I BEGAN TO UNTANGLE the thirty-two Dods, Carter, Morton, and Aubin letters. More than half had no year; some only indicated the day of the week. It felt as if Dods was trying another tack to keep her secrets. But the key to unraveling these sixty-five pages turned out to be Dod's own nemesis: unpaid bills and accounting records.

Among the photocopied Morton papers were seven pages of accounts. Two small sheets in Dods's handwriting dated 1815–19 and 1819 listed debts she ran up while living in Swansea, Wales; the remaining neatly ledgered accounts were in Aubin's handwriting, and listed both receipts and payments for 1819, 1820, and two months of 1821. The watermark on Dods's lists was 1820, proving that her summary was not compiled in 1815–19, but in 1820 or later. On the left-hand column of one sheet, she listed her creditors: Vindin, Baker; J & N Gardener; milk; Robertson; Padgett; coals; washing; rent; Properjohn, butcher; Dixon & Co. After each, in pounds, shillings, and pence, was the particular debt, in all adding up to 105 pounds, 16 shillings, 9½ pence. At the bottom of the same page, another list, but this only words:

Add. Debts at Swansea
Mrs. Carter's Debts.—
Allowance unaccounted for.
Board of an Inmate—
Profits of personal Industry
promised: quaere if attempted?

The last line was a puzzle. *Quaere,* an obsolete form of *inquire,* means "one may ask," "it is a question," or "question." In the context of the list, *quaere* might imply some money is already owing and more may be earned through additional personal industry. The nature of the prior personal industry was unclear at this point, but the new industry might well refer to Mary Diana Dods's life as David Lyndsay.

The second page of Dods's accounts has three roughly drawn columns: year, creditor, amount owed. The two first items, listed under 1819, showed a debt to Shirley of £14.13.2½ and a second debt of £4.17.4 to someone whose name, written over, was unclear. Following is a list from 1815–19 that included debts to Sylvester for £8.12.0 worth of medicine; Rees for £7.4.8 for rent at Windsor; Padby, £21.5.0, but no indication for what; Patten's, £47.0.6 for rent at Southampton Street; and Roll. Pianoforte, £9.0.0. To this subtotal of £132.12.8½, Dods added Mrs. Carter's debts of £15.14.0. The total, £148.6.8½.

Milk, coal, washing, rent—Dods's lists gave an idea of the ordinary details of her life. She had an allowance; she lived in Swansea for some period of 1815–19, for which she still owed £47 that could be estimated to cover anywhere from nine to twelve months' rent; and during the same period, she visited at Windsor for some four to six weeks; she owed money for a piano.

Aubin's payments/receipts of 1819–21 added more of the story, including establishing that the earl of Morton had been providing his daughters with a set allowance at least as early as 1815. Perhaps it was no coincidence that these allowances followed the earl's August 1814 marriage and protracted honeymoon tour. It also may have been the beginning of a new life for Dods. The earl was fifty-four years old; his bride, Susan Elizabeth, twenty-one years old. Mary Diana Dods in 1814 was approximately twenty-three. Dods's presence in Morton's home may have been unacceptable to her young stepmother—or unacceptable to Dods herself. In either case, it seems likely that this marriage precipitated Dods's departure from the comforts of her father's home. Allowance in hand, she was out on her own.

Aubin's accounts are specific only from 1819, when Carter received a lump payment of £50 in April, while her sister received varying amounts of allowance over varying periods, sometimes weekly, other times monthly; as little as £5, as much as £25. In 1820, these irregular payments continued until February, when Dods's allowance began to be doled out to her at £5 every two weeks, with the exception of a payment at the end of March of £35.5, and the end of June of £45.18.3. These larger amounts were to pay Dods's rent. In contrast, in 1820 Carter continued to receive lump payments every half year or so. Clearly Morton kept the twenty-nine-year-old Dods on a very short tether, but trusted Carter to manage her own money as a responsible adult.

In December 1820, Aubin's accounts indicate that he paid a number of the bills that appeared on Dods's list, at the same time identifying what the payment was for. Shirley, unidentified by Dods, turned out to be Mrs. Shirley, Dods's dressmaker. In January 1821 Padgett, also unidentified, was given his money. This turned out to be for supplying her with Madeira wine. In January–February 1821, Dods's biweekly allowance was raised to £10. In March another dressmaking bill of £14 for Dods is also paid and debts of £53 to Miss Charlotte Figg and £30 to Mrs. Sandby are both paid, though without explanation. However, in March Mrs. Carter's allowance, like her sister's, begins to be paid at the rate of £10 biweekly instead of lump sums. The Figg and Sandby debts may be the direct cause of the earl's new restraint on his other daughter.

The accounts give yet another insight into the relationship of the earl and his daughters, this time on the receipt side of the ledger. Apparently, the earl sent funds to cover the payments for his daughters quite irregularly. November 1819, £100, March 1820, two payments of £100 each, totaling £300 for the period. But Aubin's accounts show that £421.10.8 had actually been paid out. Between December 1820 and March 1821, £120, £100, £200, totaling £420, were provided to cover expenditures paid out during 1819 to August 1821. Somehow, at the end of all the receipts and payments, the earl still owes Aubin £33.1.11. And either the earl asked for these accounts from Aubin as proof he still owed his agent funds—or Aubin sent the accounts, with the same objective in mind.

Numbers in hand, I turned to the letters to fill in the missing narrative of father, daughters, agent. The first letter set the stage for all that followed. Written by A. Aubin to "My dearest Lord," dated July 5, 1807, addressed to his home at Park Street, London, it was some eleven years earlier than the remainder of the letters. It was also the only letter in the collection from A. Aubin. All the other Aubin letters were from J. Aubin. From context, A. Aubin proved to be J. Aubin's wife. She is most polite to the earl. She knows he is nearly ready to depart for Scotland, but hopes he may have time just to answer to say he and his mother, "dear Lady Morton," continue well. Will he also promise to write immediately on arrival at Dalmahoy to say how they fared on their journey? And before he leaves, she begs him to "enjoin my young Friends to write regularly" to her once a fortnight in case of sickness during the earl's absence so she may have them properly attended to—and he has not written one word of his "intentions respecting their removal or not." As for the Aubins, they are well and hope Lord Melville will assist them in leaving their present home in Chatham, where they have very little congenial company ". . . God bless you my dearest Lord . . . Yours most sincerely & gratefully . . . We rejoice to hear your Law suits go on so well."

This one letter revealed that Morton's reputed daughters lived with their father in London, that they remained there for long durations without him—Mrs. Aubin asks they write "regularly"—"once a fortnight"—and that sometimes he arranged for them to live elsewhere, possibly with him in Scotland. Lyndsay told Blackwood he had studied with the finest language masters. Apparently Dods did. And she and Carter no doubt were also accustomed to other advantages of title and wealth: private carriages, servants, large homes, fine clothing. A.

Aubin's letter makes clear that as of 1807, the Dods sisters lived in the midst of their father's aristocratic London life.

I add this to evidence in several David Lyndsay letters to Blackwood that Doddy as an adult occasionally lived with her father in Scotland.[1] The first clue was that Lyndsay's November 1822 letter was sent from Aberdour. Of course, he might have been in Aberdour and not at the family home. Another letter, dated July 2, 1823, told Blackwood, who was then in London: "I am this time really far away, being in close attendence upon my Papa, who now and then draws largely upon my filial piety." At first, this looks like an excuse offered for not at last meeting the publisher. The local London postmark on the letter might confirm this—except that the letter is dated July 2; the postmark, July 7. Doddy would not have held a letter to Blackwood, whom she was always anxious to contact, five days before mailing it. Indeed, this gap between letter date and postmark is the only one in the Lyndsay correspondence. The likelihood is that *Lyndsay* was with his father, and had asked someone else en route to London to mail the letter or had left the letter to be mailed, perhaps by Mrs. Carter. Lyndsay's next letter, addressed to Blackwood in Edinburgh on August 3, has no postmarks, indicating it was hand-delivered and thus further suggesting that Doddy was in Scotland with the earl. (Another letter to Blackwood also provided a link between Lyndsay and the earl of Morton. Lyndsay's October 10 letter was mailed free of cost under "Douglas of Lochleven's" Parliamentary franking privilege. It was a common practice for members of Parliament to provide free mailing for family and close associates. If Blackwood noticed the postmark on the cover sheet, he would likely take it as an indication of David Lyndsay's social circles.)

When parent and daughters were not within the same household, it was apparently Mr. Aubin who for many years served as go-between. But Mr. Aubin was not Morton's employee: Rather, he was in the service of Lord Melville, First Lord of the Admiralty.[2] In 1807 he was unhappily posted at Chatham, a major naval shipyard. In Mrs. Aubin's letter there is just the glimmer of a suggestion that the earl of Morton might perhaps put in a good word with Lord Melville. In fact, since

Aubin was in Melville's service, it is possible that it was Melville who suggested that Aubin serve as intermediary for the earl of Morton.

The second letter in the record-office sequence was written by Georgiana Dods Carter to her father at Dalmahoy on September 28, 1818. In the years between, the sisters had grown up. The India Office records showed that sometime between late 1808 and early 1810, Georgiana Dods married Captain John Carter and went with him to live in India, first at Bombay, then at Surat. Their first child, Georgiana Isabella Douglas, was born in June 1811, baptized at Surat in November 1812, buried at Bombay April 6, 1815; an infant son was also buried at Bombay on April 4, 1815. Where Doddy spent the intervening years is not entirely clear, only that her debt list, dated from 1815, indicates that she was for some duration in Swansea as well as Windsor.

By 1818, Georgiana Carter was again in London. With her is her little boy named George and a very young baby. In 1989, another letter—found by David Brown of the record office in a miscellaneous series of undated seventeenth- and eighteenth-century Morton papers—added to this story. On August 30 Aubin wrote to inform his lordship that he had just received word that morning from Mrs. Sandby to say that "Mrs. Carter is safe, in Bed, with a little boy, both likely to do well." The announcement of his second grandson has no year, but Georgiana Carter's September 28, 1818, letter informs her father that her "little Son is growing a fine fellow and I have no doubt will do very well." Her speculation about the child, together with her own "unwell" condition, suggest that the child is newborn. When she does write, however, her main subject is not the child but his father. Her letter to "My dear Lord Morton" begs him to write to the new governor of Bombay on behalf of her husband:

> . . . . if this opportunity is lost we perhaps may never have another, and Captain Carter may think I neither care for him, or wish to serve him . . . pray my dear Lord M. oblige me . . . my poor Babies want me and I

must go . . . I'll write to you soon . . . present my
Compts to Lady Morton . . . Yours very affectionately
Georgiana Carter

Georgiana Carter addressed her father not as a daughter
but as any acquaintance of the powerful might, begging of him
his support for her husband's position, possibly for a promotion,
a home furlough, or a home post. Whether Morton complied
with his daughter's pleas remains uncertain. India Office records
do indicate, however, that John Carter again went on leave in
late 1818, but died on December 7 at Bombay, possibly en route
home. Georgiana Carter, widow, with two sons, remained in
London, but not at any of her father's homes. She was an adult
woman. She married and was widowed. Of her four children,
she had buried two. Life had provided Georgiana Dods Carter
with a series of its harder lessons. But it had omitted the lessons
that would have enabled her to earn a living for herself and her
two young sons.

The third letter in the sequence, written on August 25 from
her lodgings at 3 Hans Place by Mary Diana Dods to "My dear
Lord" opens the subject of the financial need of both daughters.
There is no year on this letter, but it is likely written in 1819
because in it Dods reports that her sister "is very unwell and out
of spirits from the contents of her last Letters from India, having
only received the particulars of her poor Husbands death a few
days ago." As John Carter died in December 1818, one can assume the details would have reached her by that next August.
Dods tells her father that because Aubin left town earlier than
they expected, the sisters are placed in "a very awkward sort of
a dilemma." She sent Aubin their landlady's bill for rent, nearly
twenty pounds, contracted before he started giving them their
allowance weekly. Until those weekly payments, Aubin generally paid them in notes every one or two months, which meant
they had to pay a fee to have the notes cashed and they took so
long in getting them cashed that the interest on their bills accumulated, generally being doubled before they could pay them—
by that consequence they continued in debt—when Mr. Aubin
decided on weekly payments, it left them with six weeks' accu-

mulated bills—not dischargeable out of five pounds a week—
some of the creditors are now clamorous—landlady placed her
bill in hands of another person who declares he will arrest them
if the bill is not paid tomorrow—she does not like to send the
fellow to him but will if he will permit—if he will have the goodness to advance them a couple of month's income it will relieve
all difficulties—they have another reason for wishing this—they
moved so a friend could reside with them who pays half the rent
and something more for her board—wish a little money to pay
off old debts—purchase a few necessaries such as sheets &c—
pray My Lord advance the money—the man is remarkably insolent—pray return an answer by the bearer of this—the advance
of two months will be forty pounds as far as their town difficulties are concerned—in the meantime My dear Lord pray
grant her request and observe they are not in advance of their
weekly allowance at present, five pounds becoming due to them
tomorrow—"if you will add an advance of seven weeks you will
greatly oblige your affectionately [sic] MD Dods."

Not the first nor the last letter an offspring writes to a parent for money. The letter begins to explain why Mrs. Carter
received her allowance in lump sums semiannually while Miss
Dods received small, varying amounts, occasionally ranging as
high as £25, £35, even £40. Aubin's figures and the letters themselves made clear that the larger amounts for Dods were for her
quarterly rent payments. Doddy, old enough to live outside her
father's home, was not regarded as responsible enough to pay
her own rent. The question was, had she lived irresponsibly,
squandering her money on silk gowns and delightful evening
suppers and theater and holiday jaunts?

Contents, Aubin's accounts, and partial dates suggest that
the next letter and the nine that follow were written in 1820,
beginning with J. Aubin's August 20 letter to the earl of Morton. Opening and closing with the customary polite, effusive language of the era, this is in fact a business letter. Aubin will leave
town on Thursday, and so has "taken the liberty" of sending the
earl the account of disbursements made for Mrs. Carter and
Miss Dods since the last accounting—he would be obliged if
Morton would cause £200 to be paid to his account to enable

him to continue their allowance and to pay Miss Dods's Swansea debts for which "the creditors are very clamorous having discovered her residence" and being referred to him—to prevent mischief he agreed to pay some £90.14.10. "I have the honor to remain always Your Lordships most devoted & obliged. . . ."

Apparently Doddy had handled her outstanding Swansea 1815–19 debts by moving to London and hoping she wouldn't be found. The next letter was written on November 15, 1820, from Georgiana Carter to the earl. It is a pained, suffering letter. On the previous day, to prevent arrest for debt, Georgiana Carter had borrowed twenty pounds from Miss Figg, but the money did not satisfy because she owed an additional three or four pounds for interest for which she was "obliged" to give the man the watch given her by her "too sincerely regretted Husband," the watch intended for her little George—if the earl would set things right she gives her solemn promise it shall never happen again—they are without heat because they can get no credit after "the affair of yesterday"—forgive her but indeed if the money he is kind enough to give them was paid regularly all this would never have happened—they are obliged to run in debt which is impossible to pay on the five pounds per week—must not deceive him—she borrowed another £33 from Miss Figg for the house since he called in the past bills which in all adds up to £54—which she herself now requires. "I shall be most grateful— My poor Sister expects her bills from Swansea every day" and when received they will be sent off to him—she would have told the earl about the watch and the debts before but she always feels "so depressed and unhappy" in his presence—do not be "very angry with us—and we both sincerely promise such a thing shall never happen again."

Aubin's accounts show that on November 18, 1820, he paid £3.18.0 to recover Georgiana Carter's watch. And ten days later, he paid £37.12.6 for the quarter's rent. The money begged to repay the debt to Miss Figg goes unpaid until March 3, 1821. To the sisters' distraught letter, Aubin adds his businesslike counterpoint to My dear Lord. On November 20 he informs the earl that Mary sent her Swansea bills—her milkwoman called in person being much distressed for the payment of the £4.6.3 and

might proceed to extremities, so he paid her—receipt enclosed—Mary also sent two London bills, one for her dressmaker, another for the hire of a piano.

Aubin's accounts reveal that pressed as he felt by these
creditors, he let more than a month go by before paying Mary
Diana Dods's Swansea bills. The lapse in time gives credence to
the sisters' ongoing complaint that Mr. Aubin is habitually late
in giving them their allowance, forcing them into a vicious cycle
of buying on credit and further adding to their debts. Four days
later, Aubin writes again, this time with a "very pressing de-
mand" from the grocers, who threaten immediately law proceedings against Mrs. Carter—he therefore paid the bills; he
finds there is also three months' rent due—". . . with very respectful regards. . . ."

It seemed the sisters had reason to be unhappy with
Aubin's money management. But the next letter, and those that
followed, made clear that the problem lay more with My dear
Lord. Aubin could pay out only what the earl instructed his
banker to send. And the earl apparently took a good long time
before responding to either Aubin's or his daughters' appeals.
Between December 3 and 11, 1820, Dods wrote to plead her
sister's case because she was too ill to write herself. Dods reminded his lordship that he is then "a fortnight in arrears to her,
and will be three weeks" next Saturday—she paid the £15 he
gave her when he last visited to pay small bills "contracted *while
without* Money"—sister now again contracts debts for expenses—she is also very uneasy about debts to their friends Mrs.
Sandby and Miss Figg, who herself owes the money—"if your
Lordship will be good enough to reply to my Sister . . . Mr.
Aubin . . . advised her addressing your Lordship—"

Aubin on December 5, 1820—tradesmen continue very
pressing—some more threatening he paid—landlord called for
rent, would not wait—takes the liberty of submitting bills to enable him to pay—send money to Aubin lest if the sisters received it themselves they might appropriate it to some other
purpose— On Friday, December 22, Georgiana Carter begs his
lordship's pardon but five weeks have gone by since she received
the fifteen pounds—he said it would be paid regularly—cannot
get credit from tradespeople—requested sister to write

. . . but my Lord you did not condescend to notice her
Letter . . . wrote to M^r Aubin . . . desired me to write
to you indeed my Lord I am almost broken hearted
. . . Miss Figg in very great want . . . also M^rs Sandby
. . . was there any thing in the world I could do to rid
you of so detestable a plague as myself I would gladly
do it . . . I have . . . not health . . . low and depressed. . . .

The following evening, Doddy picked up the correspondence, thanking My dear Lord for that morning's letter that
promises to protect them from "Lawyer's Letters &c"—they
have no wish to keep him in the dark about their debts—would
have sent earlier if he encouraged them—sister's are not many,
hers are more but of longer date and she is too happy at the
prospect of being rid of them—Georgiana anxious to repay
friends—will send bills in creditors' own handwritings—her own
two principal debts are also for borrowed money though some
tradesmen's bills likewise—even then they are compelled to borrow money as they have no credit and have only the two guineas
per week their friend pays for her board and they must provide
for her—

. . . the accounts shall soon be laid before you my dear
Lord and if you will clear us with the World and pay us
our allowance *regularly* afterwards—you shall never
again have reason to complain of us, and you will confer no triffling [*sic*] blessing upon Your affectionate
Children. . . .

In a day or so, Doddy sends the tradesmen's bills—but only
from the people in London—"much pain in sending . . . best to
shew at once the worst." She omits her sister's "private debts"
as well as her own Swansea ones, which "shall be sent also but
as you wish'd to know how contracted, I have written for memo-
randums of them"—will soon arrive—sister's shall be sent separate "as you desir'd"—observe that except for two dozen of
Bronti Maiderra [Madeira], a cheap wine they had for their
friends who visit rather than their own drinking, they do not

indulge themselves—"may we hope your early attention . . . at this moment borrowing. . . ."

Doddy must have persuaded My dear Lord, or worn him out. Aubin paid the bills sent, including the wine bill, in the last week of December 1820. Doddy's explanation about the wine brought to mind David Lyndsay's chronic liver problem, and Mary Shelley's 1828 comments about Walter Sholto Douglas's deterioration in Paris. Perhaps by 1820, Mary Diana Dods had an alcohol problem; seven years later, deeply in debt, despairing over "his" marriage, Walter Sholto Douglas might have become an obvious drunkard. Or perhaps the father was sincerely concerned for the health of his daughter who had a non-alcohol-related liver ailment. Either way, the trouble Doddy took to explain away this "cheap wine" suggests that her father needed to be convinced that neither of his daughters tippled. Apparently he was; but Morton was not yet convinced to send Aubin the money to reimburse him for payments made. On January 17, 1821, between kind regards to the earl and Lady Morton from himself and Mrs. Aubin, Aubin all but begs for the £100 promised reimbursement. Then on January 23, 1821, he responds to Morton's letter of the twentieth requiring clarification of monies spent—Miss Figg—Mrs. Sandby—Miss Dods's dressmaker—gave them also £25 due at Morton's departure and £30 in advance to keep them from running into debt—enclosed amount of bills—"Your most obliged. . . ." On February 3, Aubin begs leave to refer My dear Lord to his last letter—account of sums disbursed—expected to receive remittance by this time—is suffering much from advances made in addition to Saturday allowance due of £10. . . .

Finally, on February 20, 1821, Morton sends Aubin £100, which leaves a substantial amount still owing. Still, My dear Lord is a powerful man, and Aubin responds with gentlemanly gratitude for the partial repayment of monies long overdue and spent from his own slim funds. He goes on to indicate he has tried to convince "the young ladies" to move out of London to keep costs down, but "Mary says she has Scholars which she would not get in the country" and Georgiana is trying to get a post as a companion to a lady—Aubin continues to look for a place where Georgiana and her little boys might board in the country.

Scholars. Companion. Women pursuing women's careers. Doddy, like other educated women of the era in need of money, gives private lessons. Her scholars are no doubt girls of middle- or upper-class families who may be studying French, Italian, German, or Latin. The bill for piano rental suggests they may also be taking music lessons. On Doddy's list, she had written "Profits of personal Industry." Apparently before Mr. David Lyndsay wrote for *Blackwood's,* Miss Mary Diana Dods gave lessons.

From Dods's accumulated bills, it appears that those lessons were none too profitable. My dear Lord had his own doubts about those lessons. On March 8, 1821, when Aubin thanks Morton for sending the owing £200, he assures the earl that he will take an early opportunity of visiting Hans Place to make the enquiries his lordship wishes respecting Mary's scholars—Georgiana tells him Mary is soon to return to town from the country where she went for her health—". . . with most respectful regards. . . ."

The widowed Georgiana Carter will resort to the other "career" open to poor middle- or upper-class women: companion to the mistress of the house or governess to a daughter. At best, one might find such employment with a kind family. But whether the employer was kind or not, companions for women or girls were just a cut above servants. In exchange for a roof, food, and some small remuneration, companions and governesses were required to look, act, and speak like ladies, but serve at the beck and call of their employers.[3] And a good many women, faced with no choice, eagerly sought out this dependent way of life as their only hope.

There is a gap in the correspondence until, six months later, on September 11, 1821, Georgiana Carter again writes to My dear Lord who will be much shocked, perhaps offended—trust her, her heart is truly grateful—she is presently living in solitude—must move on October 18—if My dear Lord will lend her £20 she could put her younger son as a day boarder at the same school that Georgy attends—the lady asks £27 per year each—

this would free her to board with some genteel family for £2 a week, or £100 a year—allow her to pay back at Christmastime when she receives her pension—or the greater favor of paying back £10 at Christmas and £10 midsummer—she has no security—gives her word—should she get money from Bombay, Mr. Aubin will pay him back immediately—she knows she should be careful how she asks for money after what he said about the coronation—feels distressed—parted with all gifts from her poor husband—". . . write me a line just to say if you will oblige me or no . . . do not be angry . . . greatly obliged . . . remember my dear Lord . . . it is only a *loan* . . ."

A familiar-sounding letter from Georgiana Carter explaining her distress and begging her father for his aid, but two new pieces of information are added to the puzzle of the relationship of the Dods sisters to their father. Georgiana Carter's promise that should she receive money from Bombay she will return Morton's loan at once is commonplace. What appears not at all commonplace is that she will not return the funds directly to her father. Mr. Aubin will pay him back. A. Aubin's 1807 letter linking the daughters' whereabouts to the father's, together with the evidence of the sisters' privileged upbringing, make it almost certain that Morton raised his reputed daughters in his own household, mainly in London. The remainder of the letters indicate Morton continued his relationship with them into adulthood, provided funds for them, and that the sisters knew their stepmother. It earlier appeared that Aubin was an unpaid agent who handled the monies from father to daughters to save the busy earl the time and trouble of doing so himself. But the fact that Georgiana Carter promises to return monies through Aubin suggests something new: the earl wanted no easily traced paper trail to his daughters.

The other piece of new information concerns Georgiana Carter's remark about the coronation, which no doubt referred to the George IV ascension to the British throne in January 1820. Morton may have participated in the coronation ceremonies in June 1821, perhaps at great expense. It appears likely that the earl had pointed out to his daughter, who struggled to live within relatively narrow means, that the festivities had been costly and he was financially pinched as a result.

Unfortunately, Aubin's accounts do not cover the fall of 1821, so Morton's response to Georgiana's pleas remains at least a temporary mystery. But there is no mystery about Georgiana Carter's letter to her father written two months later, on November 12, 1821. She is disappointed that though he promised to write to her after visiting her and her children, he has sent not a word—and little Georgy has been very ill—and her own heart feels like it will break—and she was evicted from her lodgings at Brompton and moved to George Street, Portman Square, but now is to be turned out again because a wealthy nabob from India has offered her landlady far more money for the rooms— her landlady treated her with impertinence—her maid then took the opportunity of being insolent—she has spent the last three weeks looking for lodgings and must take some at two guineas a week—she is fretted to death—but took the lodgings until March—then she will place her little boys at the school and board with a family—if he has no objection, she would like to board with her sister—they may be of use to each other—and her sister will allow her children to stay there at times—and "Will you dear Sir give me your promise that should any thing happen to me, you will not let my Children go to a Workhouse as you once said . . . I know you would not . . ." She is so depressed she can scarcely keep from crying even with kindest friends—Mr. Aubin is in town and very well—the king is in town and she hears in very good health and spirits.

More pieces fall into place. That Georgiana Carter would mention Aubin's presence in town and his health to her father is quite expected, given their mutual interaction. That she as familiarly reports on the king's presence and well-being confirms the closeness of king and earl, which in turn substantiates the possibility that George IV's coronation costs were the earl's excuse for being financially pinched. Still, Morton must have agreed to lend the precious twenty pounds because Georgiana Carter could not otherwise plan to have her children start school at Brompton in March. Most important, this letter begins to explain the various addresses that David Lyndsay sent Blackwood.

When David Lyndsay opened "his" correspondence with Blackwood in August "he" gave "his" mailing address as c/o Mrs. Carter, 5 Sloane Street, Brompton. Perhaps by that time,

Dods and her friends had given up their 3 Hans Place residence and were moving between temporary lodgings. Fearful that Blackwood's letter might not reach her, she gave her sister's address. Once resettled sometime after August at 10 Somerset Street, Portman Square, Dods indicated that Blackwood could write directly to Lyndsay at that address. Thus, the eminent editor of *Blackwood's Edinburgh Magazine* and the ordinary postman delivering mail both lent credence to the existence of Lyndsay. This easy acceptance of her pseudonym by sophisticated publisher and His Majesty's Official Mail was almost certainly an important step in Dods's eventual transformation into Walter Sholto Douglas.

It is at this point that David Lyndsay's self-assured letters to Blackwood overlap with the Dods sisters' pleading letters to the earl. Like an operatic ensemble, the male voices of the earl, Aubin, and David Lyndsay, and the female, Mary Diana Dods and Georgiana Carter, range between counterpoint and harmony. And Mary Diana Dods must remember which role she was assigned at birth, and which one she elects to play.

The next letter, from Aubin to the earl, thanks him for the honor of receiving a hundred pounds for the credit of the ladies' account—Mrs. Carter is very well—so too her boys—she is kind enough to allow her eldest to play with his son—Mrs. Carter has not found a family to board with—he questioned her about Mary who has no doubt she is doing much better than if in the country—"the *firm* is prospering, Miss Figg has many Pupils for the Piano & Miss Aleworth for singing, & Mary writes for the Newspapers & Magazines, she lately received £5 from the Editor of the Edinburgh Review"—Georgiana does not do as well since she must pay Mary the full one hundred pounds a year his lordship allows her for rent.

Aubin's description of Dods's and her friends' firm makes clear as never before their struggle to maintain themselves in the only business open to respectable women. They have combined their talents and their monies to educate young ladies. If successful, they will remain in London as accepted members of cosmopolitan society. They would attend soirees and teas; occasionally there might be an evening at the theater. Certainly for Dods, the firm allowed her to live within the culture in which she had been raised. Failure would mean deportation—not to the prison colonies of Australia, but to the confined life of a country village, a sentence of slow death for Miss Mary Diana Dods. Better establish a business. Or become a man.

Aubin's proud report that Dods received five pounds from the editor of the *Edinburgh Review* recalls other letters about "pecuniary acknowledgements" from Blackwood. But they were from David Lyndsay to Blackwood. In those early months of their association, Lyndsay's letters always sounded as if the money was welcome but rather of secondary importance in "his" life. In contrast, it was of immense importance in the life of Miss Mary Diana Dods. Money earned as a writer could make the difference between freedom and life in country isolation or as a lifelong supplicant to her father. Lyndsay's aloof attitude toward money was more than a comfortable, gentlemanly pose; for Dods, it must have been a relief at least for a brief while to pretend she was not haunted by debts, bills, creditors, and weekly allowances.

Aubin's next letter, written four days later on November 23, 1821, once more shows the need for the weaker to remain on the good side of the powerful—will "my dear Lord" assist Mrs. Aubin's nephew, in civil service at Bombay, favorably mention his name to the present Governor—just "a few lines . . . a very meritorious young man . . . with most respectful & sincere Attachment. . . ."

Morton's daughters must also remain in their father's good graces. When Morton wrote to Georgiana Carter that her decision to board with her sister appeared to him to be done behind his back as well as Aubin's, Georgiana hastily defended herself in a letter of November 29—she agrees she has bad qualities but deceit is not one of them—her letter of November 12 informed him of her plan to board with Mary if he had no objection—no one else will allow her to have her children with her at any time—had not seen Mr. Aubin till the other day for many months—they talked of her plan—she labors most dreadfully under a depression of spirits—My dear Lord's letter did not raise them—her little men are both well—she again suffers from toothache—hopes she will not lose all her teeth—has no news and should not have written so soon but that she was vexed and hurt at some parts of his letter—she wishes he and Lady Morton may long enjoy health and happiness.

After a gap of four months, perhaps months when Morton was in town so there was no need to write, Aubin writes to the earl on February 6, 1822, this time as a supplicant for himself—will My dear Lord refer to Aubin's letter of January 29 to which he has not had the pleasure of receiving an answer—"everything is prepared" and awaits only his lordship's sending "the private letter to Lord Melville" to have Aubin's application forwarded—no doubt of his lordship's already having done so as he has already experienced My dear Lord's goodness but should he not, Aubin entreats—"return of Post . . . as every moment lost is most prejudicial to me—With my very respectful Regards. . . ."

In the next letter, written March 9, 1822, Aubin appears to be trying to get a pension after all his years serving under Lord Melville, first the father, then the son, in the admiralty office: Many thanks for having written to Lord Melville—nothing yet transpired—probably because the king was away from town Aubin's request was not acted on—he encloses the ladies' accounts—begs a remittance immediately in consideration of his present inadequate circumstances—Mrs. Carter was obliged to put eldest boy in preparatory school at Brompton—"we trusted your Lordship would have no objection"—£2 provided in addition to the £10 fortnightly allowance, which she promised to repay from her twice-a-year pension payments.

This is Aubin's last letter in the sequence. Georgiana Carter's letter of March 18, 1822, explains why: Mr. Aubin's mind has been very uneasy for a long time past and now he is dangerously ill—she fears for his life—seized on Friday with apoplectic fit—"pray write to poor Mrs. Aubin"—Mrs. Aubin told her that Mr. Aubin had written some time ago and she was hurt that My dear Lord never replied—appears that Mr. Aubin's pension request has not yet been presented to the king, probably because the king continued to stay at Brighton—she regards herself as most unfortunate in all this because she was beginning to love Mr. Aubin as a father—may the Almighty restore him to his health and senses again—as for herself, she has once more moved, now to 42 Duke Street, Manchester Square—she knows he is angry because she hasn't paid him pension money promised—soon—her little men, thank God, are pretty well—hopes the earl will soon be in town as everybody is here except the king—P.S. Mr. Aubin quite deranged—threw open windows at five o'clock in the morning declaring the bailiffs were coming for him and he had no place to go.

Carter reports her move from Somerset Street in March 1822. But as early as January 1822, David Lyndsay told Blackwood he was leaving Somerset Street "to avoid for a few weeks the rigours of London frosts on a constitution much weakened by suffering," asking the editor to write under care of James Weale, 19 York Buildings, Baker Street, where he will stay for some time after his return from the country. On February 8, 1822, and apparently through August, Lyndsay still receives mail from Blackwood under Weale's address, suggesting Dods may not have been in London during that period.

But Georgiana Carter's letters that spring tell Lord Morton a different story. On April 1 she informs My dear Lord that Mr. Aubin is considered out of danger—his mind still wanders—constantly talks of debts and bailiffs—he needs something to employ his mind—an idle life must be dreadful for a man who has been constantly employed for forty years—the memorial has been presented to the king—Mrs. Aubin had Morton's draft changed and gave the one hundred pounds to a Mr. Baxter, a friend of Aubin's, who promised to let them have the money as Aubin did, one payment in each fortnight—Baxter was a solicitor and, of course, a gentleman. As for her sister, she desired her to send best love to My dear Lord—she is living not far in Somerset Street and doing very well—"my Boys are dancing about me—write to me if you please. . . ." But Lyndsay's letters, under care to Weale, suggest he was not at Somerset Street that spring and early summer—that Doddy was in the country or in Scotland.

Not until June 26, when Doddy writes My dear Lord from 8 Duke Street, Manchester Square, are her whereabouts clear.

She writes to say she accepts his decision not to comply with her request to help get a pension for her friend Miss Figg whose father, Captain James Figg, honorably served the king sixty years; his two sons are well off, his other daughters married, only "her friend and Partner" is left unprovided for—Miss Figg has nothing during her mother's life except what she can earn by teaching music—and "God knows the money is not easily made."

Dods would not trouble My dear Lord again except that a remark in his letter implies he doubts Dods's actual employments—"let me give it to you my dear Lord Morton once for all under my hand, that we teach music, that we had seven Pupils last winter, but few now, owing to them leaving town during this quarter of the year . . . that if you would recommend us any"— that she sometimes, about once a quarter, writes criticism for the reviews upon some popular work that happens to be the fashion for which she is "esteem'd one of the cleverest and keenest of that race of Vipers"—she is paid "tolerably well— ten guineas per sheet—but this not under my own name" as she fears if the angry authors knew the reviews were her work they would return the compliment and maul her in return—she only wants to get into a cheaper house by buying some necessary furniture—three guineas per week being a heavy rent but for an "Academy in London we can get nothing cheaper"—the house near Windsor is offered for half its usual rent because a lady was murdered there last year—she considers that safe as it is unlikely a second murder would be attempted—the men were hanged . . . .

In Charlotte Figg's story of need there is yet another variant of how females in that era, though of successful families, could find themselves virtually abandoned. Unmarried, respectable, Figg's only recourse was to become a lady's companion or join with her friend Dods and open a London girls' academy. In the course of describing Figg's need, Dods talks more about her own. Seven pupils meant the difference between financial success and failure. But they were not dependent on that alone. Not only had Dods published stories and poems as Lyndsay, she was also one among that band of anonymous critics who reviewed—and dissected—other authors. With some pride, she informed her father she is considered among the best "of that race of Vipers." Payment of ten guineas per sheet proves the truth of her statement. There are hundreds, thousands, of anonymous reviews in newspapers, journals, anthologies; of the dailies, weeklies, monthlies, and annuals. Whatever else is unearthed about Doddy, where she published those viperous critiques, whom she attacked, whom defended, will almost certainly remain her secret. Still, even the secret adds to her story. Here is another medium in which a woman successfully published; her caustic, knowledgeable words no doubt accepted as written by a man.

Doddy's letter, for all its requests for her father's assistance, has an air of independence about it. She seems to tell her father he is wrong. In contrast, Georgiana Carter's next letter, written the same week, on July 1, 1822, is all confusion. She would have replied to My dear Lord's letter earlier but she dated it wrong and sent it to the wrong address—postman had it in his pocket for a whole week—she has been very unwell—violent pain caused her to neglect thanking him for his kindness to Master Georgy who is happy to go to school—on the twenty-second she will send her young gentleman off—thanks him for solving money matters for them—weight off her mind—her pension—or rather—his pension becomes due the next day—she pays an agent to go to India House to get the money because she does not like to be stared at by a parcel of young men—her agent takes eleven shillings sixpence for his trouble—surely My dear Lord won't begrudge that—what is she to do with the money?—should the agent send it to him?, "next time you write pray direct to Duke Street 42 . . . God bless My dear Lord Morton. . . ."

So Georgy will go to school. In exchange, Georgiana Carter's pension will go entirely to her father. But the pension does not quite reach him. On July 30, 1822, Georgiana Carter writes another somewhat muddled letter about address and recipients and postage and her failure to send the pension. She must first take an oath that she has not remarried since the death of her beloved Carter—she has been so busy with preparing Georgy for school she hasn't really had time to go take the oath—and the rainy weather prevents her as well—brought Georgy to school last Thursday at Brompton—ashamed she has not paid my dear Lord his twenty pounds he lent last July—intended returning it—but cannot do it even now—now Georgy is off she shall begin to hoard all the money she can for him—sincerely. . . .

By September 6, 1822, Georgiana Carter, in response to her father's letter, manages to send him the pension money owed—though poor Georgy was brought home ill last week—her sister too is very ill—very unhealthy time.

On September 30, 1822, it is Doddy's turn to write to her father. It is no surprise that the subject is money. But it is a surprise to learn that her immediate need is to pay Swansea bills—1815–19 bills that according to Aubin's accounts had been paid in 1820–21. Padley himself came to town—she daily expects two other visitors in the "formidable, unlucky shapes of Swansea Creditors"—if she could have raised enough money to pay these through her own industry, she would have but her utmost exertions (too great for her health and strength) did not accomplish this—unhappily for them, now it is the fashion for people to send their children for education abroad—no employment in the schools—many literally going to ruin—teaching in private families doesn't pay sufficiently the expenses of hired pianos and furnished lodgings which are necessary for respectable people to employ them—rent and pianos cost 172 guineas a year—if they had their own furniture they could get a house for seventy pounds and then make money rapidly as ten pupils would make them rich—last year they had that number but their profits were devoured by expenses—in spite of all their better hopes and exertions they will be "compell'd to give up the profession" they have adopted. Her friend has gone to Paris to ask her Mother's assistance to furnish a house for them—if this plan works, they will continue "our business"; if not, they will give it up—when her "Partner" returns, they will settle matters one way or another—"but the idea of giving up our profession now" frets her cruelly and has increased her habitual illness—in the meantime as the creditors are angry at Mr. Aubin but take it out on her, let her entreat My dear Lord's attention to the bills—the same creditors as she sent to him from Hans Place—she is afraid all the bills are unsatisfied. . . .

The line between truth and fiction blurs when comparing Lyndsay's letter of early August to Blackwood with Dods's letter to her father. Her distress is genuine. So are her efforts to raise the money needed. On June 22 David Lyndsay wrote to William Blackwood, offering to write on a variety of subjects, and mentioning that "he" is obliged to make a respectable appearance "upon a very moderate allowance" from "his" father. Between June and August that year, David Lyndsay sent Blackwood five such projects, each finally rejected. In early August, Lyndsay informed Blackwood "he" is about to go to France with a friend, a clever, somewhat bitter man, for amusement. While the friend diverts himself at the expense of the Parisians, Lyndsay will "collect material for serious subjects in verse and prose." That cynical male friend was actually Miss Figg. But it is uncertain whether Dods, without telling her father, in fact accompanied Figg to Paris that August, returning alone while Figg remained to treat with her mother for the furniture money, or if Lyndsay simply told Blackwood "he" was going in order to excite interest in the new material "he" would write about as a result of "his" journey—a journey that perhaps would take place only in Mary Diana Dods's imagination.

Five weeks later, on November 7, 1822, Georgiana Carter writes to My dear Lord about her own new financial crisis—a bill from a doctor for ten or eleven pounds that Mr. Aubin said he would pay—never dreamed it had not been settled until that morning mail brought her the enclosed letter—she just paid the Brompton doctor £12.15. And her sister's bill is about two pounds—thought Mr. Aubin had paid that as well—she thinks it a little unkind that he didn't inform them he hadn't—My dear Lord cannot conceive how it vexes, torments, teases her, but he can have no idea how one feels "to pay away one's last shilling boasting I am quite out of debt and then to have a bill start up that one never dreamed of"—like struggling for nothing in the world but misery—she knows she has no husband to stand between her and prison—she asks his forgiveness for thus troubling him—with best wishes for his own and Lady Morton's future happiness. . . .

Morton may have responded to these pleas, because for three months there are no letters about further monetary emergencies. This may mean there were none or that Morton was in London and his daughters pleaded their cases in person. But on February 13, 1823, Georgiana Carter is again in trouble. She tells Morton she would hide her face were he there in person—she relies on his good nature to pardon her the miserable scrape she has now got into—she was extremely ill—ague—fever—a young lady came to stay with her a few days to care for children—while she was confined to her sickbed the pension money she owed him arrived—her friend put it aside—unfortunately Georgy's governess called—indicated she would appreciate being paid early so she could pay her own bills at Christmas—her friend paid her the pension money £14.9.6—has receipt, which she will show him—she told her friend she had ruined her—"what excuse or apology can I offer to you my dear Lord indeed I have none to offer not the shadow of an excuse that I can see"—she can see no way to repay it soon—children always want something—can my dear Lord ever trust her again?—pray write her a few lines but do not write unkindly for she is not well—and one more subject for my dear Lord—please ask Mr. Greig to be a little more regular in sending the money you are kind enough to give us—whole week now gone—obliged yesterday to borrow a pound from landlord—could he send a bill on house in that neighborhood as the city is far and very expensive and very troublesome—she asks forgiveness—Little Georgy is back to school and Hastings is pretty well—"God bless you my dear Lord, write to me, a few lines . . . Your very Affectionate Child Georgiana Carter."

On February 22, 1823, Morton drafted a response to his daughter's latest explanation. The copy is the one letter in the Morton papers from the earl to either Georgiana Carter or Mary Diana Dods, the one opportunity to hear his own voice directly, his own attitude toward his reputed daughters. To begin with, he is not at all satisfied with Georgiana's logic. If she paid out the money for Georgy's schooling that should have been repaid to

him for money advanced by Mr. Greig, and she knew money
would be due to Georgy's teacher at Christmas, how comes it
she was not prepared to meet that bill out of her allowance?
And what does she mean that the bill will be soon due again? At
what rate per annum is she educating him now? Does she mean
to educate Hastings hereafter? Surely she has not forgotten that
it was only because she promised to ask no more of him that he
agreed to allow the fourteen pounds for George. In sum, if she
intended to remit the pension to Scotland in repayment of
money advanced and to leave the school bill unpaid, he considered this as dealing insincerely with him!

No doubt to his daughter's surprise, despite this reprimand,
My dear Lord decides he will further assist her. The most he can
do is make up her income to £200 a year by adding £160 to her
pension of £40 and allowing £14 for schooling. He reminds her
that it was in consideration of her having a family that he gave
her more than her sister and if she cannot manage on £214 a
year she must move to a cheaper residence than London—fortunately many such are to be found. He will, of course, direct
Mr. Greig to deduct the pension's £40 from his remittances of
£214 for her and £100 for her sister.

And now, a warning. He has often told her how pressed he
is because his rents for several years have been falling—that at
his death she will have less than she now has—and from his heir
she can expect nothing. As for method of payment, her remittances from Scotland must continue to pass as usual through the
hands of Mr. Greig and his Scottish banker's correspondent. Finally, though she may find this letter unpalatable, "the wisest
kindness I can show you is to tell you the plain truth" which is
that he knows "many Women of Birth & respectability who live
with families on no more than you have . . . I am, my dear
Georgiana, Yours most sincerely."

Georgiana Carter no doubt welcomed her father's additional support, however couched in dire warnings of a difficult
future. Nor, after all these years, could she have been surprised
that the money from Scotland would continue to come to her
through the route established years earlier: from Morton to Mr.

Greig, to Greig's banker in Scotland, to his Scottish banker's correspondent in London.

The last three letters in this sequence are all from Georgiana Carter to My dear Lord. The first two, July 26, 1823, and October 20, 1823, express her gratitude for all that My dear Lord does for her—school bills—her continued problems with her teeth—and the "very very great kindness" it would be if My dear Lord would write to Mr. Greig and beg him to be regular in the payment of the remittances he has so kindly settled on her—she has written Mr. Greig herself but it does no good—the money coming late forces her to borrow and pay heavy interest—do forgive her—oblige her by writing him a line—"God bless you my dear Lord. . . ."

Though Georgiana Carter must still struggle with late payments and credit payments, for the moment her major financial pressures seem eased. Not so Mary Diana Dods. Georgiana Carter's last letter, written February 23, 1824, is a long, sorrowful plea written on her sister's behalf. Georgiana Carter tells my dear Lord that if he exactly understood Mary Diana Dods's circumstances his own kind heart would feel for her. Georgiana Carter has already told him that her sister was in greatest distress—the day before she saw her—she has no money at all, having given up her income to Mrs. Figg, Charlotte Figg's mother, in exchange for an advance of two hundred pounds eight months ago—most of the money should have been returned, but because Mary Diana Dods has no income of any kind, Mrs. Figg has been obliged to lend her a great part of her own money back again, to pay board. Mrs. Figg is willing to advance her another one hundred pounds which would "make the poor Soul quite happy as it would enable her to pay the rest of her debts and have money in her pocket for her board" provided My dear Lord will say "should Mary die before it is paid off" he will pay off the debt to Mrs. Figg. "Should even the worst happen and Mary die before the next two years" it would mean paying back over a period of two years after her death, "but we are to hope the best, and I do confess I think the only way to keep her alive is to keep her mind easy, I wish my dear Father you would think of this, it would be a kind piece of

Charity and in your own Family." She told Mary he was angry about her debts—but they were from Swansea, which Mr. Aubin had promised to pay—Georgiana wishes he would appoint a day to see Mary and assures him her sister is very wretched.

The remainder of the letter explains to her father what he well knew: In that era, the recipient of mail paid the postage unless the sender chose to pay. She therefore asks Morton if instead of Mr. Greig paying her allowance once a month, might she have it once a quarter?—she pays rent regularly every quarter—do not smile but poor people are obliged to be economical and receiving the money once a quarter would save on the 2s.2d postage, saving £1.6.5, almost enough in a year to buy clothes for her sons—"Yours Ever Affectionately. . . ."

Georgiana Carter's description of Doddy's wretched financial situation startles. But not as much as her sister's view that in two years, that is, sometime in 1825–26, Mary Diana Dods's disease might kill her. It is difficult to judge whether Georgiana believed this or exaggerated the situation to gain their father's sympathy. With no direct correspondence from Mary Diana Dods to her father, I decided to double-check her situation by looking at David Lyndsay's letters written to Blackwood during this same period. Lyndsay wrote on December 23, 1823, February 16, 1824, and March 16, 1824. Brief letters, reminding the publisher of articles sent—no acknowledgments—no responses. No overt sign of illness. Perhaps, on second thought, one, born of desperation or madness. Lyndsay asked Blackwood about the sales of *Dramas*—is there any chance of a second edition? In fact, short of a miracle that reversed the past, Lyndsay knew *Dramas* had not sold at all well. Indeed, the sales were so poor as to convince Blackwood not to continue publishing Lyndsay, even in *Maga*.

But the end is not at hand. Did My dear Lord agree to guarantee his destitute daughter's loan? Perhaps he did. In any case, Mary Diana Dods did not die. On the contrary, Lyndsay's next letters to Blackwood tell us of a phoenixlike restoration. On January 16, 1825, Lyndsay sent that long, self-confident letter announcing to Blackwood that the book of *Tales,* some translated, some original, that he rejected, will be published in London. Lyndsay announces the possible establishment of a quarterly magazine for young persons that "he" might go into with some friends—"he" sends gossip about Byron, Southey, Medwin—and most important, "he" reports "he" is now well acquainted with Mrs. Shelley.

The Dods-Carter-Aubin-Morton letters stand in almost dismal contrast with the Lyndsay letters. The supplicating, struggling daughters, whose lives are measured by the pound, shilling, and pence, live in a world apart from David Lyndsay, whose writings were meant to establish "him" in the world, a cosmopolitan "man" well known in Lady Byron's and Mary Shelley's circles. The Dods sequence of letters shows that Mary Diana Dods met Mary Shelley after years of physical suffering, financial distress, and mental anguish. Stretched behind her, as far back as 1815, were angry creditors and frustrated attempts to develop a profession as writer and educator by which to gain financial independence and a secure place for herself.

So here emerged a new, composite portrait of the women who secretly agreed to transform their lives and history. At the outer edges stood Georgiana Dods Carter and Charlotte Figg, with their own stories, their own struggles to survive. Closer in, Mary Shelley, author, mother, widow, forced to live in the England she had always found spiritually and politically bleak, carrying with her the fame of *Frankenstein,* the stigma of her elopement with Shelley. Parallel to her, Isabella Robinson, young, beautiful, willing to use and discard people. In front of their mothers, Carter's two sons and Percy Florence. Off to a side, in a wicker bassinet, Adeline Douglas. And posed in the center, overshadowing all, a dual vision of Doddy: a middle-height, dark-haired, somewhat misshapen woman wearing a limp white dress, staring outward. But overlaying that image, the same figure, now fashionably attired in the tailcoated jacket, contrasting trousers, and abundant cravat worn by the gentlemen of the day, top hat at a slight angle, walking stick in hand.

## CHAPTER 18

# NEW QUESTIONS/NEW ANSWERS

FINALLY IT WAS TIME to piece together the story of Doddy-Lyndsay-Douglas, Isabella Robinson, and Mary Shelley; time to dig into the strange, still partially camouflaged world these women created for themselves. Now I would reconstruct the way of their world—and of their individual spirits—that turned Mary Diana Dods into Douglas; Isabella Robinson into Mrs. Douglas; and Mary Shelley into marriage broker extraordinaire. Compiling the story to date, a number of critical questions arose.

The uncertainties mostly centered around finding out when the marriage charade ended—and why? Was there a record of the Douglases' passport in France that would show how long the couple lived there? Was the truth of the "marriage" ever suspected by their Parisian friends? Did Mary Diana Dods, David Lyndsay, and Walter Sholto Douglas die at the same time? Where were she/they buried? Where did the widowed Isabella Robinson Douglas live after her husband's death and before her marriage to the Reverend Mr. Falconer in 1840? Did the Douglases' daughter, Adeline, know anything of her "parents'" story? And finally, who was Adeline's father?

Fitting piece to piece, the story revealed new secrets as it took on a life of its own. There were days the trio's motivations seemed clear, only to have conflicting evidence arise. Was Dods a transvestite? a lesbian? Robinson bisexual? Mary Shelley experimenting with being a lesbian? The uncertainties about their sexual penchants, beyond any other questions, seemed the crucial barrier wall that stood between them and me.

That wall began to chip away in working through the lists of books that revealed the Britain of the nineteenth century. But the real breakthroughs came from the answers to "fishing" letters to record offices and libraries in Paris, Scotland, Italy, and England. Among the *nons* from the Parisian cemeteries (one letter undeliverable because the cemetery had moved) was a *oui*. The Mairie de Paris (city hall) reported that Georgiana Carter had been buried on August 21, 1842, in Montmartre Cemetery, but in a temporary grave. They had no idea where her remains were moved to. Nor had they, or any other Paris cemetery, any record of Miss Dods or Mr. Douglas. The Scottish record office didn't know where the earl or his daughters were buried. The Edinburgh newspaper *The Scotsman* did not provide search services and there was no copy anywhere in the United States of July–August 1827, which certainly would have carried an obituary notice. Some of the executors' legal records were on deposit in Scotland, but not indexed and therefore requiring a personal search. There was no record showing that Adeline Douglas was born in Ramsgate, or Maidstone, or Glace Hill; in Aylesbury, Delapre Abbey, or Dover. The Drummond-Wolff archives held nothing. The incumbent Lady Drummond-Wolff chatted with me by telephone from her apartment in Switzerland, but no, she had not the portrait of Isabella Robinson once rumored in her possession. And yes, Fanny Wright's letters to Mary Shelley were at the Bodleian—copies sent.

Aberdour's parish minister, the Reverend John Scott, warned of considerable difficulty in such a search, as "the aristocracy are not too keen to acknowledge the existence of any 'reputed' offspring" nor can he help beyond recommending sources—records not in record office at Edinburgh—Aberdour House itself about to become part of a complex with retirement homes and apartments built around it—might write to the present earl (the twenty-second) John Douglas, who lives at Dalmahoy—Dods's mother might have been a servant in the fifteenth earl's house—chances are she would have been given a cottage rent-free on the estate or married off to one of the estate workers with some financial settlement—not unusual for young aristocrats to test their sexual prowess on housemaids.

So I wrote to the present earl. Perhaps Mr. Scott was right about the acknowledgment of reputed offspring, because there was no response.

From Pistoia, word came that Isabella, daughter of Giuseppe Robinson and wife of Guglielmo Falconer, died at 24 Porta San Marco on February 7, 1869; that she was fifty-nine; that she was born in England; that she lived for many years in her own villa, situated near S. Allesio—because the record office was moving, they couldn't check further—write again. From Florence came word that the consulate records covering the time Adeline Douglas married Drummond Wolff had been sent to the central record office, St. Catherine's House, London.

It grew increasingly clear that many of the missing pieces were to be found only in Paris, London, and Edinburgh—if at all. At the end of May 1989, I went to Europe to call on the Douglases in person to see if they had left other clues; and if I knew enough about them to find and recognize those clues.

In Paris, the first stop was at the National Archives to search for records of the Douglases' passport, a will, or any other papers left by Georgiana Carter. She might lead to Mr. and Mrs. Douglas, who I all but lost track of in Paris after Mérimée's last reference to them in February 1829. Three long days at the National Archives, with side trips to the Police Archives and the Bibliothèque Historique; lists of notaries, passport records, foreigners in Paris, prison records, and newspaper accounts of court proceedings added to the story by explaining something that hadn't even seemed a problem.

Both had to do with the passports Mary Shelley arranged for the Douglases. Passport archives for British travelers in the early nineteenth century are sparse among French records because at the time neither Britain nor France required them of

British subjects. From this came the realization that the trouble to get the Douglases' passport—Mary Shelley's deceit, Payne's and his actress friend's impersonations—was not to permit international travel; it was for intercultural, intergender travel. The passport, which gave the Douglases their only legal identification, takes on special significance for Dods's ambition to join the diplomatic corps. Mr. Douglas would find it impossible to establish appropriate credentials in Britain. "He" would certainly need to establish a past history in the kind of British circles that eventually would trip "him" up. Even abroad, if Mr. Douglas approached British officials to offer "his" services, they would still likely require introductions, letters, and possibly, official papers from home. But Europe offered another prospect. With the presence of his family providing living credentials, and "his" mastery of foreign languages and sophisticated learning, Mr. Douglas could shape a career in the diplomatic corps of France, Germany, or Italy, countries that in that era employed foreign nationals in their missions.[1] "He" had the documentation of a British passport to prove who "he" was, and the imagination to explain why "he" had no other documents to certify "his" existence.

The archives of the Bibliothèque de l'Institut de France more than verified that existence and "his" wife's—in the letters of a very jealous woman. Suddenly, both Mr. and Mrs. Douglas reappeared as they were in France in the late 1820s, along with important clues to what happened to them afterward, in the story of Mary Clarke and Claude Fauriel. Published biographies and memoirs revealed that the young Mary Clarke had been in love with the older Claude Fauriel, but that he had only been in like with her. While Fauriel maintained a close friendship with Clarke from 1821 to his death in 1844, during those same years the much celebrated author had a number of love affairs with other women. Because both Fauriel and Clarke—as the famous *salonnière* Mrs. Mohl—have respected places in French history, their papers are preserved in l'Institut. Among Fauriel's are some of the letters exchanged between author and *salonnière*. A recurring topic of these letters—at least from Clarke's view—is Fauriel's relationship with a certain married woman with whom he is apparently having an affair. Mary Clarke, who asked Fauriel to marry her in 1823,[2] was openly jealous, hostile, and hurt. The woman in question is Mrs. Walter Sholto Douglas.

The surprise was not that Isabella Douglas was a flirt. The Garnetts, in May 1828, entered her in the lists of flirt and co-quette. In July they declared that Fauriel had taken the place of an earlier suitor as Mrs. Douglas's favorite, but to their wonder Mary Clarke did not seem to mind. Three months later, Mér-imée informed Mary Shelley that Fauriel "continues his woman-izing regularly with your friend." But none of these comments, voiced in the polite terminology of the day, prepare for the ex-tent of the "womanizing" and the "manizing"; or, contrary to the Garnetts' observations, the extent to which Mary Clarke cer-tainly did mind. As a result, the Fauriel-Clarke letters give a remarkable description of the seductive Mrs. Douglas; of her "husband's" situation; and of how very jealous Clarke was.

In mid to late May 1828, Mary Clarke sent Fauriel a brief, complaining note. She will not see him that evening because she will not attend the salon. She writes because she knows it would be impossible to be alone with him without picking a quarrel; she prefers to avoid it but she cannot forget that for two months she has asked him to go with her alone to the Louvre and he never had the time, but the moment it was a question of going with Madame Douglas to the Jardin des Plantes, he found the time. Imagine how he would feel if he asked her the same kind of thing for two months, she refused under some pretext, and went instead with another man.

This note may be a condensed, controlled version of a longer, far more bitter, draft of another letter in the 1828 folder. Or perhaps the longer letter was sent on another occasion, when Clarke was even more provoked. In the amplified letter, Mary Clarke reminds Fauriel that though she has asked him for two years, spring and fall, to go with her just once to the Bois de Boulogne, he always declined with the excuse of not having the time. But he very quickly found time to visit another young woman—and also found time to go to Madame Douglas. For the hurt he has given her, Clarke is resolved to tear out what she feels for him for he doesn't deserve it and he doesn't understand her and never will understand her. She is miserable and weak and pleads with Fauriel to help her have the courage to break off with him and never see him again.

Clearly, she did not keep her resolve. Possibly not even long enough to send the letter, for only the draft survives. On August 3, 1828, while on a visit to England, Clarke tells Fauriel that she will say nothing about Madame Douglas for fear of getting in a bad mood, but for her interest and the interest she takes in him, she tells him to use his time instead of seeing Madame Douglas to see people for whom he has sympathy instead of scornful pleasantry. To Clarke's growing frustration, he does not take her advice.

On November 4, 1828, Clarke has been back in Paris for three nights. All three nights, Fauriel has chosen to go to Madame Douglas's. As Clarke has something she must get his advice about, and as she doubts she will ever see him alone to discuss the matter, she has decided to write to her Dear Dicky. The matter concerns Madame Douglas. Clarke assures Fauriel that she does not want to hurt that "poor woman," but in light of the story she will reveal, she does not know if she should invite Madame Douglas to her salons. The fact is that M. Jacquemont told Mérimée that on his second visit (and Clarke does not know how Jacquemont and Madame Douglas got along so well together) Jacquemont kissed her. Clarke blushes to write this—she would prefer to tell him—but when does she see him? Mérimée himself blushed when telling this, and beat around the bush a long time before coming to it, but indicated he told her because he thought it would be bad for her not to know. He added that she was "not obliged to believe Jacquemont but I believe him like myself." It appears Jacquemont's tattle didn't stop there. The incident has become the subject of considerable gossip. The Lafayette family has also heard about it; and Madame Le Breton, at whose house Jacquemont and Madame Douglas met, also repeats the story. It seems Madame Douglas made Jacquemont the most extraordinary speeches. Clarke remembers Fauriel once prevented her from meeting another woman whose reputation might sully her own. Should she invite Madame Douglas or not? She asks that he put aside his friendship for Madame Douglas, be fair to her, and also believe the truth that Clarke has no feeling against her.

Clarke says, unlike Fauriel, she does not believe that a woman is fit to throw out the window if she isn't honest in the ordinary sense of the word, and for fear of hurting Madame Douglas, she hesitates not to invite her. If Clarke were well settled and in other circumstances, it would be different and she would be more concerned about afflicting Madame Douglas than with her own reputation. Unfortunately, all that was done with Jacquemont does Madame Douglas singular harm because Jacquemont, not being at all in love with her, gave it all such an ugly color—it all happened, he says, while Madame Douglas was walking peacefully, her husband being in the other room, and she coming and going with the doors wide open.

Clarke gives Fauriel her word she would not have had the courage to tell him all this if she were not in an embarrassing position about her own conduct. Also, a certain speech Madame Douglas made was so singular that Mérimée couldn't repeat it to her. Clarke thought that Mérimée alone knew *them*, the Douglases, but that day she has heard almost the same things from the Garnetts, who got it from Madame Victor de Tracy, so unfortunately it is not a secret. Therefore, will he think and be good enough to advise? P.S.: He realizes she was careful not to tell the Garnetts what Mérimée had told her, but at the first opportunity, he is capable of telling the Garnetts. . . .

Clarke undoubtedly hoped her reports would disenchant the multiamorous Fauriel with the multiamorous Madame Douglas. This woman who was "not honest in the ordinary sense" made speeches that could not be repeated in polite company. She kissed a man she had only twice met, while her husband was in the next room and the doors were open. She had betrayed both Fauriel and her husband. Her scandalous behavior was the talk of Paris. Fauriel, Clarke's beloved Fauriel, surely would not continue his friendship with such a woman.

This letter reveals two important pieces of information. First, neither Clarke nor the others knew that the husband observing "his" shameless wife in the other room was a woman. Second, that despite her continuing hostility toward Madame

Douglas, Mary Clarke still referred to her as a "poor woman" whom she would not want to hurt. This called to mind Mary Shelley's descriptions of the couple in June 1828: Isabella Douglas is a poor child whose sufferings transcend all that imagination can portray; what D now is, she will not describe in a letter—she only "trusts that the diseased body acts on the diseased mind, and that both may be at rest ere long." Apparently, Mary Diana Dods in the course of their year's existence as a married couple changed from the anxiously awaited *"Sposo,"* the loving husband of his little wife, to a man sick enough for a jealous woman to still feel sorry for her rival; sick enough for Mary Shelley to consider herself "as in some sort" the cause of the poor wife's present suffering in her marriage, pledging to devote herself to "extricate her."

At that time, Mary Shelley was unaware of the snide stories Mrs. Douglas told about her to the Garnetts and probably to others as well. Nor could she guess the basis of Mérimée's condemnation of Mrs. Douglas as an unworthy friend. Or even consider what might have been Mr. Douglas's sufferings at "his" wife's hands. But apparently during the following years, Mary Shelley's angelic Isabella Douglas disappeared, her place taken by the real Isabella Robinson. Here was the sad explanation of Mary Shelley's *Journal* entry at the end of November 1830. Seeing her again, Mary Shelley finally and painfully recognized that Isabella was "ever false yet enchanting" and that because she "can no longer serve her" Isabella took no more trouble to please. Trying to console herself with the thought that surely Isabella "is not the being she once was," Mary Shelley's own enchantment ended.

But what happened to Doddy? Did her chronic liver ailment begin to gnaw away at her whole being, dismantling mind as well as body? Or was Doddy suffering the incurable anguish of many a disappointed spouse? Her "wife" was a flirt. More than a flirt. In the first year of their marriage, her "wife" had openly turned her attentions to a series of men. Very possibly she had affairs—as she certainly did with Fauriel. If Doddy was actually in love with her "wife," she had occasion enough to lose her senses. Her beloved "wife" had made her the object of public humiliation time and again. Her "wife," her friend, her co-conspirator had betrayed her trust. But there is another possibility that encompasses the physical-illness-betrayed-spouse scenarios and goes beyond it. Doddy had, in a sense, rejected her entire past life when she became Douglas. Being a woman had not worked for her. Now, being a man might not work either.

From Clarke's remarks about Fauriel's "scornful" attitude toward Isabella, he may well have known exactly what her nature was. Though his remarks about Mrs. Douglas's dishonesty indicate he held to the dual standard for male versus female conduct of the era, Fauriel evidently didn't care. No response from Fauriel about Mrs. Douglas's shocking behavior with Jacquemont exists in the Clarke-Fauriel correspondence. He may have paid Mademoiselle Clarke a long overdue visit to discuss the matter, to advise her, to reassure her of his friendship. Or he may have ignored the letter entirely, which is how he handled all of Clarke's comments on Mrs. Douglas in their exchange of letters. He appears to have responded to every topic in Clarke's letters except the subject of Douglas. The Fauriel-Douglas relationship continued. And so did Clarke's complaints.

Clarke's next letter to Fauriel that refers to Mrs. Douglas was dated almost a year later. On August 28, 1829, writing to Fauriel while he was at Brussels and she in England, Clarke says that she had looked for a volume of his work among his books but couldn't find it. Mérimée told her he saw it at Madame Douglas's. Clarke tells him that she suspected if Fauriel loaned Madame Douglas any books, she would lose them. She reminds him she wrote him that opinion the year before but . . .

Three months later, on November 24, 1829, Clarke turns her attention from Mrs. Douglas to send extraordinary news about Mr. Douglas. She tells Fauriel that Mr. Douglas is in prison, for debts. But Douglas apparently doesn't care. In fact, he has asked Mr. Fisher to buy him black mustaches and sideburns, probably to impress the jailers. But Mr. Douglas gave an incorrect address. Mr. Fisher went to the women fashion merchants for the aforesaid objects and they laughed at him. Mr.

Fisher got furiously angry and wants nothing more to do with Mr. Douglas.

Mary Diana Dods, in debtors' prison in Paris. Unlike the early 1820s when she pleaded with her father to send her the money to keep her out of debtors' prison in London, she is now indifferent. More than indifferent: She sends a friend to purchase for her false mustaches and sideburns, then just becoming the rage in fashionable Paris. For men unable to grow their own in stylish abundance, false mustaches and sideburns were available.[3] Clarke's conclusion that Mr. Douglas wished to impress others by being in the very height of fashion seems reasonable enough. Miss Dods, on the other hand, would have other reasons to want false facial hair. Within a day or two of imprisonment, it would become apparent to those around her that Mr. Douglas, unlike the other adult male prisoners, had no need to shave. But that kind of thinking would be more like the careful planning of the summer of 1827, when Dods first married. Besides, the money for the false hair would have bought a daily razor and basin and pretense for some time. The description in this letter goes beyond debts and fashions; it is about fantasies shattered. Mary Shelley's 1828 description of Dods's mental health, Clarke's sympathy for poor, suffering Mrs. Douglas, together with Dods's indifference to being in prison, suggest that by this time, Mary Diana Dods had all but lost her mind. And having lost her mind, perhaps no longer knowing whether she was a man or woman, why not adorn "him self"?

Clarke's letter proves that Doddy was still in Paris—and still a married man—at the end of November 1829. It may also shed some light, however oblique, on David Lyndsay's last letter to William Blackwood, in which Lyndsay confessed that "he" was the author of material submitted a month earlier under the signature "X." In the wake of Blackwood's rejection, "he" now offers a fifteen-year-old, 171-page poem celebrating Scottish history. The letter is dated September 11, 1829, and supposedly was written from Grosvenor Square, London, where Lyndsay invites the publisher to respond. The tone and contents of the letter are consistent with Lyndsay. And the fact that Douglas is in debtors' prison two months later indicates the ever-present need for money. Possibly Dods had gone over to England to try to raise some money, as she had years before gone to Paris for the same purpose. Perhaps she did remain in London some short while, running up more debts before returning to her "wife and daughter" in Paris. But unlike all the other letters written by Lyndsay to Blackwood, this one is not in Mary Diana Dods's handwriting. Of course, she may have been too physically ill at the time to write. Or perhaps she never left Paris, instead sending a draft of the letter to a friend, who lived in the rather choice area of Grosvenor Square, to copy and forward to Blackwood. Wherever Doddy was, the idea that Blackwood, who had consistently rejected David Lyndsay's writing over a number of years, would now undertake to publish a 171-page poem may itself speak of madness or desperation or both.

In early January 1830, Clarke has more to say about Mrs. Douglas in the course of again complaining of Fauriel's behavior. Now the object of her resentment is a Madame Arcanti. Fauriel goes often to Madame A.; seldom to her. He appears to prefer Madame A. Clarke, who says she hid her sorrow about Madame Douglas the year before, realizes she should have talked to Fauriel about it right away. He continues to hurt her and she tearfully asks if all sympathy between them has gone. Clarke believes Madame Douglas is finally out of Fauriel's life, only to be replaced by Madame A. The 1831 letters that survive make no mention of either Douglas. Temporarily, it appears Clarke was right. But the 1832 folder holds two letters, one dated early September, the other, twelve pages, undated, both anguished, suffering, imploring letters. One was written out of the torturing pain Clarke felt at what she calls her silent suffering during Fauriel's liaison with Madame Douglas; the other, at the idea that Fauriel spent the summer of 1832 with Madame D.; neither letter mentions Mr. Douglas.

The Douglases' story comes to an end for Clarke with these 1832 letters. Later I would find the Fauriel and Clarke correspondence between 1822 and 1843 published—but with Clarke's marriage proposal and the most revealing Douglas letters omitted.[4] It is difficult to determine how long Madame Douglas's liaison with Fauriel lasted, or whether she had other liaisons, as

Fauriel did, during the same years. There is a gap until 1840, when, only then thirty years old, Mrs. Douglas, widow of the late Walter Sholto Douglas, their young daughter no doubt by her side, married the respected Rev. William Falconer and established a new home for herself in Italy and England.

How did it end for Mr. Douglas? "He" suffered severe mental and physical deterioration in 1828 and 1829. At the end of 1829, thrown in debtor's prison, indifferent, "he" madly tried to enhance "his" image, with no evidence of "his" wife trying to rescue "him." These last, bleak scenes played out by Mr. Douglas explain Mary Shelley's statement that by November 1830, she can no longer be of aid to Isabella Robinson Douglas. So long as Mr. Douglas was alive, Mrs. Douglas could certainly have made use of Mrs. Shelley. Only Doddy's death, sometime between November 1829 and November 1830, would have released her widow from fear. In the course of almost two and a half years, no one had discovered the secret of the Douglases' marriage. The widowed Isabella Douglas knew that Mary Shelley and Georgiana Dods Carter could not expose her without ruining themselves and their sons. All the evidence argues that by November 1830, Mary Diana Dods had died, leaving the stage free for her widow to get on with the next act.

But where was the body? With Doddy's death, Mr. Douglas disappeared in Paris. Finding no more there, I followed "his" trail backward to London and found more new pieces to the puzzle.

One piece confirms David Lyndsay's continued existence and literary status into the early winter of 1829. The *Literary Blue Book* for 1830,[5] a guide to literature, science, and art, includes among its lists of prominent living authors a number of those in this story: Mary Shelley, Eliza Rennie, Lord Dillon— and D. Lyndsay. The introduction to the book, dated December 21, 1829, expresses the publishers' belief that their lists are generally correct and complete, but asks readers to send in any corrections or omissions for a proposed next edition. There was no further edition, no way to check if Lyndsay had been moved from "Living Authors" to the category of deceased "Eminent Persons" in the next year or two.

Another link to Doddy also appeared in a lengthy series of letters written by the fifteenth earl of Morton, dated between 1782 and 1786, and one from 1820.[6] According to Lyndsay's self-description to Blackwood, which seems to be corroborated by descriptions given by others of her age at various times, Mary Diana Dods was born a few years after Lord Byron, which means circa 1791. Perhaps the earl's letters might offer some clues to his daughters' mother. There were none. The 1820 letter dealt with his ongoing interest and continued heavy investment in the Dongola breed of horses; the earlier letters described Morton's career ambition. Traveling in Europe, learning many foreign languages, his ardent aim was to enter the diplomatic line in His Majesty's service. Perhaps Walter Sholto Douglas's own ambition for a career in diplomacy was influenced by "his" father's early ambition.

But the most crucial and unexpected facts materialized from the holdings of the British Record Office: two death certificates; one marriage certificate; and a second, conspicuously missing, marriage certificate. The first death certificate, a British consular record, simply confirmed the Italian municipal record that Isabella Falconer, born Robinson, fifty-nine years, wife of the Reverend William Falconer, died at the Villa Falconer near Pistoia on February 7, 1869. The second death certificate, however, narrowed the period in which Adeline Drummond Wolff had been born. My earlier information was that she died in the second quarter of 1916. But though her death was registered on April 1, placing it in the second quarter by one day, her death certificate specified that, as a result of infirmity of age, congestion of the lungs for twenty-four days, and heart failure, she died at the age of eighty-nine on March 31, 1916.

Something was wrong. Adeline's age on her death certificate did not agree with her age on the marriage certificate of Mr. and Mrs. Henry Drummond Wolff, who were married on January 22, 1853. The bride is described as Adeline Douglas, "minor," spinster, residing in Villino Gaspericini, Florence, "daughter of Walter Sholto Douglas, an officer in HM's Service." Here was a work of fiction, this time almost certainly written by Mrs. Isabella Douglas Falconer. Not only was Walter

Sholto Douglas listed as father of the bride, he was promoted into the ranks of His Majesty's Service—which seemed quite appropriate, as the bridegroom himself was then attaché to His Majesty's legation. Bride and groom were thus of a rank. The third fiction was the bride's age.

If she was a minor on January 22, 1853, it meant she was born sometime after January 22, 1832. But her death certificate—and the story of her parents—testify to an earlier birth. Her death at the end of March 1916, age eighty-nine, means she was born sometime between April 1826 and March 1827, which would make her some three to four years older than her husband, who was born in 1830. That might be reason enough for tampering with the facts; but there was another, more compelling reason for fiction here. British law did not require the civil registration of births, marriages, and deaths until 1837. Before that time, family records would be entered in local parish registers—or not at all. A woman of legal age to marry would prove her majority with a birth record. A woman who claimed to be a minor, with or without a certificate, required parental approval to marry. The Reverend Mr. Falconer's wife certainly approved.

And after fifty-five years of marriage, the bridegroom indicated by omission that he knew about this final act of the marriage of Mr. and Mrs. Walter Sholto Douglas. In his two-volume, 1908 memoirs dedicated to "My wife Lady Wolff for so many years my constant comrade," in which he gives plentiful and specific details about friends, their families, and their social station, he disposes of his wedding in three sentences:

> While living in Florence I became engaged, and we were married very quietly at the consulate at Leghorn. My best man, as I said before, was Mr. Lytton. Sir Henry Bulwer gave away the bride, and her brides-maids were the two daughters of Lady Walpole, Miss Du Boulary, and an Italian lady.[7]

Particulars about the bridal party; not a word about the bride's family. And on the facing page, a photograph of the Victorian lady the marriage gave final legitimacy to, adding legitimacy in the process to Isabella Douglas as well. She was now recognized in rather fashionable circles not only as the wife of the Reverend Mr. Falconer but the mother-in-law of Sir Henry Drummond Wolff.[8] The calculating Isabella Robinson had done well for herself.

One wonders what Mary Shelley's feelings might have been had she lived beyond her fifty-three years to learn of the Drummond Wolff marriage two years after her death in 1851. Or another thirteen years and heard news in 1869 that Charles Robinson informed his friend Alexander Berry, Mary Shelley's cousin-in-law and correspondent to whom she introduced Charles Robinson, that he has just lost his sister, "Mrs. Falconer, the wife of Mr. Falconer, Rector of Bushey in Hertfordshire . . . she died at Pistoja [sic] near Florence where I left her but 3 months back in pretty good health—she has left one daughter (Lady Drummond Wolff)."[9] Or how Mrs. Shelley would have reacted if she saw the Drummond Wolffs build a home on the land adjoining Boscombe, the estate of her beloved son and daughter-in-law, and become their friends, and attend her son's semiprofessional theatrical performances at the theater he built attached to his home.[10] Perhaps she would have told her children about other performances, many years earlier, in which she was a backer and supporting actor; Lady Wolff played a minor though pivotal role; but it was Mrs. Falconer who reaped the box-office receipts as coproducer and costar.

Searching for the wedding certificate of Mrs. Falconer's second marriage, the one referred in the *Dictionary of National Biography,* I found the irrepressible Isabella Robinson may have padded her role a bit further. There was no English marriage certificate for the reverend and his wife in 1840. Or in 1838 or 1839, 1841, 1842, 1843. Possibly they married in Italy and the consulate failed to send forward the records. Subsequent checking of the marriage records in the Anglican Chaplaincy of Florence indicates the couple was not married there,[11] though Florence and its environs appear to have been where Mrs. Falconer made her home. But with this cast of characters, it is also possible that the well-respected reverend, the man of a distinguished, famous family, and his wife, widow of W. S. Douglas, despite the authority of the *DNB*, never legally married.

I shifted scenes to Scotland, and it was Mr. Douglas who again took center stage. I had hoped the burial place of the fifteenth earl could be located and perhaps his daughters might be buried nearby. And in the vast mountain of mostly business papers in the Scottish Record Office might lurk more shadows of the fifteenth earl and his daughters; and in the National Library, there might be more about David Lyndsay and his Scottish publisher.

Perhaps even the Dods sisters' mother would appear, comfortably situated in her own cottage, deeded to her by the earl, somewhere on the family estates. The Morton papers might tell such a tale. They might also fill in other gaps in Doddy's story, including information about the death of the fifteenth earl and his family.

Before that first night was out, reading through the microfilm of *The Scotsman* for July and August 1827, I found the obituary of the fifteenth earl. On August 1, the newspaper reports that the earl, having died at his seat of Dalmahoy upon the seventeenth instant, his lordship's remains were on the thirtieth instant interred in a vault belonging to the family in the parish church of Ratho.

> The Funeral was, by his Lordship's express directions, conducted in the most private manner, there being present—George Sholto Douglas, Esquire, now Earl of Morton, Chief Mourner, John B. Y. Buller, Esq. and the Hon. Douglas Gordon Hallyburton, Lord Meadowbank, the Lord Advocate, and Robert Dundas, Esq., his Lordship's trustees; the Right Hon. Sir Robert Liston and Sir John Hope, the vice-Lieutenant of the County . . . The servants upon his Lordship's estates, with the labourers, preceded the hearse . . . His Lordship's titles were. . . .

I recognized the names of the trustees from the earl's will, and was not surprised that, although Mary Shelley's letters indi-

cate Mary Diana Dods was at Dalmahoy at this time, she was
not listed among those attending the funeral. Neither was Lady
Morton nor, in keeping with current practice, any other women.
The parish "mort-bell" announcing that the earl was dying and
the "soul-bell" after death were no doubt rung, but public
mourning was men's work.[12] The important information here
was that the earl was buried in a vault belonging to the family in
the parish church of Ratho.

A family vault would be the burial place of centuries of
Mortons. Could the Dods sisters be buried there as well? It
seemed highly doubtful. They were, after all, reputed daughters.
On the other hand, they were Mortons, with "the finest Scottish
blood" running through their veins. There was another possibility. Georgiana Dods Carter, whose body was removed from
her Paris resting ground, and Mary Diana Dods, who very likely
died in Paris—perhaps in debtors' prison or a madhouse—might
be buried not in the vault but nearby in the churchyard.
Dalmahoy, Doddy's sometime home; Ratho, Doddy's sometime—perhaps all-time—church.

More eager than ever, I worked through the Morton papers
at the Record House and also checked the *Register of Deeds* to
see if the earl's outright bequests and trusts to his wife and his
daughters were registered. Two separate volumes indicated that
the estates, the London Park Street house, furniture, diamonds,
wardrobe, carriages, oil paintings, books, are all duly deeded to
Susan Elizabeth, countess of Morton. Not a word about the
trusts to his daughters. Parties were not legally obliged to register their transactions.

Though the boxes of Morton legal documents made no reference to Doddy, in combination they explained a part of her
story. Vast sums of money flowed in and out of the Morton coffers. One bundle of "Incidental Accounts 1827" held two expense vouchers for the earl's funeral dinners. The first was for
the five Aberdour tenants' dinners: food £3; plus wine 9s., toddy
£1.12.6, whiskey porter and beer 10s., horses' corn and hay 13s.,
and coachman 1s.6d., added up to £5.16. The second dinner was
for the gentlemen: food £2.10.0, servants £1.10.0, wine £4.0.0.,
toddy £2.0.6, brandy 7s., ale 4s., porter 4s., beer 1s., horses

15s., adding up to £11.11.6. The cost of these ritual dinners stands in marked comparison with the earl's March 1827 annual contribution of £7 for coal for the poor—and the £7.15.1 paid the schoolmaster for the year 1826–27.

A series of large, neatly kept account books reveals even more about the earl's life-style. His income from Aberdour, crop and rental, in 1826 was £12,700.5.4; expenses, including £11.13.0 for Mr. Alexander Greig, accountant; 16s.9d. contribution toward the yearly salary for the schoolmaster at Inverkeithing; £8.8.0 for hunt dues; building assessment of £86.15.0; totaled £12,833. The annual books, back to 1821, appear, whatever the income and expenses, to almost always nearly balance. If the bottom line of these accounts is accurate, poor Lord Morton had nothing left for himself. Debits equal credits. The earl must get by on his annual income of approximately £12,000 a year from Aberdour. But one should not feel too sorry for the earl. In an era when the coachman's salary for driving the tenants the twenty-six miles roundtrip from Aberdour to Dalmahoy was 1s.6d.; when schoolteachers in the earl's employ would be expected to live on £7.15.1 (housing provided); when average weekly wages in cotton factories was 9s.10d.; for northern agricultural workers 9s.2d.; coal miners, at its 1825 peak of 5s.3d. per day; the select rank of London highly skilled craftsmen, 36s.6d. per day, while their provincial brothers earned 25s.; when ladies of good families might be expected by their relatives to live on £100, which would place their income above laborers and artisans, but on the average well below clergy, doctors, engineers, and lawyers, £12,000 was a fortune.[13]

A closer look at the actual expenses listed against income gives more evidence of the earl's wealth. The income provided not only for all the earl's living expenses in Scotland, whether at Dalmahoy or during sojourns at Aberdour—repairs to mansions, coaches, servants, food, tailors, horses, hounds—it also included costs of living at his fashionable residence in London. All expenses are itemized and explained—hounds, horses, coal, meat, gardening—verified by the little slips of paper in the little bundles—except for one category: cash payments. Each year, cash is drawn from the income and given to Morton's accountant to dispense. In 1821 through 1825, Mr. Greig managed an average of £1,222 per year above and beyond all living expenses. What he spent it on is not spelled out in the accounts. But one expense is clear: the Dods sisters' letters show that their allowance came to them via Mr. Aubin, via Mr. Greig. No doubt, separate accounts were kept. These are not in the files. Nor are the books that would report Morton's additional income from his other vast estates.

From 1820 to 1826, Morton's Dalmahoy housekeeper paid out on the average approximately £859 per year for food and drink alone. In 1825, Morton paid £5.17.0 for two years' worth of newspapers. In the same year, he had bound 112 volumes, plus a catalog of this library in folio morocco, at the cost of £123.16.7. And 1820–25 were the very years when My dear Lord's daughters wrote their letters begging their father to supply the funds that would allow grandsons to be sent to school; a girl's academy to operate with some hope of income; a widow's watch retrieved; shopkeepers and rent bills accumulated over five years to be paid; the women kept from debtors' prison. Their debts, overexpenditures, and infants' needs accumulated from 1815 through 1824 required approximately £250 to settle. Some he settled; others not. Aubin's accounts indicate that between April 1819 and September 1821, with a gap in his books from mid-September through October, a period spanning three years and five months, the earl provided a total of £924.11.1. The letters from Dods, Carter, and Aubin in 1820 place Morton in town during August at least through November. They also show that Morton personally gave Georgiana Carter £15. It is unlikely that he gave his daughters other sums, as these are the months when both are threatened with arrest for nonpayment of bills and they complain about the irregular payments of their allowance that threw them into further debt. The combined allowance he provided during this period was £200 a year, meaning Morton gave them an additional £80 per year meant to cover their full living costs, rents, debt payments, and childrens' expenses, in total approximately £270 per year. For each pound given, the daughters paid a special toll. They must beg for timely payments. They must be grateful.

They must also understand that the earl has great expenditures to maintain his accustomed life-style. Georgiana Carter, prototype of the Victorian standard model of obedient daughter or wife, demonstrates that she did understand. When she appeals to him to advance her £20 in September 1821, she tells him that she knows she "ought to be careful" how she asks him "for Money after what you said about the Coronation and *nothing* would have made me do so, but that I feel distressed and uncomfortable, and have in some way or other parted with all the gifts of my poor Husband." George III, king of England from 1760 through 1820, monarch during the American and French Revolutions, monarch during more than a decade of his own madness, died on January 29, 1820. There was no question that he would be succeeded by his son, Prince of Wales, Prince Regent, and roué. The royal ceremonies were scheduled for July 19, 1821, and the new king personally directed that the event be marked by an extravaganza of pageantry and antiquarianism. Among the earl's papers are the invitations and precise directives that would ensure the overweight, dissipated king a majesty he lacked in his own person.

The earl of Morton, together with all the barons, viscounts, earls, marquesses, and dukes of the realm would all attend, all in correct regalia. To insure that each noble was "furnished and appointed as to your Rank and Quality appertaineth," exact instructions ranging from crimson velvet robes and satin underclothing to silver coronets and carriages, were sent by the king's deputy marshall. A careful game plan, informing those in attendance of the order in which to line up, coronets to be held in their hands; who would serve the dinner, and what they would wear; and, before the second course of dinner was served, the ceremony of the challenge of the king's champion, a knight in bright armor especially appointed who would enter on horseback into the hall accompanied by pages to ceremonially challenge anyone who contests or denies "Lord King George the Fourth."[14]

In August 1822, the earl had additional expenses connected with His Royal Majesty when the king visited Edinburgh for some two weeks. The earl's papers hold a variety of memorabilia of that visit: the letter informing the earl of the impending visit, and his responsibility to do his best for a proper reception; nontransferable tickets to a ball in honor of His Majesty; receptions by the Highland Society of Scotland, the Board of Green Cloth, the Corporation of the City of Edinburgh, and a host of other events to celebrate the king's visit.[15] No one can argue that the earl did not have great expenses. But by Mr. Greig's accounts, the earl, with negligible personal sacrifice, had more than enough to meet those expenses; more than enough, had he chosen, to protect his daughters and grandsons from lives of constant financial fear and threat.

The opulent life of the earl described in the papers at the register house cast the struggles of author David Lyndsay into an even sadder and braver light. Searching through the Blackwood papers for new pieces of information, for possible suggestions that Dods/Lyndsay/Douglas wrote for *Blackwood's* under yet another name, I realized that success in Scotland would have had special significance to Dods. If her works had been acclaimed, if she had become a *Blackwood's* luminary, she could announce to her father that she was the celebrated David Lyndsay and had made her own mark in the land of her ancestors, a land that knew her not as the daughter of the fifteenth earl of Morton but as that odd-looking though exceptionally brilliant commoner, Miss Dods.

But that was not Lyndsay's fate with *Blackwood's.* Instead, in addition to the Lyndsay-Blackwood correspondence, there are only a few other traces of Lyndsay among the hundreds of documents of the publisher. One "Stock Book 1820–24," page 46, lists the printing costs of the one thousand copies of "Lyndsay's Dramas," to be sold for 7s. each in unbound sheets, as £115, plus a payment of £50 to the author on December 17. What is odd about this entry is that when Blackwood wrote to Lyndsay on January 3, 1822 informing him of the cost of printing the volume, he set down the price of printing at £122. Even odder, in that letter Blackwood was negotiating with the author about paying him a commission of £75 at the completion of sales or a lesser payment in advance. In early January, Lyndsay indicated he preferred a payment of £50 in advance, which Blackwood sent him on January 12, almost a month after Blackwood set that amount down in his books.

A second "Stock Book" of "Magazine Contributions" indicates cash payments as well as other Blackwood publications sent to *Maga* authors. Lyndsay's account records: August 30, 1821, to cash: £5.5.0; November 30, books in the amount of £1.19.0; a November payment of £10.10.0; in 1822, cash payments of £10.10.0 in March and September; in 1823, books in September for £1.5.0. In total, for the seven contributions Lyndsay made to *Maga*, he was paid £39.19.0. Each contribution earned him about £5.5.0, which was in keeping with going rates of the time for an unknown author. A third book, a "Manuscript List of Early Contributors to Blackwood's Magazine," includes Mrs. Douglas and William Godwin, Jr., Mary Shelley's half brother who was just establishing a writing career when he died of typhoid fever in 1832. Both David Lyndsay and Mary Shelley are conspicuously absent.

A trip to Dalmahoy presents a mansion and an estate that keeps its grandeur, despite the fact that its one thousand acres, at the foot of the Pentland Hills, has been a country club for some years and is not being further "developed." At the entry, a churchyard holds the remains of six rows, three by three, of Mortons. Some are marked with headstones, others by sepulchers. They are the generations of Mortons who followed the fifteenth earl, tucked in near a church built in 1850 by the Mortons. The mansion itself is a gray stone Adams house built in 1725 for the thirteenth earl of Morton, who launched Captain Cook on his discovery voyage of Australia. Scaffolding abuts one side of the house, and billboards announce ANOTHER QUALITY REFURBISHMENT. Inside, only the magnificent stone fireplaces amid the all-but-gutted interior tell of room after room of past opulence.

Ratho Church is only a mile away, over the stone bridge that spans the Ratho canal. The church, dedicated to the Blessed Virgin, dates from the twelfth century and lies within a churchyard north of the village. Much altered and remodeled in the seventeenth century and subsequently, the oldest tombstone there dates from the fourteenth century. Both church and grounds are now part of the Historical Monuments (Scotland) Commission.[16]

On the wall of the east gable, a stone announces: HERE LIE THE REMAINS OF THE RIGHT HONOURABLE GEORGE EARL OF MORTON KT. DIED 17TH JULY 1827. The stone is apparently modern, and is partially hidden by a wooden wall with two doors. The east gable, the burial place of the Morton family, now houses the large, handsome church organ. Somewhere behind that wall, entombed beneath that organ, are the original memorial stones to the Mortons. And the Mortons themselves. There is no way to know whether the remains of either Dods sister was there.

One other source of Morton history was located at Dalmahoy Farms: the present earl of Morton and Lady Morton.[17] The twenty-second earl, like the fifteenth, is a Representative Peer with the same responsibility of greeting Her Majesty upon arrival and helping arrange appropriate ceremonies in her honor as Doddy's father had for George IV. In the Morton living room, there is another relic of an earlier time. Among the family portraits is one of a young child, barefoot, striding, dressed in a one-shouldered gauzelike dress, a dark green cloth draped over one arm and reaching out behind him like an angel's wing. Despite the dress, the portrait is of either the fourteenth or the fifteenth earl, Doddy's father or grandfather; in nineteenth-century England and America, dresses were the normal clothing for boys until as late as age five or six.[18]

The Mortons also indicate that the Scottish National Portrait Gallery holds a portrait of James Douglas, thirteenth earl, his wife, and their five children; a little boy in that portrait they say looks just like the child in their painting. It turns out that not only the two sons, but the two daughters and the infant on its mother's lap, looked exactly alike. The 1740 date of the painting and *Burke's Peerage* proved that the Morton painting was likely that of the grandfather. On the other hand, with such strong family resemblances, the angelic boy in the Morton living room might have been some other Morton, even Doddy's father, and perhaps the Dods sisters had the same family features. Piece by piece, after so many years, I was close to a secret knowing of Mary Diana Dods that went beyond all the individual facts accumulated.

That knowing gained new depth the following day in the 1815–1850 Ratho Kirk Session Records and Minute Books at the record office. Neither the Mortons nor the Dodses are mentioned. But the Church Session Records tell other stories, of sinners guilty of "fornication" before marriage or while married to others or unmarried. Session after session, from 1815 through 1850, sinners are made to stand before the assembled congregation. Their sins are proclaimed aloud. At times, the proclamation was redundant as with one Agnes Law, whose apparent state of pregnancy—her "shame"—was quite evident and so recorded. The elders ask the sinners if they confess, and who is the sinner they have partnered, and are they truly penitent. If the elders believe the sinner is penitent, they so note. The confession is written out in the book and signed or "X'd" by the sinners. Publicly rebuked, their crime inscribed for all time, the sinners may remain within the church. But when the elders' questions go unanswered, or they suspect insincere repentance, the fallen are publicly barred from the church, excommunicated at once and forever from church and community.

The fifteenth earl of Morton attended this church. He and his ancestors are buried there. But no Kirk Session called the fifteenth earl of Morton to stand before the congregation to bare his shame, to confess, to repent. And even if the elders had believed him once, what chance had he facing them with a second bairn born out of wedlock? Condemnation. Excommunication. This was not to be the earl's fate. On the contrary, the fifteenth earl remained a Lord Commissioner to the General Assembly of the Church of Scotland. He had successfully hidden the truth of his reputed daughters or, like other wealthy Scottish sinners, he had purchased church silence. He was George Douglas, fifteenth earl of Morton, Representative Peer of Scotland, Baron Douglas of Lochleven, chamberlain of the household to the queen consort, Knight of the Order of the Thistle, lord lieutenant of Fifeshire and of Midlothian, vice-president of the Royal Society, Lord High Commissioner of the Church of Scotland. It was in his power to educate his daughters and clothe them; teach them aristocratic manners; accustom them to aristocratic expectations; and at the same time, at will, he could make his daughters invisible.

# CHAPTER 19

# ENTER, MARY DIANA DODS

BUT THE SISTERS are not invisible to me. They lead me back to the house of mirrors, where there is partial light but infinite possibilities. Moving back and forth one hundred and fifty years across time, that may be all one can expect. I stand behind Doddy; at a different angle I find a different image. It is the earl of Morton, in his scarlet-and-ermine coronation robes, clutching in each hand the center of a wooden cross. Not religious relics, they control, suspended on almost indiscernible strings, two female marionettes. One, dressed entirely in black, has two little boys fastened to her skirts; each time her strings are jerked, the boys feebly bounce along. The other, shorter, somewhat misshapen, in a limp white dress, feverishly hacks at her strings with the point of a quill pen.

Could Doddy, or any other daughter of the age, break those strings? The reality was, the earl of Morton's power over his daughters was little different in that century from the power of other men over their female relatives. There were exceptions in theory and practice, Godwin most prominent among them. But English society by the 1820s anticipated the Victorian-held "truth" that every woman, however clearly an adult in appearance and age, remained a child incapable of directing her own life. Every man was as a father, who by law and right controlled his wife's or daughter's or sister's destiny. How much power men exercised depended on them, tempered only by the degree to which their women complied. As a result, many adult females held a shared, perhaps only partially realized, secret and a shared ambivalence: Being human, they thought; thinking, they knew themselves to be adults. Still, their society insisted otherwise.

To play their assigned roles, they had to hide their selves; to become, to an important degree, invisible. They could hide by throwing themselves into charity or society or fashion. They might drink more wine than was ladylike; or develop one of the many illnesses for which laudanum's sweet opium brought hazy solace. The more fortunate made friendships in which they could share, openly or tacitly, their secret. Some of the talented might dare to write. And the most imaginative and courageous might break the code of the realm—and risk the consequences. Among those most daring women were Mary Diana Dods, Isabella Robinson, and Mary Shelley. And, at last, I understood how each had her own complex reason—her own mirror—that drew her into an extraordinary bond of defiance and risk.

Because I knew the most about her, Mary Shelley came into focus first. It was clear that she had least to gain from public acceptance of the Douglas "marriage" but, from her viewpoint, everything to lose if it was exposed. Mary Shelley could again be open to attack in the public, possibly the legal, arena of gossip and notoriety. Disgraced and poor, she could not prevent Sir Timothy Shelley from gaining custody of Percy Florence from his renegade son's detested widow. How bewildering it would have been for Sir Timothy to learn that one of Mary Shelley's prime motives for helping the Douglases resulted from the very scandal that in the first place provoked her father-in-law's undying wrath.

The ground was laid thirteen years earlier, when Mary Shelley, out of "Love, youth, fear & fearlessness,"[1] defied society by eloping with the married Shelley and set the gossips of London to work. The fact that Mary Shelley's stepsister accompanied the elopers only aggravated matters: It was whispered that Godwin had sold his two daughters to the rich young squire.[2] After Shelley's death, when Mary Shelley was forced by

Sir Timothy to return to England, "correct" society exacted its toll for her youthful daring. Sentenced to remain in England by her father-in-law's power, she lived in a culture that grew increasingly intolerant toward feminine audacity, remembered or recent. Mary Shelley learned her lesson. When she came to the aid of the Douglases, she knew too well the importance of secrecy.

Why help them at all? Mary Shelley's letters and journals tell that story: Isabella Robinson was the lure that drew her in. Like Mary Shelley, like Mary Wollstonecraft, Isabella was an unwed mother. She had not even her lover to protect her and her child from the wounds of an austere, middle-class social code. Mary Shelley, as mother and daughter, bore such scars herself. Through the Douglases' marriage, she could safeguard another social outcast and, at the same time, in some degree avenge herself and her mother for past and present injuries.

What Mary Shelley did not recognize during most of the Douglas union was that the young, lovely "bride" was adept at deceit. Setting the Mary Shelley, Fanny Wright, and Garnett letters side by side, adding to them Mérimée's letters, it is clear that Isabella betrayed Mary Shelley within months of pretending the deepest friendship—love—for her. Isabella used Mary Shelley—something Mary Shelley barely brought herself to admit in her 1830 *Journal* entry. That Mary Shelley felt herself "partly responsible" for Isabella Douglas's situation was certainly Isabella's intention. But if Isabella was a practiced cheat, Mary Shelley was a perfect victim.

Mary Shelley was in part preconditioned to the role by the trauma of losing her mother at birth, as well as by the tales of her mother's own unusual ardor for helping females in need. Possibly as a result, Mary Shelley, even when happy with Shelley, longed for an idealized female relationship. The accepted socialization of an era that approved of, and encouraged, loving relationships between women would make her longing all the more natural. Mary Shelley's life was marked by a series of such friendships, gained and lost.

Ironically, her first beloved friend was also an Isabella, forced from her by Isabella Baxter Booth's family in the wake of the Shelley elopement. After Shelley's death, the childhood friends were reunited, but it was never the same. Mary Shelley's captivity by Isabella Robinson was certainly made easier through the accident of sharing her name with that earlier Isabella. And the accident of shared names may have also played a role in the unequivocal love Mary Shelley ultimately found just three years before she died. Jane Hogg had betrayed her; Jane Shelley, her daughter-in-law, made amends by worshiping her. Mary Shelley not only returned that love, she joined in yet another conspiracy.

If the wife was Mary Shelley's first reason for helping the Douglases, the husband could also awaken her sympathies. Mary Shelley, like Mary Diana Dods, struggled against her male-dominated world. Feeling she was the prey of "masculine insensibility" not for defects of her own character but because she was a woman "poor & unprotected," Mary Shelley privately declared, "Most women I believe wish that they had been men—so do not I [sic]—change my sex & I do not think that my talents would be greater—& I should be like one of these— unselfish unkind. . . ."[3] If not for the memory "of those matchless lost ones" who "redeem their race" she "should learn to hate a sex who are strong only to oppress—moral only to insult—"[4] Why not assist Dods into making that magical transformation that she herself, in the depths of her depression, had written about?

Even with these circumstances, and Isabella Robinson's wiles, perhaps Mary Shelley might still have hesitated to play the dangerous role of broker to the Douglases. But Jane Hogg surely supplied the catalyst by her betrayal that took from Mary Shelley the illusion of that beloved angel, resurrecting in its place the guilt and loss she suffered at Shelley's death. Through Mary Shelley's generosity to Isabella Robinson and Mary Diana Dods, through their mutual affection and sacrifice for each other, Mary Shelley could find restoration in her own eyes. She would prove to herself and to those who counted to her that she was a true "heroine in friendship,"[5] worthy of love.

Some of Mary Shelley's reasons were no doubt conscious; others, perhaps less so. Everything seemed to fall into place, but a nagging question remained. Did Mary Shelley's friendship with the Douglases include experimenting with lesbianism? It was time to tally up what I actually did know about Mary Shelley's sexual life. The first realization was that the answers were not so simple or clear-cut as they had earlier appeared. Yes, Mary Shelley had had a passionate and enduring sexual life with Shelley, apparently even when their relationship was troubled.[6] And though almost certainly unconsummated, there was her youthful adventure with Thomas Jefferson Hogg.[7] Nor, after Shelley's death did "the spoiled child of my beloved—young & affectionate of heart"[8] turn away from other men.[9] Rather, she was afraid that should "the elastic feelings of youth" lead her "to form other prospects, they would be blighted" as her life with Shelley had been.[10] The "companion of Shelley companionless,"[11] torn between the bitter pain of loss and the recognition that she was still "young & affectionate of heart," longed for a second Shelley or someone as remarkable. Finding none, unwilling to compromise, like Frankenstein's creature she suffered a deep, particular loneliness. It was that loneliness she tried to lessen through female friendship and love.

But had those friendships crossed over into sexual attraction and fulfillment? We today label such relationships lesbian and homosexual, but just as neither word existed then, so, too, the idea that ladies could have those feelings for other ladies was equally nonexistent.[12] In fact, as the nineteenth century unfolded, it taught its ladies that they didn't have sexual feelings toward men either. How real, how successful, how universal, was this conviction among the ladies of Britain? How real for Mary Shelley, who after all had broken a number of sexual mores: her elopement with Shelley; her experiment with Hogg; her novella *Mathilda,* a story about incest in an era that considered the subject taboo even to discuss; her satisfaction when the Reverend Mr. Collyer, who had attacked Shelley as being immoral, was publicly accused of sodomy[13]—the contemporary term for homosexuality; her bravado years later when she told Claire Clairmont that she "was never afraid of loving a man who does not love me—and if I am suspected of liking him" her own "steady conduct soon puts that out of people's heads."[14]

Did she depend on steady conduct to put her female loves out of people's heads as well? In our world, our beliefs argue that all love has some degree of sexuality in it—it is a matter of degree as well as conduct. But what about Mary Shelley's world and their beliefs? There is no question that Mary Shelley loved Jane Hogg. But although evidence in both women's lives—including Shelley's and Edwin Williams's interaction with the women and the fact that during the widows' close friendship Jane and Hogg had already become lovers—strongly suggests that the women did not engage in a sexual relationship, that doesn't mean that Mary Shelley's feeling for her angel were non-sexual.

In her pain at Jane Hogg's betrayal, Mary Shelley went out of her way to assert her continuing affection for women—now Isabella—as well as her rejection of men in rather sexual language. She is grateful for

> . . . several things, but for nothing so much as my gender—in fact, dear, except the feminine what is amiable except our pretty N——— the word is too wrong I must not write it, but I shall certainly decline only haec & hoc dilecta vel dilectum Jeff. *must not* see this.—"[15]

"N" appears to stand for one of the dozens of slang words for the female pudendum;[16] her erudite Latin promises that she will use the verb "to love above all others" only in the feminine and neuter genders. Seven years later, reflecting on this period, she admitted to John Trelawny that at the time she was "so ready to give myself away" and "afraid of men," she was "apt to get *tousy-mousy*" for women.[17] *Tousy-mousy* ranges in meaning from "pulled about" by women to a reference to the female pudendum.[18] Was Mary Shelley not only sexually involved with these women, but open about it as well? In fact, these two letters indicate the contrary. If Mary Shelley and Jane Hogg had been sexually engaged, she would have had no need to tell Jane to conceal the letter from Hogg: So open a statement would have taken that letter to the fire many years ago, if not by Jane Hogg than certainly by Jane Shelley. Mary Shelley's warning indicates not that she had been engaged in sex with another woman but that even mentioning anything to do with sex was taboo and would embarrass her if Hogg knew. So, too, it is almost certain that Mary Shelley was unaware of the slang connotations "tousy-mousy" or she would not have used it in a letter to Trelawny, who was not only a man but who had already shown himself to be less of a friend than she once thought.

In also revealing to Trelawny her feelings about their mutual friend Caroline Norton, Mary Shelley gives a critical clue to her own sexual self-identification: "Had I been a man I should certainly have fallen in love with her—As a woman—ten years ago—I should have been spell bound & had she taken the trouble she might have wound me round her finger." But that was years earlier. In the interim was the crushing disappointment of Jane Hogg followed by Isabella Robinson, after which she wrote in her journal that her "exclusive life with women" nourished only a "feverish restlessness" and she planned to dismiss that style of life.[19] Now, she tells Trelawny, she is "more wrapt up in myself—my own feelings—disasters—& prospects for Percy—I am now proof as Hamlet says both against man & woman."[20] Was she proof? Despite her declaration, she continued to form new friendships, female and male, some of them with the same ardor of her younger days. And her language referring to those friendships might sound to the modern ear to be the language of love. It was. But lesbian? Bisexual? At some time? To some degree? Given the times and Mary Shelley's interactions with men and women, her reports of herself, and other's reports of her, it appears that her love relationships with the women she loved were nonerotic.

In many ways, Mary Shelley's part in the Douglas marriage is consistent with traditional biographical accounts of her efforts to assist women in difficult social situations. She went to the aid of male as well as female friends, accurately reporting of herself that "sacrifices have been made."[21] As a heroine in friendship, she also fits the character of the proper, sympathetic female assigned to women in the Victorian era and carried through to our day. But the Douglas story also dramatically challenges the old, standard image of Mary Shelley as unremittingly conventional and ordinary after Shelley's death. Her role in brokering the Douglas marriage required "fear and fearlessness" as well as her lifelong "companion" imagination and her "darling sun bright dreams!"[22] Breaking her out of her confined biographical crypt, together with other recent insights, should help liberate both her life and her works from reductive assumptions that have largely blinded modern scholarship to the full value of the woman and her art.

Did Mary Shelley ever refer again to the Douglases after 1830? Perhaps once she did. In an August 16, 1842, letter in which she talks about the possibility of Claire Clairmont and a mutual friend Elizabeth Hammond living together, Mary Shelley's comments may refer to the events of 1827–1830 as well:

> I am sorry for what you say with regard to Hammy . . .
> I am sorry you sacrifise your personal independance—
> it the last dearest good of those who have no other.
> You have I know thought me selfish for clinging to
> mine—I could not help it—the sentiment was plus fort
> que moi—It is hazardous for a woman to marry a
> woman. . . .

Mary Shelley's responses to the social structures were those of a complex artist, born to the middle class and introduced through marriage into the upper class. Isabella Robinson—or should we not give her her chosen married name, Isabella Douglas?—was also born into the middle class, but there was nothing of the artist to mediate between her and the rules that governed her society. Her father was one of the builders then making money through the housing boom that turned London into its neat squares of Regency buildings. The Robinsons hobnobbed in literary and artistic circles; one son became a banker; a second went to find his fortune in Australia; one daughter married an officer in the East India Company; another married the widower Sir Aubrey Beauclerk. In 1827, a seventeen-year-old unmarried mother would bring to this middle-class family not political defiance but shame.

But there were different ways to bring shame to a family, even more unthinkable then: Was Isabella Douglas a lesbian? Mary Shelley's letters in 1827 indicate that the wife is pining for the *sposo*. Did she elope with Mary Diana Dods because she, after falling victim to a male's wiles, found true love with Doddy? Putting together the letters of Mary Shelley, the Garnetts, Mérimée, Clarke, and Fauriel offers a different scenario. Isabella Douglas emerges from these reports as a woman who, from her mid-teens, was actively heterosexual. Her attraction to Doddy appears not to be sexual but rather an attraction that resulted from Isabella's recognition that Doddy was her passport to propriety and freedom.

Still, several scenarios are possible: She might have been bisexual; or she might have gone through a phase of homosexuality with Doddy after her disappointment with her male lover; or her active sexuality—hyperactive in the eyes of observers—might have been a cover to fool others—and herself. Perhaps the marriage ruse might have been less of a ruse after all. But the fact is that Isabella Douglas, besides attracting and being attractive to men, had other apparently consistent characteristics that better explain her relationships with both Mary Diana Dods and Mary Shelley: Isabella Douglas used, deceived, and betrayed people.

Might her actions have been in vengeance for her own betrayal by the father of her child? Against men, possibly. Of course, this is to assume the man and not she was the seducer. And possibly Isabella Douglas's behavior may also have arisen from a sense of being trapped; of desperately wanting to free herself from the restrictions of middle-class English life by any route she could find. But none of this justifies her treatment of the two women who did so much to aid and protect her. Which raises again one of the central mysteries in the Douglas story: Who was the father of Isabella's daughter?

Rennie's memoirs link her story of a girl in Mary Shelley's company, a girl of the greatest beauty she ever saw, directly with the story of a another girl whose *real* vivid and startling romance would prove Byron's words: "Truth is strange—stranger than fiction." This second girl is a great coquette, who that evening flirts outrageously with Graham, the editor of a weekly journal. Young, handsome, very attractive to women, Graham and the coquette only a few months after that particular evening enacted an "*all* but *fatal* tragedy," which led to his departure from England to America.

The only person among Mary Shelley's friends who fits the description of that girl was Isabella Robinson. Rennie's reasons for not giving the girl's name seem apparent. The incidents took place some thirty-five years earlier and besides, Isabella Douglas, now the respectable Mrs. William Falconer, was still alive. But Rennie could not resist this titillating story, as well as other seemingly personal anecdotes, that would draw more readers to a book she desperately relied on to earn some money.[23] She included it, but veiled its "*all* but *fatal* tragedy." What else did Rennie veil? And what could the "*fatal* tragedy" have been?

Some of the answers were in an 1842 memoir. Eighteen years before *Traits,* a Mrs. Walker wrote about her experiences during "An Evening at Dr. Kitchener's" for the *Friendship's Offering.* Again dusty records proved their worth. Mrs. Walker turned out to be the married name of Eliza Rennie.[24] There is no question that both memoirs are versions of the same story. In this first version, Rennie says she met Kitchener some fourteen years earlier, brought there by a friend. She again comments on Kitchener's own oddities, and also lists the names of some of the more prominent guests, among them, the poets Miss Landon and Miss Benger, Alaric Watts, Mr. Croly, and Lord Dillon; Graham, editor of a London journal; the singer Braham and his wife, and Mrs. Percy Bysshe Shelley. In this telling, written while Mary Shelley was alive, Rennie offers a different version of her anecdote about Mary Shelley and her Frankenstein creature. This time, it is not Mary Shelley who unsympathetically remarks that an ugly poet stalking the rooms reminded her of her creature. Instead, "one of the ladies remarked to Mrs. Shelley [he] must have suggested the idea of the Monster in question." Nor does Rennie claim Mary Shelley as a close friend, as she does after Mary Shelley's death. These earlier details appear far closer to the truth.

Rennie also returns to the story of Graham, he of "the

insouciant manner." Again, he is reported to have died in a duel in America a few months after this party. But in this earlier telling, it is not a coquette with whom he converses but a "young lady whom his talents had captivated, and who, a short time afterwards, in a fit of despair at his indifference, took laudanum, and cut her throat in a hackney-coach!" The result of this tangled affair? "*He* sleeps in death, and *she* is now well and happily married—such is human life!"

If both tales are put together, we have the story of a love affair between a flirtatious young woman and Graham. She becomes pregnant; he refuses marriage. Perhaps she threatened to have her father sue for breach of promise. Graham escapes her claims by rushing off to America. She, abandoned, takes laudanum and cuts her throat as much in despair over her feelings for him as the need, for herself and her family, of a husband. What of this Mr. Graham? At that point, he was only a name, a not-uncommon one at that, and editor of an unnamed journal. But slowly, through nineteenth-century biographical accounts, I uncovered a considerable trail that brought the dubious Mr. William Grenville Graham to life.[25]

Born in upstate New York in 1793, Graham died in a duel in America sometime in October or November 1827. He is consistently described as a young man of enormous gifts, talents, looks, charm—and as a profligate, a spendthrift, and a womanizer. After "misconduct" forced him to leave college, he settled in New York City. Living beyond his means, he presented a forged check at a bank. Only through the influence of friends did he escape prison. In 1814, at twenty-one, he decided to try his fortunes in Europe. In England, he had the unusual luck to attract the patronage of a philanthropic man of fortune, who supported him at Trinity College, Cambridge, where he studied for the law. But again, through his own lack of "self-government" he destroyed the benefits of this friendship. Having squandered a considerable amount of money, both inherited and won in gambling, he found a position in London as translator for the famous Italian writer Ugo Foscolo. But the two came to fight a duel when Graham had an affair with one of Foscolo's servants—with whom Foscolo himself was having an affair. The duel over, with both protagonists alive but unreconciled, Graham found new employment as editor of Whittaker's *Weekly Museum*. However, "it was in his character to go to the utmost excess in his sensual pursuits."[26] To pay for them, he again forged checks. The law hot in chase, he barely escaped back across the Atlantic; found work as an editor, and died in a duel that resulted from an argument over a game of cards.

Why the two versions of this story? Very possibly, because all Eliza Rennie actually knew in 1826 was the story of Graham and of Isabella Robinson's suicide attempt followed by her subsequent marriage to a Mr. Douglas. Both Eliza Rennie's letter to Thomas Moore and Moore's response indicate both of them at the time believed there was a *Mr.* Douglas. Clearly, neither had been made privy to the Douglas charade by the conspirators, who for their own protection let only a few intimates know. Despite Rennie's published claims of friendship, the evidence of Godwin's journals, Mary Shelley's records, and her own exchange of notes with Moore indicate that Rennie was not an intimate friend of any of the conspirators. Most likely, both of Rennie's accounts of Graham and the young woman were pieced together from what she, as a member of London's small literary world at the time, would know, enlarged from secondhand stories told her by someone who knew a great deal more about the actual Douglas "marriage." And this quite likely leads back not to Mary Shelley, but to Mary Shelley's unreliable friend, her "angelic" Jane Hogg.

There is no absolute proof that it was Jane Hogg who told the story of the Douglases' marriage and of the "wild and wonderful" career of Mary Diana Dods to Rennie, but for a number of reasons she appears to be the one plausible link between the parties. Mary Diana Dods's two letters to Mary Shelley show that Dods knew and was delighted with the "wicked" Jane Hogg. Mary Shelley's disguised reports in her letters to Jane Hogg also make it clear that only Jane Hogg was kept informed, closely informed, of the details of the Douglas story by Mary Shelley herself. After the events, Mary Shelley had every reason to keep the Douglas story secret. But Jane Hogg had earlier broken her trust in spreading "every idle & evil tale"[27] about

Mary Shelley's intimate life with her husband to their mutual friends, including Isabella and Dods. And it was Isabella who told Mary Shelley of Jane Hogg's betrayal, causing the break in their friendship and making Isabella the object of Jane's anger and thirst for revenge.[28] She might well have been willing, even anxious, over the years to defame Isabella Douglas by revealing the details of this strange intrigue.

If Rennie learned more of the truth—but not all of the truth—from a third party after the 1842 version of her story, that would explain the differences between Rennie's accounts of an evening at Kitchener's as well as her inaccuracies. It also would explain the quotation marks Rennie put around her statement that Dods "resided many years at Paris, where 'she died and was buried.'" That is what someone told her. Rennie's references in *Traits* to a beautiful, flirtatious girl whose life is stranger than fiction and Miss Dods's "wild and wonderful" career leave no doubt that decades following Miss Robinson's marriage to a Mr. Douglas, she had found out the true identity of the groom. In her narrative, she kept the actual facts a secret as much to protect the players as because, in so many ways, they remained a secret to her as well.

Is there any trace of Graham in Mary Shelley's life? One—in a footnote to a scholarly essay on Foscolo in 1835,[29] Mary Shelley refers to the story of Foscolo's challenge to "one Graham, an American" over one of his household servants; Graham was at the time a reporter to a newspaper—"afterwards got into difficulties, committed a forgery, and was obliged to leave this country. Soon after, he fell in a duel in America." Why bother to include this unnecessary anecdote, one of the very few footnotes in the entire volume, except perhaps as a covert reminder to a particular reader? All the circumstances—Jane Hogg's knowledge of the story, the contextual prominence as well as the differences in Rennie's two stories about Graham and his young lady-cum-coquette, Mary Shelley's seeming aside about Graham, and the complete absence of any other evidence that in any way identifies Isabella Robinson's lover—circumstantially suggest Graham may well have been Adeline Douglas's actual father. But Graham bolted to America and died there.

Exit Mr. Graham—not fleeing from a weeping, pregnant young woman, but from the more compelling arms of the law and a jail sentence for forgery.

Enter Mr. Walter Sholto Douglas. Husband in name only in 1826, a year later Mary Diana Dods donned *les culottes* and provided Isabella Douglas with a husband in appearance as well. But what caused Mary Diana Dods to take both wife and child to herself? Mary Diana Dods wrote under a man's name and dressed like a man: Was Mary Diana Dods a lesbian? a transvestite? both? or neither? Were her suit and top hat the passports to a life she had always yearned for, a maleness so important to her that she would risk all to shed that white linen dress and replace it with the clothing of her true sexual self? Originally it seemed that answering these questions would unlock all the complexities of Dods's character and her actions. But, as with everything else in the Douglas marriage, it is not so simple.

From centuries of ignored, hidden, buried, overlooked, or brushed-aside historical records spanning the sixteenth century through the present, in Europe and America, increasing numbers of examples are being retrieved in which women successfully passed as men. The profile of the vast majority of these women shows they were almost always members of the working class; they mostly went into the armed forces, getting away with their disguises for varying lengths of time in service, including combat duty (perhaps using the commonly seen painted-on mustaches that young male soldiers wore until they were old enough to grow their own);[30] or they entered other male, and therefore higher-paying, occupations. What is significant here, besides their numbers and the daring of their actions, is that only a small minority of these women appear to have been lesbians.[31]

Depending on where their masquerade took place, and when, their discovery brought them banishment, the pillory, jail—or honors. In the eighteenth century, when the deserted Hannah Snell enlisted as James Gray to search out her deceitful husband, she earned a reputation for exceptional courage in combat. Even after she left the army, remarried, and revealed in her memoirs her true identity, she continued to receive her army pension until her death. Other English ex-soldiers Christian Davis, Phoebe Hessel and Mary Anne Talbot lived from money received for their military service. In England, the king and members of the nobility extended favors to various cross-dressers who had served in the military campaigns against Napoleon. The German Antoinette Berg, who in the English service fought the French on Dutch territory in 1799, was specially celebrated in the 1814 peace festivities in London.[32]

Though the female military "men" were mostly working class, stories of cross-dressing are also found among middle- and upper-class women.[33] Legend, if not history, has fascinated us with accounts of transvestite women. From medieval times, we have the tales of the third-century Saint Eugenia, who is said to have entered a monastery as a man, risen to abbot, and only to prove her innocence at the accusation of attempted violation of a woman, for "God's Honor" opened her garment to show her true sex.[34] And, on circumstantial evidence, there's the ninth-century Pope Joan.[35] Centuries later, we have the historical fact of the celebrated "Ladies of Llangollen," discussed earlier. And the less known, even more extraordinary Dr. James Barry, who when he earned his degree in medicine in 1812 at seventeen appended to his thesis: "Do not consider my youth, but whether I show a man's wisdom." If his professors had followed his forty-year career in the military in which he rose to the rank of Inspector General of Hospitals, to the day he died in 1865, they would have better understood that quotation. As the nurse who laid out the deceased Dr. James Barry informed the world, he was "a perfect female."[36] In 1988, the jazz musician Billy Tipton, saxophonist and pianist, husband for nine years and stepfather to three sons, died at the age of seventy-four and gave up his secret to his apparently unsuspecting family and the world: He was a woman.[37] We probably will never know as much about middle- and upper-class women who dressed as men, because their wealth and social position better protected against discovery—witness the Douglases. But, past assumptions to the contrary, current historical research about lesbians and transvestites plainly demonstrates that the two categories cannot be equated.

Given this evidence, for all her masculine mode, Dods's

transvestism in itself does not necessarily give proof of motivation. Still, there remains the question of whether she was a lesbian, and how that might have influenced her. Were there lesbians in Dods's Britain? Britain had an antihomosexual statute, stemming from Leviticus 20:13, first legislated in 1533 and operative until 1967, that decreed the death penalty for sodomy (until 1835) as well as a number of other penalties. But homosexuality was believed to be a fundamentally male activity, and the sodomy laws were construed not to refer to cases of female homoerotic acts. On the Continent, however, with some exceptions, lesbian relations had been recognized and legally regarded as the same crime as male sodomy. Both were subject to the death penalty—until it was abolished under the French National Assembly in 1791—and later incorporated into the Napoleonic Code.[38]

Why the difference in Britain? Contemporary beliefs held that a man could be attracted to another man, a woman could be attracted to a man, but it was thought ridiculous that a woman, who in that society was accounted as an inferior being, could be attracted to another woman. Not that rare instances of prosecutions for such aberrant behavior are unrecorded.[39] But British law[40] held that the offending woman's crime was impersonating a superior being, making her guilty of fraud, not the male-designated crime of sodomy. Under these circumstances, if Mary Diana Dods was a lesbian, assuming a man's clothing and a man's prerogative to have a wife, while the Douglases were in England in 1827, was the most dangerous thing she could do. Dods would have far better protected herself by continuing to dress as a woman, thereby disguising her homoerotic activities from a society that communally agreed to turn a blind eye to the existence of female homosexuals. And even on the Continent, she would have been far safer as a lesbian if she wore female clothing.

Why did she run the risk? Before answering that question, one other lingers: Is it possible that Doddy was a member of that comparatively rare breed of true hermaphrodite? Did she have male as well as female characteristics? Could she actually have been Adeline's father? Earlier it seemed possible—but the appearance of Mr. Graham, together with a host of other reasons, led to dismissing Dods as father. Among the most important were Mary Shelley's letters, which once deciphered make it clear that the Douglases' was a marriage between two females. Mary Shelley might have been deceived, but Dods's own life pattern suggests she was not.

Until Miss Dods became Mr. Walter Sholto Douglas, there is no evidence that she was anything but a female. True, she wrote under two male pseudonyms, and one of her works dealt autobiographically with the development of a boy into manhood. But while she wrote as Mr. Douglas for *Blackwood's,* it is quite possible that the works forwarded as by Mrs. Douglas were also Doddy's. To confuse the role-playing even more, Mary Shelley's letter to the editor Watts in September 1827 almost certainly indicates that Doddy was at times using the name Mrs. Douglas while in London;[41] and Lord Dillon's letter shows she was still submitting works as Miss Dods—all four names being used during the same years. As William Blackwood indicated in his first letter to David Lyndsay, disguises with editors in the opening stages of publishing relationships were not unusual. Other women—wives and mothers among them, including the Brontës and George Sand—increasingly used male pseudonyms as much for the additional earnings a man would command as for the ever-growing attitude in the nineteenth century that careers, including that of writer, were improper for ladies. Mary Diana Dods's male pseudonyms appear less a sign of sexual preference than a sign of social and economic pragmatism. Where she was unusual—perhaps unique—was in the remarkable success and duration of those disguises.

Dods provides additional evidence that she self-identified as a female in her 1820 letters to her father that describe her struggle to earn income through the legitimate female career of establishing a girls' school. Nor in 1827 was it a given that Dods would dress as a man when the Douglas entourage embarked on their European adventure. Otherwise Mary Shelley would not have particularly announced to Jane Hogg the news that Dods "now seriously thinks of les culottes." By that time, Doddy was about thirty-six years old. If there was some genetic ambivalence for Dods, the circumstances of her father's death could have allowed her the new freedom to fulfill a biologically based longing to become a man. Rennie's report of Dods's appearance comes to mind: Her short hair more resembled "that of a man than of a woman"; at first glance, Dods looked like "some one of the masculine gender" who had "indulged in the masquerade freak of feminine habiliments, and that 'Miss Dods' was an *alias* for Mr. ———." From this description, one might argue for a possible genetic basis. But present authority indicates that hermaphrodites would also have the characteristic of facial hair.[42] Given Rennie's delight in describing the odd Miss Dods's male features, we can reasonably assume she would not have omitted the even odder mark of facial hair. A further perspective is provided by modern medical research, which though still in the early phases of exploring female and male sexuality, suggests that androgynous children generally adapt themselves into the sex in which they were raised—and Mary Diana Dods was raised female.[43]

Another modern sexual category remains. Could Doddy have been a transsexual—that is, someone who believes, like Jan Morris[44] in our era, that appearances and genes to the contrary, they were born to the wrong sex? Perhaps. But her transmogrification to Mr. Douglas can be explained in terms that better fit the spirit of her age. She was raised in a century when enraptured romantic attachment between women was not only accepted, it was celebrated as "noble and virtuous in every way." At that same time, female eroticism, particularly in ladies, was considered by British society to be nonexistent.[45] So when Mary Shelley, Fanny Wright, Fanny Trollope, the Garnett sisters, Isabella Robinson, and Mary Diana Dods exchanged affectionate endearments, they implicitly understood their love for each other, however effusive, as nonerotic. Were there subconscious sexual desires? People in the nineteenth century, given their socialization, would not have been able to understand the question, much less answer it. Still, modern thought, in hindsight, suggests such desires did exist. Evaluating their influence remains in a realm yet to be explored.

Is it possible that Dods may have been out of step with her

age and genetically or otherwise consciously been homoerotic? In a story as strange as hers, that would seem the least odd part to the modern reader; in her era, in her society, it would have been the most difficult to accept. After many years of following her path back in time, I end where I began on this issue. I am convinced that Dods's sexual preference is in fact very important in her story, but to my own surprise, not for the reasons I first thought. If she was a lesbian, the necessarily clandestine nature of that preference reinforced what was a far more significant question central to her life: In her own eyes, who was Miss Mary Diana Dods?

Here the legal documents preserved in the Edinburgh National Record Office again offer clues. From the financial papers of the earl of Morton and his accountant, his banker, his London representative, and his executors, it is clear that the earl kept his daughters at a legal arm's length. Even Morton's will separates his bequest to Lady Morton from the codicil providing an annuity for his illegitimate daughters. In this way, the will could be and was separately administered and perhaps separately read. The Dods sisters' letters found among the Morton papers were not cataloged as written by Morton's daughters. On the contrary, many of them were filed with letters from other supplicants for the earl's favors. Quite likely, those letters would not have been preserved if members of the Douglas line, who deposited the Douglas documents in the Record Office sometime late in the nineteenth century, had realized who the Dods sisters were. This secret, with its hidden trail, was no doubt also hidden from the world in Scotland. To what extent did the father hide his daughters themselves as well?

The codicil that held the secret of Morton's paternity of the Dods sisters clearly indicated that the earl of Morton recognized his daughters. And Aubin's letters, as well as other Douglas papers, make it clear that Lady Morton knew her husband's daughters, that the sisters had been raised by their father, and that father and daughters maintained their familial ties until the end of the earl's life. But the critical question is: Did the earl of Morton hide his daughters at the same time that he raised them, keeping them an open secret in London, where illegitimate children of the nobility were generally no disgrace, but a closely kept secret in Scotland, where the Church would not wink at the living evidence of two such infractions of the laws of God and State?

From their father, the Dods sisters knew the meaning of luxury and upper-class life-style. He made it clear that he regarded his daughters as "women of birth and respectability," despite their illegitimacy. And Mary Diana Dods, as David Lyndsay, proudly informed Blackwood that she was of the finest Scottish blood. But the sisters also knew, and were constantly reminded by their father's complex legal devices, as well as by their second name, that in an important sense they did not exist. Nor, among the Douglas papers, is there any evidence that their mother existed. Not one document among the hundreds of Morton papers mentions a woman named Dods. Were there support payments to the mother, but under a different name? Was a cottage granted to her? Had a marriage been arranged that conveniently separated the girls' name from her own? Did the young girls know their mother? Or, given the absence of any document naming the mother, together with the fact that the earl did raise them, did Miss Dods die when both her daughters were quite young?

There are no birth records for the Dods sisters; nor is there a trail to the implementation of the annuity left to them by the earl after his death. For all the apparent acknowledgment these daughters enjoyed from their noble father, in an important part of the real world they were illegitimate and were hidden. The absence of these papers is a major loss in piecing together Mary Diana Dods's life, but that same absence is symbolically significant. To be female and nonconforming brought with it its own dilemmas. To be physically deformed and unattractive was another challenge for self-esteem. With these obstacles, to be illegitimate and constantly recognized as such would have added burden enough. But Mary Diana Dods had the further, even more acute psychological burden of conflicting position. She was of prestigious, wealthy, aristocratic lineage, except when her father and their society decided she was of no lineage. In the confusion of being and not being, how did either of the sisters come to recognize herself? Georgiana Dods Carter found her way out of her conflicted role through marriage—the only truly legitimate occupation for a nineteenth-century female. Her apparently sincere letters show that Georgiana Carter understood the earl's perspective. She fully accepted that her father must spend the kind of monies he did on carriages and homes, travel and appearance: He was, after all, the fifteenth earl of Morton. Just as David Lyndsay's letters to Blackwood placed himself among the Tory aristocracy, Georgiana Carter was also of the Tory aristocracy. That she had not the wealth was beside the point. Neither she nor Doddy was a radical upstart. They respected God, King, and Father; the status quo; order. Which made Doddy's charade, and Georgiana Carter's part in it, all the more irreverent.

Georgiana had exchanged the name of unacknowledged Dods for the respectable married Carter. When she became a widow, her lack of her sister's unusual intellectual achievements handicapped her financially but helped retain her social position in the mainstream of society's designated role for women. When Georgiana Dods married John Carter, she established a legitimacy of her own. But how could Doddy establish hers? The motivating force that drove Mary Diana Dods, subsuming sexual genus as well as writing genius, surely must have centered in her longing for identity.

It was Dods who was odd person out: of the finest Scottish blood, yet unacknowledged; raised and highly educated by her wealthy, noble father, but publicly a Dods, not a Douglas. Physically unappealing, her chances of marriage were slight; and in the Britain of the 1820s, already prefiguring the constricted attitudes of Queen Victoria's reign, Dods's remarkable learning would have been viewed by men as yet another handicap. But a learned man could marry; and, as the Garnetts' comments show, a deformed man could marry a lovely young woman. It is not difficult to imagine that the unmarried, somewhat misshapen Doddy sought more than anything else her own legitimacy, her own identity, and was willing to part with name and gender in exchange.

There was certainly a financial incentive for Doddy's transformation. When the fifty-four-year-old earl of Morton married the twenty-one-year-old Susan Elizabeth Buller, Morton's bride and his illegitimate daughters were about the same age. Probably it was this marriage that forced Mary Diana Dods to live on her own, trying to get by on the hundred-pound allowance provided by her father beginning in 1815. But the years before, with their homes in elegant Park Street and visits to Dalmahoy and Aberdour, their language masters, carriages, and servants, did little to prepare Dods to live on a tight budget, which helps to explain her 1815–1819 debts. Contrary to her father's opinion, and his life-style, it was impossible for a lady—and Dods had been raised a lady—to live on the hundred pounds a year her dear Lord deemed sufficient.

When she and her business partners tried to earn income through their girls' school, the venture did not prosper, and new debts were added to old. But at the same time that Miss Dods failed, Mr. David Lyndsay was quite a success: two books published in three years; poems and articles in the popular journals of the day; a play, perhaps produced; and anonymous book reviews. If David Lyndsay, only a name, a persona, could achieve so much, what might be achieved by a Mr. Walter Sholto Douglas, who combined Lyndsay's writing abilities with superb language skills, urbane conversation, and world knowledge? Disappointed in her life as a woman, it is little wonder she was willing to make a place as a him self.

I believe that Mary Diana Dods was disposed to change roles because, in a sense, she had no self-role to begin with. In becoming Lyndsay in name only, she experienced real satisfaction. She earned not only money but stature. Could one argue that that stature was enhanced for her because she was a lesbian and therefore identified with men? Not in the face of modern research, which indicates that lesbians do not necessarily identify with men.[46] The idea that they do is a holdover from nineteenth-century beliefs that women could not be sexually attracted to other women because they were a lesser species. Besides, Dods left ample clues that she intended to live as a female. She established a girls' school. She had Lyndsay announce that "he" was "a short-lived man." Almost certainly,

Doddy took pride in her Lyndsay role not because she felt sexually a man but because the sickly, brilliant, financially mismanaging Mary Diana Dods was at last successful at something—in what was then even more of a man's world and on a man's terms. For Isabella Robinson's sake, she took on the name of Walter Sholto Douglas and, while she was at it, again used that name to enter *Blackwood's* pages. The successes she had as Lyndsay and Douglas enforced the message of male opportunity.

In her full-fledged male incarnation, when she put those *culottes* on to become Mr. Walter Sholto Douglas, husband and father, she broke with the deformed, confusing reflection of Miss Mary Diana Dods, spinster. With the earl's death, she no longer had to answer to anyone. She could go to the Continent, where not only was it cheaper to live, but fewer questions would be asked. It was quite common for partners in irregular liaisons—though hers was certainly more irregular than most—to live abroad. In a sense, Mary Diana Dods aborted her own life in favor of Mr. Douglas's. The final irony, the final insult, was that because of Isabella, Douglas failed to provide her with the unambiguous social position for which she must have longed: "His" wife's liaisons denied the man, and in denying "him" denied Mary Diana Dods as well.

In the beginning, Dods was probably as blind to her "wife's" character as was Mary Shelley. Isabella was exceptionally good at deception. She was also good at selecting vulnerable prey. Doddy, not wanting to know the truth about Isabella, could set aside the multiple frustrations of the narrow female life assigned by contemporary standards. When she became Douglas, for the first time she found a socially honored role: She became the head of her own family; she had a seemingly devoted "wife"; she became a parent. By dropping the name of Dods and openly assuming her father's name, she gave herself legitimacy. Perhaps it was for the same reason that Georgiana Dods Carter's death certificate gave her maiden name as Douglas.

As Mr. Douglas, Dods could establish a life and a career for herself on the Continent. Leaving behind the years of financial and identity struggle, she instead became a person who attracted attention, admiration, and affection. Mr. Douglas could also offer a man's protection to the widowed Georgiana Dods Carter. Each sister would benefit by going to France. The one could establish a more economical life for her family; the other could become, however disguised, herself.

As Douglas, she let her new circle know of her aspirations to the diplomatic corps. Once successful, she could announce to Douglas's friends that "he" was also a published writer—to protect the privacy of the family, "he" had written under the pseudonym of David Lyndsay. It is clear that the Douglases had entered a marriage of mutual convenience. The "little wife" escaped the stigma of bearing an illegitimate child and Dods escaped the gender that barred her from the career that "his" intellect could attain. But was it, as the Garnetts said, also a love match as far as Doddy was concerned? Quite possibly. That love might well have included erotic desire for another woman, although, as we have seen, records of nineteenth-century female friendship and love show that such desire was not an essential factor.[47] But what happened to that love once the Douglases established themselves in Paris?

Isabella Douglas's coquettish behavior, her open search for a male partner, was a grievous betrayal for her "husband." Dods, having come so close to attaining an identity that was real in everything but, perhaps, actual sexual identification, stood in daily danger of losing that self if Isabella Douglas should leave "him" or, worse, reveal the truth of their marriage. Doddy may well have feared what historical records demonstrate: In cases of female marriages, the "wife," especially when young, could and often did claim to have been deceived and victimized, leaving the "husband" to suffer the legal consequences and the social stigma.

Could Isabella Douglas get free of her husband through this route in that sophisticated Parisian world of shifting liaisons of the heart and body? Mérimée, Stendhal, Fauriel, cosmopolitan men of the world, believed from first to last that the Douglases were a married couple. Mary Ann Clarke, who grasped at any gossip to discredit the couple out of jealousy of Mrs. Douglas, thought them a couple. The more reserved Garnetts, who spent a great deal of time with the Douglases and came to thoroughly disapprove of Mrs. Douglas because of her coquettish behavior, believed them a couple. In a circle that surely could be expected to know the difference, Mary Diana Dods successfully and amazingly crossed the gender-identity line, no doubt greatly aided by audience expectation. Douglas dressed like a man; had a wife and child; spoke with the learning of a man; had a sister who deferred to "him" as a brother. Ergo: Douglas was a man. What Dods probably did not realize was that the same code of social assumptions that helped her pass as Mr. Douglas would prevent Isabella Douglas from telling their truth. Mrs. Douglas's married role allowed for flirtations, even sexual liaisons; but after actively engaging in such extramarital relations, she could not pose as a victimized waif, deceived by a male impersonator. Nor could she reveal that she was involved in a relationship that could be interpreted as sexual. Isabella Douglas was locked into the Douglas marriage and it appeared that only death would them part.

And that death almost certainly took place a short time after Doddy broke another gender line in November 1829 when she was thrown in debtors' prison as Mr. Walter Sholto Douglas. Her attempt to purchase mustaches and sideburns was no doubt an effort to maintain her male pose for public consumption. But, at the same time, it was likely an attempt to keep her pose for herself as well. Mary Shelley's words of June 1828 about the Douglases echo of an Isabella whose

> . . . misery to which she is a victim is so dreadful and merciless, that she shrinks like a wounded person from every pang—and you must excuse her on the score of her matchless sufferings. What D. now is, I will not describe in a letter—one only trusts that the diseased body acts on the diseased mind, & that both may be at rest ere long.

Isabella Douglas's appearance in London in 1830, without husband, and no longer pretending to be Mary Shelley's friend, because she no longer needed her help, certainly indicates that the disease that Georgiana thought might claim Doddy as early as 1823, when she implored her father to assist her sister, and in 1828, when Mary Shelley thought Doddy's death imminent, finally claimed her.

But where is the body? Doddy's remains, like her sister's, were probably put in a temporary grave for thirty years from which, if no permanent grave is paid for, in accord with French regulations governing interment,[48] the remains would have been removed to lie, unmarked, in a mass repository for the bones of the dead. Mr. Walter Sholto Douglas—or perhaps, in death, Miss Mary Diana Dods—disappeared into time.

When I first discovered that Lyndsay and Douglas were both Doddy, I thought her story was rooted in sexuality. Her sexual orientation, or disorientation, appeared to be the critical factor, perhaps an outgrowth of female envy. But this approach, preconceived in our post-Freudian era, turned out to be conditioned by as pat a set of beliefs as were those of the society that accepted Doddy as a man. Both are generalizations that may not be valid, and are at best based on statistical data and social blinders, not individual lives. At the end of this journey, I ask myself, What appears to be true for Mary Diana Dods? And for that matter, for Isabella Douglas and Mary Shelley as well? The answer, I believe, is linked to both sex and gender. What each in her own way searched for most, and lacked most, was an existence where she would be recognized for what she was; where she could see her self in the mirrors that are other people's eyes. Of the three, Doddy was the most displaced. In becoming a man, she was like an immigrant to a foreign country: Though she might miss her native habitat, she went with the hope of finding living conditions and opportunities not available at home.

And each time Dods crossed the gender barrier, she did. She almost fulfilled her dream of recognition—as a writer, as a person—in the strange trail she left through history. Despite her own prediction, she did not become a short-lived man. On the contrary, she left a series of questions from her time to ours. David Lyndsay, who wrote *Dramas,* was a woman, not a man; the anonymous *Tales* was long believed to be written by George Borrow, an important Victorian novelist and, again, a man. Can one know from a work itself if a man or a woman wrote it? The *Dictionary of National Biography,* biographies, passports, marriage certificates, and death certificates connected with the Douglas story—all wrong? The perceptions of a sophisticated Anglo-French circle, all based on conventional assumptions? Giddy questions, given Doddy's story.

Leaving in her wake the need for rigid definitions, Doddy's life insists on the mysteries and complexities of existence that are so often oversimplified in the name of order and control. Of course, she knew about order and control. Living through the early years of the nineteenth century, Dods experienced the political, economic, social, and scientific change in Britain that began the extension of male power and its image from throne and church to everyman as the metaphoric microcosm of the universe. At the same time, Doddy learned through experience that in male protection and cultivation of that new universe, men increasingly relegated women to lesser, dependent spheres. Had she lived later, Dods probably would have joined womens' collective efforts for an expanded metaphor of humanity that would encompass their selves as well. Her special legacy is a remarkable chapter in the history of women—and of men.

Doddy's striving for individual self-ness was not isolated, or confined by time or sex. Rooted in eighteenth-century enlightenment philosophy, Mary Wollstonecraft's impassioned voice argued for that philosophy for women as well as men. Her claims are echoed in women's works now being retrieved from the hidden crannies of history and literature. They are at the core of the networks of nineteenth-century women, who preserved their sense of individual value and potential beyond the restricted roles they were assigned. And they are central to the story of Isabella Robinson Douglas, who chose not to accept either the stigma of illegitimacy that would mark her and her child or the society that would so brand them; central to Mary Shelley, whose entire life was lived in a world of imaginative possibilities and who, in assisting the Douglas intrigue, added to her repertoire another myth that, untangled, changes the way we think; and, most of all, central to Mary Diana Dods, who in searching beyond her life as the illegitimate daughter of the fifteenth earl of Morton, created a mirror in which to see reflected a self—what matter, if dressed as a man.

# NOTES

PROLOGUE

1. William Kitchener (1775–1827, *DNB*) and his soirees have been described in a number of memoirs of the era. All agree on his eccentricity though not always on details. See:

Alaric Alfred Watts, *Alaric Watts: A Narrative of His Life* (London: Richard Bentley and Son, 1884), 2 vols., Vol. II, pp. 302–308.

[Eliza Rennie], *Traits of Character; Being Twenty-Five Years' Literary and Personal Recollections,* By a Contemporary (London: Hurst & Blackett, 1860), 2 vols., Vol. I, pp. 105, 195–198.

Mrs. Walker [Eliza Rennie], "An Evening at Dr. Kitchener's," *Friendship's Offering* (Cornhill: Smith, Elder, 1842), pp. 243–249.

William Jerdan, *Men I Have Known* (New York: G. Routledge & Sons, 1866), pp. 282–287.

*The Works of Thomas Hood* (London: Edward Moxon & Co., 1862), Vol. I, pp. 2–4, 210–216.

Arnold Constable, *Personal Reminiscences* (New York: Scribner, Armstrong, 1876), pp. 209–214.

**2.** The standard charge during the 1820s and 1830s for two-horse hackney carriages transporting passengers one mile or less was: 1s. 0d. (one shilling, no pence); 1 to 1½ miles, 1s.6d.; 1½ to 2 miles, 2s., with 6 pence per ½ mile afterward. After 8 P.M.

and before 5 A.M. and beyond 5 miles, full return fare was required. See *The Literary Pocket-Book* (London: C. & J. Ollier, 1820–22); the *Post Office Directory of 1840,* "Abstract of the Acts for Regulating Hackney Carriages and Metropolitan Stage Carriages enacted 5 January 1832."

**3.** Brian R. Mitchell, *Abstract of British Historical Statistics* (Cambridge at the University Press, 1962).

English money in the early part of the nineteenth century can be roughly approximated to dollars by first multiplying by five, then by forty to adjust for inflation (Julia Prewitt Brown, *A Reader's Guide to the Nineteenth-Century English Novel* [New York: Macmillan, 1985]).

**4.** For Mary Shelley's life, as well as the Shelleys' lives together, I have drawn on the many volumes and documents cited in my edition of *The Letters of Mary Wollstonecraft Shelley,* 3 vols. (Baltimore: Johns Hopkins University Press, 1980–88), herein cited as *MWS Letters,* most especially the Abinger manuscripts of Mary Shelley, Shelley, William Godwin and their circle (Bodleian Library) and Mary Shelley's letters and related documents in the Carl H. Pforzheimer Collection. *MWS Letters* is the major source of material regarding Mary Shelley's life, except when otherwise noted, supplemented by Mary Shelley's Journals in manuscript and *The Journals of Mary Shelley, 1814–1844,* eds. Paula R. Feldman and Diana Scott-Kilvert, 2 vols. (Oxford at the Clarendon Press, 1987), herein cited as *MWS Journals* together with Mary Shelley's published and unpublished works. For Shelley's life, I particularly relied on:

Edward Dowden, *The Life of Percy Bysshe Shelley,* 2 vols. (London: Kegan Paul, Trench & Co., 1886).

Newman Ivey White, *Shelley* (London: Secker & Warburg, 1947).

*The Letters of Percy Bysshe Shelley,* ed. Frederick L. Jones, 2 vols. (Oxford at the Clarendon Press, 1964).

Kenneth Neill Cameron, *The Young Shelley: Genesis of a Radical* (New York: Macmillan Co., 1950).

*Shelley and His Circle, 1773–1822,* eds. Kenneth Neill Cameron and Donald H. Reiman, 8 vols. (Cambridge, Mass.: Harvard University Press, 1961–1986).

For Godwin and Wollstonecraft, the best source, in addition to manuscripts and their own works, is William St Clair, *The Godwins and the Shelleys* (London: Faber and Faber, 1989).

CHAPTER 1: THE SEARCH BEGINS

1. Elie Halevy, *England in 1815* and *The Liberal Awakening* (New York: Barnes & Noble, 1961).

E. J. Hobsbawm, *The Age of Revolution: 1789–1848* (New York: Mentor, 1962).

Harold Perkin, *The Origins of Modern English Society: 1780–1880* (London: Routledge & Kegan Paul, 1969).

E. P. Thompson, *The Making of the English Working Class* (New York: Vintage Books, 1963).

2. Elizabeth Longford, *Queen Victoria* (New York: Harper and Row, 1964), pp. 32–33.

3. Alaric A. Watts (1797–1864) was editor and proprietor of *The Literary Souvenir,* one of the fashionable illustrated annuals that flourished in England in the 1820s and 1830s. See Alaric Alfred Watts, *Alaric Watts: A Narrative of His Life,* 2 vols. (London: Richard Bentley and Son, 1884).

4. For a discussion of the annuals of the period, see Ian Jack, *English Literature: 1815–1832* (Oxford at the Clarendon Press, 1963), pp. 173–175.

5. Rudolph Ackermann (1764–1834), London publisher and bookseller, who among his many other diverse art and literary publications first introduced annuals to Britain in 1822 (*Dictionary of National Biography*).

6. Henry Colburn (d. 1855), publisher of the *New Monthly Magazine* and of many novelists of the day, including Mary Shelley, Bulwer-Lytton, Lady Morgan, and Horace Smith (*Dictionary of National Biography*).

CHAPTER 2: OLD FRIENDS

1. Mary Poovey, *The Proper Lady and the Woman Writer* (Chicago: University of Chicago Press, 1984).

Helen Heineman, *Restless Angels: The Friendship of Six Victorian Women* (Athens, Ohio: Ohio University Press, 1983).

Helen Heineman, *Mrs. Trollope: The Triumphant Feminine in the Nineteenth Century* (Athens, Ohio: Ohio University Press, 1979).

Carroll Smith-Rosenberg, "The Female World of Love and Ritual: Relations Between Women in Nineteenth-Century America," *Signs*, Autumn 1975, Vol. 1, No. 1, pp. 1–29.

**2.** See, for example, *MWS Letters*, Vol. I, September 17–20, 1822, pp. 260–263; March 7, 1823, pp. 320–324.

**3.** *MWS Letters*, Vol. I, January 2, 1825, p. 462.

**4.** *MWS Letters*, Vol. I, September 27, 1825, p. 501; November 29, 1825, p. 505.

**5.** *MWS Letters*, Vol. I, June 11, 1826, p. 519.

**6.** Newman Ivey White, *Shelley* (London: Secker & Warburg, 1947), Vol. I, p. 397.

**7.** White, *Shelley*, Vol. I, p. 356.

**8.** See Edward Dowden, *The Life of Percy Bysshe Shelley* (London: Kegan Paul, Trench, 1886), Vol. II, pp. 76–95; White, *Shelley*, Vol. I, pp. 494–497.

**9.** *MWS Journals*, Vol. II, p. 438.

**10.** William St Clair, *The Godwins and the Shelleys* (London: Faber and Faber, 1989), p. 363.

CHAPTER 3: NEW FRIENDS

**1.** *MWS Letters*, Vol. I, August 20, 1827, pp. 562–566.

**2.** *MWS Letters*, Vol. I, August 30, 1827, pp. 573–574.

**3.** *MWS Letters*, Vol. II, October 1, 1827, pp. 12–13.

**4.** *MWS Letters*, Vol. I, August 26, 1827, pp. 570–571.

**5.** *MWS Letters*, Vol. I, August 28, 1827, pp. 571–573.

**6.** *MWS Journals*, Vol. II, p. 507.

**7.** *MWS Letters*, Vol. II, May 4, 1828, pp. 39–40.

**8.** Betty T. Bennett and William T. Little, "Seven Letters from Prosper Mérimée to Mary Shelley," *Comparative Literature*, Vol. 31, No. 2 (Spring 1979), pp. 134–153.

**9.** Mary Shelley's review of Mérimée's *La Guzla, ou Choix de Poésies Illyriques recueillies dans la Dalmatie, la Croatie et l'Herzegowine* and *La Jaquerie; Feudal Scenes; Followed by the Family of Carvajal, a Drama*, "Illyrian Poems–Feudal Scenes," appeared in the *Westminster Review,* Vol. 10 (January 1829), pp. 71–81.

10. *MWS Letters,* Vol. II, June 28–29, 1828, p. 51.

11. In 1978, only an incomplete published version of the *Journals* was available. Fortunately, I had a microfilm copy of the manuscripts of the *Journals* to work from. In 1987, the accurately transcribed Feldman–Scott-Kilvert edition of the *The Journals of Mary Shelley* became available, to which all *MWS Journals* references are herein cited.

12. Cyrus Redding, *Literary Reminiscences and Memoirs of Thomas Campbell,* 2 vols. (London: Charles J. Skeet, 1860), Vol. II, pp. 175–176, 332; Cyrus Redding, *Fifty Years Recollections,* 3 vols. (London: Charles J. Skeet, 1858), Vol. I, p. 227; Vol. II, p. 331; Cyrus Redding, *Yesterday and Today,* 3 vols. (London: T. Cautley Newby, 1863), Vol. I, pp. 179.

13. The Drummond Wolffs had two sons and a daughter. The daughter, Adeline Georgiana Isabel, who married Col. Howard Kingscote, was a novelist who wrote under the name Lucas Cleeve and died in 1908.

14. R. Glynn Grylls, *Mary Shelley* (London: Oxford University Press, 1938), p. 208n.

CHAPTER 4: YOURS VERY TRULY, DAVID LYNDSAY

1. Alan Lang Strout, *A Bibliography of Articles in Blackwood's Magazine, 1817–1825* (Lubbock, Texas: Texas Tech Press, 1959).

2. Thomas Moore, *The Love of the Angels* (London: Longman, Hurst, Rees, Orme, & Brown, 1823), Preface, pp. vii–x.

3. *Blackwood's* reviewer, probably John Wilson, wrote that Lyndsay produced a remarkable first book though not without its faults. Comparing the *Dramas* with the works of other modern playwrights including Joanna Baillie and Byron—and discounting Baillie's works because she "is a woman, and thence weak in many things"—Wilson believes the *Dramas* show that Lyndsay is "a man of talents and of genius . . . and that is all we know of him, except that he once or twice sent us some dramatic

sketches for this Magazine." The reviewer feels at times Mr. Lyndsay might have been more powerful, but "in other passages redeems himself nobly," sometimes "bordering on extravagance" but "not without sublimity. . . . We do not fear to say, that he is a poet with much feeling and no little imagination . . . chief fault is a dim and misty splendour indiscriminately flung over all his conceptions . . . no simplicity . . . neither is there much curious or profound knowledge of passion . . . but Mr. Lyndsay conceives situations very finely and originally; his diction is often magnificent, and his imagery striking and appropriate; he seems to write in a sort of tumult and hurry of young delight . . . bad passages bombastical . . . have given enough to prove, that if a young writer, which can scarcely be doubted, high hopes may be justly formed of him who, in a first attempt, has produced so much poetry true to nature, and belonging to the highest province of imagination." (*Blackwood's,* Vol. LIX, Pt. 2, December 1821, pp. 730–740.)

4. At this point, I telephoned three friends, Charles E. Robinson and Donald H. Reiman, both Romantic scholars, and Emily Sunstein, to tell them what I had learned about Lyndsay and to ask that they keep an eye out for any information about him or his friend James Weale. Eventually, all three played a special part in my tracking of David Lyndsay.

5. See Chapter 2 above, pp. 000–000.

6. *Blackwood's,* Vol. XVI, November 1824, p. 606, lists "David Lyndsay, author of 'Dramas of the Ancient World'" among contributors to Alaric Watts's *The Literary Souvenir* from "the pens of the most popular writers of the day."

7. Phrenology was founded by Franz Joseph Gall (1758–1828). Godwin had Mary Shelley assessed by his friend William Nicholson, an amateur phrenologist, when she was nineteen days old. In 1820, he was himself assessed, but his 1831 *Thoughts on Man* essay repudiated phrenology (*MWS Letters,* Vol. II, December 30, 1830, pp. 122–123).

8. John G. Lockhart, *Blackwood's,* Vol. XIII, March 1823, pp. 283–293.

CHAPTER 5: SOME PROGRESS?

**1.** The originals are part of the Shelley materials deposited by Lord Abinger at the Bodleian Library in 1975.

**2.** For this, and other devices for deciphering manuscripts, I am indebted to Professor Paul Zall.

**3.** David Lyndsay to Blackwood, July 2, 1823.

**4.** Charles Ollier, editor and publisher, who with his brother conducted a publishing firm from 1817 to 1823. He was Shelley's publisher and later was instrumental in publishing a number of Mary Shelley's novels (see *MWS Letters*, Vol. I, p. 41).

**5.** *Blackwood's*, Vol. LIX, Pt.2, December 1821, pp. 730–740.

**6.** Apparently Samuel Taylor Coleridge was far less happy with the work. His marginalia to page 57 contains some sharply impatient comments; and he does not cut open, and read, the pages from 65 onward (Coleridge's copy of *Dramas*, British Library).

**7.** When the princess asks the little monster how he dared select a princess of her exalted rank to share his underground hovel, she is met with a mighty tirade on rank and appearance: "'Rank!' replied the irritated little demon, 'and what is this rank of which you are so vain? an imaginary splendour bestowed upon some men by the cringing servility of others,—the weak fancy that decks one with this supremacy, gives birth to the slavish fear that ensures to him its possession. Rank!' continued the atrabilious little viper, swelling into a respectable width by the overflowing of his angry venom, 'rank! it is power gained by force, won by the sword, by fraud, by oppression! The strongest is the noblest; and if so, I am more than your equal, beautiful Brunilda, for, princess as you are, you are my captive, and I am your master.'" At this point, the angry Brunilda renews her attack, this time "commenting with great severity upon his frightful little person: she sneered at his long beard, short legs, and large head . . . and demanded if he had ever looked in a mirror. . . . At no age have ugly people borne to be laughed at, for, however hideous they may happen to be, they seldom find it out themselves, and are, in consequence, very much surprised and offended when informed of it by others; and, as vanity is usually the reigning passion of the most disfigured, they seldom pardon an offence which is mortal."

**8.** In the course of this minisaga of inheritances, swords, feasts, and beasts, Lyndsay stops the story for a brief disquisition on the structure of the spoken language: "You are aware, dear reader, that the Scandinavians of the year 112, and some time after, did not use the same simple, plain, commonplace sort of style which they have adopted to express their meaning now-a-days. If we may believe their own writers, they were always in alt [i.e., an exalted or excited frame of mind], gave their commands in a kind of heroic prose, and carried on dialogues in a sort of rambling blank verse. It must therefore be obvious to you, dear reader, that I spare you their language, and only give you their sentiments, which, to the best of my humble ability, I will translate for you into decent colloquial English, the better to carry your patience through the long-winded history which I am preparing as a trial for it." On the subject of Valhalla, Lyndsay comments that Hamlet, almost as unpopular as his father in Valhalla, continually instructs Odin, causing so much mischief that Thor "lifted up his mallet to knock out the shadow" of Hamlet's brains but was finally talked out of it. Following the 119-page "Maelstrom" are five pages of scholarly notes, identifying places and characters.

**9.** When I returned home, I found a letter waiting from Alan Bell. He has drawn a blank on Sholto Douglas—he hasn't been able to identify my man at all even with the new information sent—the Scottish Record Office has Morton papers—perhaps they can advise me—also, try the descendants of the Douglases' daughter Adeline Drummond Wolff. His note that Lyndsay, not George Borrow, wrote the *Tales* will appear in the autumn *Book Collector*—suggests I send a short note about "Lyndsay's possible pseudonymity" or, if I decide to deal with it at greater length, he will assist in any way. Nor has he had any luck with Marcus Dods. When he has time, he will check in Dods's son's autobiography.

CHAPTER 7: THE QUESTION OF A PRONOUN

**1.** I am deeply grateful to Donald H. Reiman of the Carl H. Pforzheimer Library for this important query.
**2.** *MWS Letters,* Vol. I, p. 110n.
**3.** Again, I am deeply grateful to Donald H. Reiman.

CHAPTER 8: "AN ALIAS FOR MR. . . ."

**1.** The National Union Catalog listed only the Library of Congress, Duke University, and the Library Company of Philadelphia as owning copies of *Traits of Character,* cataloged under its title rather than under its author's name. Under Eliza Rennie, I found only a book called *Poems* (London: B. E. Lloyd, 1828). But before making extensive travel plans, I telephoned Robert Yampolsky at the Pforzheimer Library, who informed me that they also owned a copy.
**2.** [Eliza Rennie], *Traits of Character; Being Twenty-Five Years' Literary and Personal Recollections,* By a Contemporary (London: Hurst & Plackett, 1860), 2 vols., Vol. II, p. 203.
**3.** Transvestism is a modern psychological term, invented in 1910 by the German sexologist Magnus Hirschfeld to define people who have an irresistible urge to dress in the clothing of the opposite sex. See Rudolf M. Dekker and Lotte C. van de Pol, *The Tradition of Female Transvestism in Early Modern Europe* (New York: St. Martin's Press, 1989), p. 54.

CHAPTER 9: THE CODICIL

**1.** I was able to identify David Lyndsay as Mary Diana Dods's pseudonym in Volume I of the *Mary Shelley Letters,* but deadlines and technicalities prevented my revealing the "marriage" of Mary Diana Dods and Isabella Robinson in that volume.

CHAPTER 10: A NEW TRAIL

**1.** The term *homosexual* was coined in the late nineteenth century. Its contemporary meaning and connotations are even more recent. The term used to denote sexual activity between members of the same sex prior to that was *sodomy,* regarded as an incidental act rather than as part of a fixed sexual characteristic. See Rudolf M. Dekker and Lotte C. van de Pol, *The Tradition of Female Transvestism in Early Modern Europe* (New York: St. Martin's Press, 1989), p. 56.

**2.** See Chapter 20 of Dekker and van de Pol for a discussion of sexual mores and the impact of the law on homosexuals during the nineteenth century.

**3.** *MWS Letters,* Vol. II, October 12, 1835, pp. 255–256.

**4.** The word *lesbian* to denote female homosexuals was introduced in the twentieth century. See Dekker and van de Pol, p. 57.

**5.** For discussions of women's education, see:

C. S. Bremner, *Education of Girls and Women in Great Britain* (London: Swan Sonnenschein, 1897).

G. S. Osborne, *Scottish and English Schools* (Pittsburgh: University of Pittsburgh Press, 1966).

Maurice J. Quinlan, *Victorian Prelude* (Hamden, Conn.: Archon Books, 1965).

Josephine Kamm, *Hope Deferred* (London: Methuen, 1965).

John Lawson and Harold Silver, *A Social History of Education in England* (London: Methuen, 1973).

**6.** From my Bodleian Library files, I retrieved notes taken years before that appeared to tie the Douglases directly to Mérimée, Lafayette, the Misses Garnett and Miss Clarke. In 1820–23, C. and J. Ollier, Shelley's publishers, published annually *The Literary Pocket-Book, or Companion for the Lover of Nature and Art,* a combination diary, London guidebook, and poetry sampler containing works by Shelley, Keats, Byron. (In

1988, I would learn that the 1823 edition published "Poetry, Painting, and Music" and "Translation, Hymn to Venus, by Metastasio," both by David Lyndsay [Vol. 5, pp. 113–114, 117–119]; with thanks to Donald H. Reiman and Hilton Kelliher, The British Library.)

7. A. W. Raitt, *Prosper Mérimée* (New York: Charles Scribner's Sons, 1970), pp. 66–71.

8. *Shelley and Mary* (London: privately printed, 1882), Vol. 4, pp. 1092–1106.

CHAPTER 11: FANNY WRIGHT, PHILANTHROPIST AND AGITATOR

1. For a comprehensive study of Fanny Wright and her works, see Celia Morris Eckhardt, *Fanny Wright: Rebel in America* (Cambridge, Mass.: Harvard University Press, 1984).

2. *MWS Letters*, Vol. I, August 22, 1827, pp. 566–568.

3. Alice Perkins and Theresa Wolfson, *Frances Wright: Free Enquirer* (New York: Harper & Bros., 1939), pp. 49–89, 151, 176.

4. See Helen Heineman, *Mrs. Trollope: The Triumphant Feminine in the Nineteenth Century* (Athens, Ohio: Ohio University Press, 1979).

5. Robert Dale Owen, *Threading My Way* (New York: G. W. Carleton, 1874), pp. 296–330.

6. Cecilia Helena Payne-Gaposchkin, "The Nashoba Plan for Removing the Evil of Slavery: Letters of Frances and Camilla Wright, 1820–1829," *Harvard Library Bulletin*, Vol. 23, pp. 221–251, 429–461.

7. Next to Julia's name is a footnote revealing that Julia was the great-grandmother of Cecilia Payne-Gaposchkin, the article's author, and an editor's note explains that in 1974, Professor Payne-Gaposchkin deposited in the Houghton Library a collection of thirty-three letters from the Wrights to Julia and Harriet Garnett. Only two thirds of that 1974 Wright deposit appear in these letters.

8. I am deeply indebted to Professor Edward Gaposchkin

and Mrs. Katherine Haramundanis, the son and daughter of the late Professor Payne-Gaposchkin, for their permission to use the family's papers. I am also indebted to Rae Ann Nager, then curator of the Keats Collection at the Houghton, for assisting me in the early phases of arranging to work with the Payne-Gaposchkin papers; and particularly to Dr. Rodney Dennis, curator of manuscripts, for all the ongoing and generous assistance he has provided.

CHAPTER 12: A POEM OF SECRET SORROW

1. R. Stanley Dicks, "Mary Shelley: An Unprinted Elegy on Her Husband?" *Keats-Shelley Memorial Bulletin,* No. XXVIII, pp. 36–41.
2. *MWS Letters,* Vol. I, April 12, 1822, pp. 231–233.
3. This copy of the *Dramas* is among the papers and library of the late Romantic scholar Frederick L. Jones, which were bequeathed to Furman University. I am indebted to J. Glen Clayton, Special Collections librarian, for all his assistance.

CHAPTER 13: THE LADIES OF 14 RUE DUPHOT

1. Payne-Gaposchkin's daughter, Mrs. Katherine Haramundanis, provided Emily Sunstein with a copy. Later, Professor Edward Gaposchkin, Payne-Gaposchkin's son, gave me a copy of the *Garnett Letters.*
2. *Shelley and Mary* (London: privately printed, 1882), Vol. 4, pp. 1096–1109.
3. See C. Willett Cunnington and Phillis Cunnington, *Handbook of English Costume in the Nineteenth Century* (London: Faber and Faber, 1970).
C. Willett and Phillis Cunnington, *The History of Underclothes* (London: Michael Joseph, 1951).
*The Connoisseur's Complete Period Guides,* eds. Ralph Edwards and L.G.G. Ramsey (London: The Connoisseur, 1968).

R. Turner Wilcox, *The Dictionary of Costume* (New York, Charles Scribner's Sons, 1969).

Claudia B. Kidwell and Margaret C. Christman, *Suiting Everyone* (Washington, D.C.: Smithsonian Press, 1974).

Claudia Brush Kidwell and Valerie Steele, *Men and Women: Dressing the Part* (Washington, D.C.: Smithsonian Press, 1989).

4. Clarke and her circle are described in Kathleen O'Meara, *Madame Mohl: Her Salon and Her Friends: A Study of Social Life in Paris* (Boston: Roberts Brothers, 1886).

M.C.M. Simpson, *Letters and Recollections of Julius and Mary Mohl* (London: Kegan Paul, Trench & Co., 1887).

Margaret Lesser, *Clarkey: A Portrait in Letters of Mary Clarke Mohl (1793–1883)* (Oxford: Oxford University Press, 1984).

5. Lesser, *Clarkey*, p. 90.

6. O'Meara, *Madame Mohl*, p. 40.

7. [Eliza Rennie], *Traits of Character; Being Twenty-Five Years' Literary and Personal Recollections,* By a Contemporary (London: Hurst & Blackett, 1860), 2 vols., Vol. II, p. 207.

8. *MWS Letters,* Vol. II, June 28 and 29, 1828, p. 51.

9. *MWS Letters,* Vol. II, June 15, 1828, p. 46.

10. *MWS Letters,* Vol. II, August 9, 1828, p. 55.

11. *MWS Letters,* Vol. II, September 9, 1828, p. 58.

12. *MWS Letters,* Vol. II, June 15, 1828, p. 46.

13. See Chapter 3 above, p. 360.

14. *La Jaquerie; Feudal Scenes; Followed by the Family of Carvajal, a Drama.*

15. Stendhal's theory is expressed in his *De l'Amour* (Paris: P. Mongie L'Aine, 1822).

16. Prosper Mérimée, *Correspondance Generale,* ed. Maurice Parturier (Paris: Le Divan, 1941), Vol. I, p. 44.

CHAPTER 14: TRANSMOGRIFICATIONS

1. *The Journal of Thomas Moore,* ed. Wilfred S. Dowden (Newark: University of Delaware Press, 1986), Vol. 3, p. 929.

2. Miss E. D. Yeo answered that as Mr. Bell was then abroad, she undertook to respond to my inquiry.

3. See *Shelley and His Circle (1773–1822)*, eds. Kenneth Neill Cameron and Donald H. Reiman, 8 vols. (Cambridge, Mass.: Harvard University Press, 1961–1986), Vol. II, pp. 923–924.

CHAPTER 15: PIECES OF HISTORY

1. I am deeply grateful to Alice G. Fredman for her assistance in this particular search.

2. See M. R. Apted, *Aberdour Castle* (Edinburgh: Her Majesty's Stationery Office, 1961; 2nd edition, 1985), for a description of Aberdour Castle.

CHAPTER 17: MY DEAR LORD AND HIS DAUGHTERS

1. For a discussion of postmarks, see *Shelley and His Circle (1773–1822)*, eds. Kenneth Neill Cameron and Donald H. Reiman, 8 vols. (Cambridge, Mass.: Harvard University Press, 1961–1986), Vols. II, VII.

2. Henry Dundas, First Viscount Melville (1742–1811), in 1782 first became Secretary of the Navy; in 1804, he became First Lord of the Admiralty. In 1805 he resigned when accused of misuse of funds, but upon acquittal was restored. On his death in 1811, he was succeeded by his son, Robert Saunders Dundas, Second Viscount Melville (1771–1851), Tory politician and statesman who became First Lord of the Admiralty in 1812 (*DNB*).

3. In 1850, there were approximately forty thousand governesses in England. Charlotte Brontë was paid twenty pounds a year, less 20 percent for laundry. Mary Wollstonecraft wrote about the demeaning position of governesses in *Thoughts on the Education of Daughters: With Reflections on Female Conduct, in the More Important Duties of Life* (London: Joseph Johnson, 1787), p. 72, and after the girls' school she and her sisters conducted failed, she became, for less than a year, a governess in Lord Kingsborough's household and there experienced the degrading role firsthand. See:

Jonathan Gathorne-Hardy, *The Old School Tie* (New York: Viking Press, 1977), p. 235.

Ralph M. Wardle, *Mary Wollstonecraft* (Lincoln, Neb.: Nebraska University Press, 1951), pp. 54–78.

Eleanor Flexner, *Mary Wollstonecraft* (New York: Coward, McCann & Geoghegan, Inc., 1972), pp. 67–84.

CHAPTER 18: NEW QUESTIONS/NEW ANSWERS

**1.** I am indebted to Donna Evleth, a scholar based in Paris, for this information and for other assistance in my research in Paris.

**2.** Unpublished letter (NS. 141, 369), Bibliothèque de l'Institut de France.

**3.** Richard Corson, *Fashions in Hair* (New York: Hillary House Publishers, 1969), pp. 402–403.

**4.** *Correspondance de Fauriel et Mary Clarke,* ed. Ottmar de Mohl (Paris: Plon-Nourrit et Cie, 1911).

**5.** Published by Marsh and Miller, London; and Constable, Edinburgh.

**6.** British Library MSS., MS. 35, pp. 526–536; MS. 19, pp. 347–348.

**7.** Sir Henry Drummond Wolff, *Rambling Recollections,* 2 vols. (London: Macmillan, 1908), Vol. I, p. 188.

**8.** R. Glynn Grylls, *Mary Shelley: A Biography* (London: Oxford University Press, 1938), p. 208.

**9.** Unpublished letter, April 22, 1869, the Mitchell Library, Sydney, Australia.

**10.** Wolff, *Rambling Recollections,* Vol. II, pp. 102–103; Grylls, *Mary Shelley,* p. 255.

**11.** Guildhall Library, London.

**12.** Bertram S. Puckle, *Funeral Customs* (London: T. Werner Laurie Ltd., 1926; reissue, Detroit: Singing Tree Press, 1968), p. 82.

**13.** Salaries quoted from the Edinburgh newspaper *The Scotsman,* 1827.

Harold Perkin, *The Origins of Modern English Society: 1780–1880* (London: Routledge & Kegan Paul, 1969).

G.D.H. Cole and Raymond Postgate, *The British Common People* (London: Methuen, 1938).

Jeffrey G. Williamson, *Did British Capitalism Breed Inequality?* (Boston: Allen & Unwin, 1985).

**14.** Register House, Edinburgh, GD150/2664.

**15.** Register House, Edinburgh, GD150/2666.

**16.** *The Royal Commission of Ancient and Historical Monuments and Constructions of Scotland,* 10th Report (Edinburgh, 1929), p. 158.

**17.** I am deeply grateful to Harry Watson and Les Duff for arranging to introduce me to the present Earl of Morton and for other assistance in this search in Scotland.

**18.** Phillis Cunnington and Anne Buck, *Children's Costume in England* (New York: Barnes and Noble, Inc., 1965); N. Hudson Moore, *Children of Other Days* (New York: Frederick A. Stokes, 1905).

Claudia Brush Kidwell and Valerie Steele, *Men and Women: Dressing the Part* (Washington, D.C.: Smithsonian Press, 1989).

CHAPTER 19: ENTER, MARY DIANA DODS

**1.** *MWS Journals,* Vol. II, p. 438.

**2.** See Chapter 2 above, pp. 30–31.

**3.** *MWS Journals,* Vol. II, p. 487.

**4.** *MWS Journals,* Vol. II, p. 488.

**5.** *MWS Letters,* Vol. II, October 1, 1827, p. 13.

**6.** *MWS Letters,* Vol. I, June 30, 1822, p. 238; July 3, 1822, p. 239.

**7.** See Chapter 2 above, p. 31.

**8.** *MWS Journals,* Vol. II, p. 488.

**9.** See *MWS Letters* for her relationships to a number of men, including Mérimée, Payne, John Chalk Claris, Bryan Procter Waller, Alexander Knox, and Ferdinando Gatteschi.

**10.** *MWS Journals,* Vol. II, p. 432.

**11.** *MWS Journals,* Vol. II, p. 484.

**12.** Lillian Faderman, *Surpassing the Love of Men: Romantic Friendship and Love Between Women from the Renaissance to the Present* (New York: William Morrow, 1981), for an overview of women's sexual orientation.

**13.** *MWS Letters,* Vol. I, pp. 382–383n.

**14.** *MWS Letters,* Vol. III, September 20, 1843, p. 92.

**15.** *MWS Letters,* Vol. I, August 28, 1827, p. 573.

**16.** *Slang and Its Analogues,* ed. J. S. Farmer and W. E. Henley (New York: Arno Press, 1970).

**17.** *MWS Letters,* Vol. II, October 12, 1835, p. 256.

**18.** *MWS Letters,* Vol. II, October 12, 1835, p. 256. According to contemporary polite usage, "to touse and mouse" meant "to pull about roughly." See *Dictionary of Obsolete and Provincial English,* ed. Thomas Wright (London: Henry G. Bohn, 1851). A variant, "towsy-mowsy," was also slang for the female pudendum. See *Slang and Its Analogues,* eds. J. S. Farmer and W. E. Henley (1st ed., 1890–1904; repr. New York: Arno Press, 1970).

**19.** *MWS Journals,* Vol. II, p. 514.

**20.** *MWS Letters,* Vol. II, October 12, 1835, p. 256.

**21.** *MWS Letters,* Vol. II, October 1, 1827, p. 13.

**22.** *MWS Journals,* Vol. II, p. 543.

**23.** The records of the Royal Literary Fund show that Eliza Rennie four times, in 1854, 1861, 1863, and 1869, applied to the fund for money they provided as a charity to needy authors. Awards were granted in response to each of her requests, except in 1861.

**24.** Records of the Royal Literary Fund, No. 1354.

**25.** Graham's story is variously told in J. Gorton, *A General Biographical Dictionary,* 3 vols. (London: Henry G. Bohn, 1841).

Henry Hill, *Recollections of an Octogenarian* (Boston: D. Lothrop, 1884), pp. 164–184.

William Charles Macready, "Biographical Memoirs of Eminent Persons: William Grenville Graham," *The Monthly Magazine* (London: Geo. B. Whittaker, 1828), pp. 206–218.

William Charles Macready, *Macready's Reminiscences,* ed.

Sir Frederick Pollock (New York: Macmillan and Co., 1875), pp. 118–119, 222–223.

**26.** Macready, "Memoirs," p. 212.

**27.** *MWS Letters,* Vol. II, June 28–29, 1828, p. 50.

**28.** *MWS Letters,* Vol. II, June 5, 1828, p. 42.

**29.** *The Cabinet Cyclopaedia, Eminent Literary and Scientific Men of Italy, Spain, and Portugal,* ed. Dionysius Lardner, 3 vols. (London: Longman, Orme, Green, & Longman; and John Taylor, 1835–1837), Vol. II, p. 387.

**30.** Richard Corson, *Fashions in Hair* (New York: Hillary House, 1969).

**31.** Rudolf M. Dekker and Lotte van de Pol, *The Tradition of Female Transvestism in Early Modern Europe* (New York: St. Martin's Press, 1989).

Julie Wheelwright, *Amazons and Military Maids: Women Who Dressed as Men in the Pursuit of Life, Liberty and Happiness* (London: Pandora, 1989).

Lynne Friedli, "'Passing Women': A Study of Gender Boundaries in the Eighteenth Century," in *Sexual Underworlds of the Enlightenment,* eds. G. S. Rousseau and Roy Porter (Chapel Hill: University of North Carolina, 1988), pp. 238–242, discusses a number of incidents of passing females, including *The Female Husband* (1746) by Henry Fielding; *Autobiography of Charlotte Charke* (1755); *The Female Review or Memoirs of an American Young Lady* (1797); *The Female Soldier; Or, The Surprising Life and Adventures of Hannah Snell.* The 1989 Augustan Reprint Society's publication of Hannah Snell's autobiography (UCLA) notes a number of other eighteenth- and nineteenth-century biographies of female warriors (see pp. v, xi).

**32.** Ellen C. Clayton, *Female Warriors: Memorials of Female Valour and Heroism, from the Mythological Ages to the Present Era,* 2 vols. (London: Tinsley Bros., 1879).

Menie Muriel Dowie, *Women Adventurers* (London: T. F. Unwin, 1879).

Nadezhda Durova, *The Cavalry Maid: The Memoirs of a Woman Soldier of 1812* (Ann Arbor, Mich.: Ardis, 1989); a second translation under the title of *The Cavalry Maiden: Journals of a Russian Officer in the Napoleonic Wars* (Bloomington, Ind.: Indiana University, 1989).

Brian Hurwitz and Ruth Richardson, "Inspector General James Barry MD: Putting the Woman in Her Place," *British Medical Journal,* February 1989.

**33.** See Peter Ackroyd, *Dressing Up* (New York: Simon & Schuster, 1979), for a well-illustrated series of accounts of transvestites.

**34.** Jacobus de Voragine, *The Golden Legend* (London: Longmans, Green, 1941).

*La Madeleine de Vezelay Guide Book and Plans* (Lyon: Lescuyer, 1985).

**35.** See Lawrence Durrell, *Pope Joan,* trans. and adapted from the Greek of Emmanuel Royidis, 1966.

**36.** Hurwitz and Richardson, "Inspector General James Barry MD."

**37.** *The New York Times,* February 2, 1989, p. A18; *Time* magazine, February 13, 1989, p. 41.

**38.** Louis Crompton, "The Myth of Lesbian Impunity: Capital Laws from 1270 to 1791," *Journal of Homosexuality,* Fall/Winter 1980–81 (New York: Haworth), pp. 11–25.

The 1986 *Immodest Acts* by Judith C. Brown, (New York, Oxford University Press, p. 6), in contrast, argued that Europeans also "had long found it difficult to accept that women could actually be attracted to other women. Their view of human sexuality was phallocentric."

**39.** See Lillian Faderman, *Scotch Verdict: Miss Pirie and Miss Woods* v. *Dame Cumming Gordon* (New York: William Morrow, 1983), in which she discusses the public case of the Woods and Pirie libel suit against Dame Helen Cumming Gordon (1811). Dame Gordon claimed that the women, who ran a successful girls' school in Edinburgh, were sleeping together and were sexually engaged. As a result of Dame Gordon's charges, Woods and Pirie were forced to close the school. After ten years, the plaintiffs won the case, based on the judges' opinion that ". . . the crime here alleged has no existence." However, the trial also brings into focus some of the attitudes toward female sexuality in the era that are counter to the generally held perception that females did not engage in homoerotic practices. Among the evidence cited was a list of literary works that demonstrated erotic behavior between women. One judge maintained that he had little doubt that women in all ages and countries had enjoyed such pleasure seeking.

**40.** *Lord Hardwicke's Marriage Act* of 1754 was instituted to punish those who "married" outside a church or without a license. Under this act, men were charged with the sexual offense of sodomy, while women who married were charged with fraud. See Friedli, "'Passing Women,'" p. 252, n.6.

**41.** *MWS Letters*, Vol. I, September 25, 1827; see Chapter 14 above, pp. 156–158.

**42.** I am grateful to Dr. John Money for providing this, and other information, regarding aberrant sexual characteristics.

**43.** Much of the pioneering research on modern sexology is the work of John Money, *Gay, Straight, and In-Between* (New York: Oxford University Press, 1988).

John Money and R. Ambinder, "Two-year, Real-Life Diagnostic Test: Rehabilitation versus Cure," *Controversy in Psychiatry,* eds. J. P. Brady and H.K.H. Brodie (Philadelphia: Saunders, 1978).

John Money and Anke A. Ehrhardt, *Man and Woman, Boy and Girl* (Baltimore: Johns Hopkins Press, 1972).

For studies of biological, psychological, and social foundations of sex roles, see:

Shirley Weitz, *Sex Roles* (New York: Oxford University Press, 1977).

Vern L. Bullough, "Transsexualism in History," *Sex, Society, and History* (New York: Science History Publications, 1976), pp. 150–161.

Candace West and Don H. Zimmerman, "Doing Gender," *Gender & Society,* Vol. 1 (Brooklyn College & Graduate Center, CUNY, 1987), pp. 125–151.

Marcia Yudkin, "Transsexualism and Women: A Critical Perspective," *Feminist Studies,* Vol. 4 (College Park, Md., 1978), pp. 97–106.

**44.** Jan Morris, *Conundrum* (New York: Harcourt, Brace Jovanovich, 1974).

45. Lillian Faderman, *Surpassing the Love of Men,* p. 16.

46. Dekker and van de Pol, *The Tradition of Female Transvestism,* p. 71.

47. See particularly Helen Heineman, *Restless Angels: The Friendship of Six Victorian Women* (Athens, Ohio: Ohio University Press, 1983). Heineman writes specifically about the Garnetts, Fanny Wright, Fanny Trollope, and Mary Shelley, referring in the course of her narrative to "Mary Shelley's friend Mrs. Douglas," who "turned out to be just another Parisian coquette" (p. 97).

48. Information provided by the Mairie de Paris, Service des Cimetières, Paris.

# WORKS BY MARY DIANA DODS

PUBLISHED WORKS
(LISTED UNDER THE PSEUDONYM USED BY HER AS AUTHOR)*

BOOKS

David Lyndsay, *Dramas of the Ancient World* (Edinburgh: Blackwood's, 1821).
("The Deluge," "The Plague of Darkness," "The Last Plague," "Rizpah," "Sardanapalus," "The Destiny of Cain," "The Death of Cain," "The Nereid's Love")
David Lyndsay, *Tales of the Wild and the Wonderful* (London: Hurst and Robinson, 1825).
("The Prediction," "The Yellow Dwarf," "Der Freischütz," "The Fortunes of de la Pole," "The Lord of the Maelstrom")

ESSAYS, POEMS, STORIES, DRAMAS

David Lyndsay, "The Plague of Darkness: A Dramatic Scene from the Exodus," *Blackwood's Edinburgh Magazine,* Vol. IX (August 1821), pp. 555–565.
David Lyndsay, "The Vigil of St. Mark: A Dramatic Tale,"

*I would be grateful for any further identifications.

*Blackwood's Edinburgh Magazine,* Vol. X (October 1821), pp. 341–347.

David Lyndsay, "The Mount of Olives," *Blackwood's Edinburgh Magazine,* Vol. X (December 1821), pp. 654–655.

David Lyndsay, "The Ring and the Stream: A Drama," *Blackwood's Edinburgh Magazine,* Vol. XI (January 1822), pp. 50–61.

David Lyndsay, "Horae Gallicae. No. I. Raynouard's States of Blois," *Blackwood's Edinburgh Magazine,* Vol. XI (May 1822), pp. 530–547.

David Lyndsay, "The Death of Isaiah—a Fragment," *Blackwood's Edinburgh Magazine,* Vol. XII (August 1822), pp. 205–211.

David Lyndsay, "Poetry, Painting, and Music," *The Literary Pocket-Book* (London: C. and J. Ollier, 1823), pp. 113–114.

David Lyndsay, "Translation. Hymn to Venus, by Metastasio," *The Literary Pocket-Book* (London: C. and J. Ollier, 1823), pp. 117–119.

Reprinted: "Translation. Hymn to Venus, by Metastasio," *La Belle Assemblée* (February 1823), p. 80.

David Lyndsay, "Firouz-Abdel: A Tale of the Upas Tree," *The Literary Souvenir,* ed. Alaric A. Watts (London: Hurst, Robinson, 1825), pp. 341–371.

Reprinted: *The Tale Book,* Second Series (Paris: Baudry, 1835).

Reprinted: *The Tale Book* (Königsberg: J. H. Bon, 1859).

[Sholto Douglas], "The Owl," *Blackwood's Edinburgh Magazine,* Vol. XX (July 1826), pp. 13–15.

[Sholto Douglas], "My Transmogrifications," *Blackwood's Edinburgh Magazine,* Vol. XX (August 1826), pp. 152–154.

David Lyndsay, "The Bridal Ornaments: A Legend of Thuringia," *A Forget Me Not for 1827,* ed. Frederic Shoberl (London: R. Ackermann, 1827), pp. 393–416.

Reprinted: *The Rose; or Affection's Gift for 1848* (New York: D. Appleton, 1847), pp. 9–30.

David Lyndsay, "The Three Damsels: A Tale of Halloween," *A Forget Me Not for 1827,* ed. Frederic Shoberl (London: R. Ackermann, 1827), pp. 79–86.

David Lyndsay, "The Beacon Light: A Tale," *The Pledge of Friendship for 1828* (London: Chadwick Healey, 1828), pp. 208–233.

WORKS LISTED IN DAVID LYNDSAY'S AND MARY SHELLEY'S CORRESPONDENCE, EITHER UNPUBLISHED OR UNLOCATED TO DATE

Translations of Alfieri
"Shade of the Bridegroom" ("Der Bräutigam's Vorschem")
*Duke of Guise*
*The Festival of the Earth,* for a book of dramas
Foscari
Translations of the *Gespensterbuch* (*Spectre Book*), by Apel and Laun
Horae Italicae
Junge's Theory
La Motte Fouqué
Les pièces justifications
"Loose thoughts on the Cardinal"
Translations of Maffei
Poem (on Scottish history, 171 pages)
Raynouard's Temples and historical notices
*The Revolt of the Wilderness,* for a book of dramas
*The Waters of Jealousy*
*The Wedding of Undine,* for a book of dramas
*Der Zauber Liebe—Magic Love,* trans. of German drama by Alarn

# INDEX